"Number me among Franklin Schneider's soon-to-be legion fan base."

—Daniel Mueller, author of *How Animals Mate: Stories*

"For the majority of you reading *Canned*, a feeling of contempt will wash over you toward the writer for exemplifying the worst in Americans. Others will read these words and show some form of remorse for the author and his ill-conceived notions as to what he is 'entitled.' In either respect, I am sure that everyone who is not a Marxist can agree, Franklin Schneider is the type of person this country can do without."

—Charles Signorile, ConstitutionallyRight.com

"Men are supposed to work. From the time they first can, until the day that they physically just can't. It's how I was raised, and it's what I believe still to this day. Men who don't work—those who are just too lazy, dishonest, or wretched—are the most pathetic excuses for men in this country. And Franklin Schneider is as big a loser as you'll ever meet. I hope he ends up on the streets. And I hope he gets beat and robbed by every other homeless guy out there. Yeah, I wish nothing short of hell for this guy."

—Robbie Cooper, UrbanGrounds.com

CANNED

How I Lost Ten Jobs
in Ten Years
and Learned to Love
Unemployment

FRANKLIN SCHNEIDER

CITADEL PRESS
Kensington Publishing Corp.
www.kensingtonbooks.com

CITADEL PRESS BOOKS are published by

Kensington Publishing Corp.
119 West 40th Street
New York, NY 10018

All Kensington titles, imprints, and distributed lines are available at special quantity discounts for bulk purchases for sales promotions, premiums, fund-raising, educational, or institutional use. Special book excerpts or customized printings can also be created to fit specific needs. For details, write or phone the office of the Kensington special sales manager: Kensington Publishing Corp., 119 West 40th Street, New York, NY 10018, ATTN: Special Sales Department; phone 1-800-221-2647.

CITADEL PRESS and the Citadel logo are Reg. U.S. Pat. & TM Off.

First printing: October 2010

10 9 8 7 6 5 4 3 2 1

Printed in the United States of America

Library of Congress Control Number: 2010925001

ISBN-13: 978-0-8065-3226-4
ISBN-10: 0-8065-3226-2

*This is how the hero of our time must be. He will be
characterized either by decisive inaction, or else by futile
activity.*

—MIKHAIL LERMONTOV, *A Hero of Our Time*

*I was the evil product of an evil soil. If the self were not
imperishable, the "I" I write about would have been
destroyed long ago. To some this may seem like an
invention, but whatever I imagine to have happened did
actually happen,* at least to me. *History may deny it,
since I have played no part in the history of my people,
but even if everything I say is wrong, is prejudiced,
spiteful, malevolent, even if I am a liar and a poisoner, it
is nevertheless the truth and it will have to be swallowed.*

As to what happened...

—HENRY MILLER, *Tropic of Capricorn*

Contents

CANNED

The Great Recession

or, This Recession Is Great!

I've been unemployed now for almost three years and I'm the happiest man alive. I go out almost every night, because why not? I've got nothing to do in the morning and the tabs aren't paid with real money, it's just unemployment checks. On Friday and Saturday, the people who still have jobs show up en masse, and everyone crams in, and you can tell the employed apart by their slightly better grooming, their slightly better beer, their palpable desperation. After all, these are people with something to lose! These are people whose credit ratings have not yet been eviscerated, who have performance reviews coming up, who have just forty-eight precious hours to captain their own ships before they're chained back to the oars. I remember it well myself, my weekends as a workingman, propelled out into the night in search of something, anything. I had no idea what I wanted, only that it was missing and would perhaps be found at the bottom of the next pint or under the skirt of the next woman or in a befogged corner of the next bar.

Of course, I've left those days far behind. The only thing missing from my life now is a job, which is to say there's nothing

missing at all. The Great Recession, isn't that what they're calling it? And really, a truer name was never coined, because it
has in fact been pret-ty fucking great, at least for us, myself
and Kyle and Haley and the other unemployed ladies and gentle-
men here on this very night, swilling the cheapest most watery
beer on tap and looking nothing like the harried poverty-
stricken desperadoes you read about in the newspaper. No,
we're toasting each other with bright eyes and look five years
younger than our ages since we get ten hours of sleep a night
while our upwardly mobile counterparts are working twelve-
hour days in hopes of surviving the next round of cuts, and
then more hours up late at the kitchen table, poring over
mortgage statements and investment portfolios and clasping
their foreheads and asking, how, how did this happen?

While everyone was scrambling madly to get ahead, I got
ahead just by standing still!

Another unemployment extension has just passed and we're
buying round after round in anticipation of the coming wind-
fall. Everyone insists they knew all along that the extension
would pass, though I suspect that more than a few had spent a
sleepless night or two polishing up the ol' résumé. There's
some confusion as to how many more weeks we're getting; it
all depends on the unemployment rate but no one has the
slightest idea what that might be.

Is it a number? Haley asks. What about seventy, does that
sound right? I read seventy in the paper the other day.

No, it's a percentage. Seventy percent is way too high. It's
more like ten.

Ten? Ten?! I thought it was supposed to be bad out there.
Ten's not bad at all. What do they want, every single person
out there slaving away?

I think that's the idea, Kyle says, and for a moment we stare
into our pint glasses, reminded of the enormity of what we're
up against, and then we all burst into laughter, because it's all
so fucking stupid...

*   *   *

Yes, as things have gotten worse for everyone else, they've gotten better and better for us. The unemployment extensions are piling up with no end in sight, one on top of the other like a ladder to heaven, and we can all breathe easy because we're funded for years. And unlike past stints on the dole, no one says a cross word to us. Because *in this economy,* we can hardly be blamed for not having a job. (Never mind that we're not trying.) *In this economy*—we love this phrase and adore working it into conversation, making air quotes with our fingers before dissolving into derisive snickering. *In this economy,* why bother paying bills? Student loans, credit cards—let 'em all go to collection. What are they going to do? There's no debtor's prison anymore. Why do we need good credit? To buy a house? *In this economy,* renting seems to be the wiser course of action.

But son, the mother says, you're just throwing your money away if you rent. If you buy you get equity!

Yes, I'm throwing money down the toilet, but would you rather me throw my best years down the toilet? Chained to a shitty job taking orders from inferior people fifty weeks a year just to make mortgage payments on some drafty prefab crackerbox in a whitebread subdivision where the neighbors will hassle me about the length of my grass? And that's if the market doesn't crash and leave me a hundred thousand dollars underwater…

As the night wears on and people become too drunk or lazy or absorbed in their attempts at seduction to put money in the jukebox, the silence that ensues always seems to induce reflection, and inevitably our thoughts turn to those who are absent. Our friends who were fired or laid off but like the songbird freed of its cage couldn't handle freedom, and sat around the house watching daytime television, whining about *I don't know what to do with all this time* and *my self-esteem hurts* and *what will my parents think?* And I was always taken aback when they said these things to me, because they didn't seem to realize that what they were really saying was *I don't know how to live* and *I don't know who I am*. And sure enough, after a few weeks they took new jobs that often paid the same or sometimes even less than unemployment, just to work, just to be able to bang that alarm clock each morning and put on the uniform and rejoin, I don't know, the circle of life or some shit. Horrible jobs at public high schools where the students threw books at them or grabbed their asses so hard it left bruises, temp gigs where the manager dumped thirty pounds of data entry forms on them the first day and they were allowed a thirty-minute unpaid lunch and even the security guards regarded them like some exotic genital growth. And when they showed up at the bar to complain about these new jobs, we sat stonefaced and unsympathetic and said, well, it was your choice, you could've sat back and cashed unemployment checks, what are you complaining about? And shortly, they stopped showing up at all...

Someone suggests pouring out a drink in their honor but no one moves to actually do it.

We're not going to waste good beer on those fuckers, someone else says, and there are mutters of agreement up and down the bar.

But no, I say, they may be lost li'l lambs and scared grown-up children (this is a familiar spiel and already some people are snickering in anticipation), but let's not forget where our unemployment checks come from. If it wasn't for their pathological compulsion to ride the hamster wheel, to lick the hand that flogs them (general applause), where would we be? We should be thanking them for the faulty parenting they haven't shrugged off, their generalized fear of life, their unwillingness to question anything, ever, because it is their misguided labors that fund our unemployment checks and, indeed, form the bedrock of this *fine* country, God bless it. And let's not forget, above all, that each of us was once like them, too, before we were liberated by the pratfalls of capitalism. So let us now gratefully raise our pints that were paid for by our gainfully employed betters and are filled in a way not with beer but with a decoction of their excellence, their righteousness, every commercial they ever believed, every résumé workshop they ever attended, every time they ever colored inside the lines or fake-laughed at a boss's joke, let us drink of their flesh and blood and be thankful!

Everyone tips their glasses back and shudders.

Whoo, that's fucking horrible!

I think I'm going to vomit...

You've got a gift, Haley says, possibly kidding. You ought to run for president.

I may just do that, I say, easing back onto my stool. And the way things in the world seem to be going, who's to say I couldn't be president someday? Wasn't it Nietzsche who said that everything sacred was once criminal? A few more recessions, a few more burst bubbles, and who knows, I might find myself securely in the mainstream...

We stumble out at bar close, four or five of us, and as we file down a quiet side street, Kyle points out a house in the moonless dark as the residence of an ex-boss. This was the job before last, where this asshole cut Kyle's hours down to the bone instead of just firing him, gave him a half-shift a week for a month straight until Kyle was broke and starving and had no choice but to quit, thereby disqualifying himself from unemployment. We all agreed this was a chickenshit move and that something had to be done to show this fellow that what goes around does indeed come around.

It's a weeknight and silence hangs over the block like a held breath. We walk across the street as steadily as we can manage and stand assembled in front of this rowhouse. Kyle coughs but quickly stifles the sound with one hand, out of something like reverence. An American flag hangs limp on the front of the house, and someone pulls it down and ties it by the corners around Kyle's neck like a cape. The face of the house is dominated by a huge cycloptic pane of glass, and while every other house on the street has a protective grate over its picture window, this house conspicuously does not.

We fan out to find a brick or large rock, but there are none around. I try to pry up a paving stone from the sidewalk, but it's securely set. Someone else suggests that we throw a nearby garbage can through the window, but it turns out to be empty and the consensus is that it isn't heavy enough to shatter the glass.

Kyle, I say, you could get in the can, and we'd put the lid on and then heave it through. Then when your boss came out of his bedroom to see what happened, you could jump out of the can screaming, flapping your flag cape, and scare the shit out of the bastard!

Someone lights a cigarette. Maybe we should burn the house down, he says, half-joking.

This guy's probably insured up the ass. We might as well just write him a check for a half-million dollars.

In the shadow of the front steps, Kyle has found an old-fashioned push mower and now he's pushing it in figure-eights through the small overlandscaped lawn, around the dwarf ferns and white lilies and multitiered miniature terrace bordered with artificially-aged bricks and filled with mauve-dyed woodchips, trundling along in the dark while singing in a low, cretinous voice, *dum-de-dum-de-dum-de-dum-de-doo.*

Let's throw it in the creek, in the park, someone suggests. It's not far from here.

No, let's rig it so that the next time he uses it, the blade will kick back into his legs!

How do we do that?

I don't know.

You're an idiot.

I like the creek idea, I say.

The creek's a mile away!

Not if we take it down through the south end of the park...
Yeah, but it's shallow there...

That's even better! It'll sit there in the mud, sticking out above the water like it's taunting him. That's perfect! We could even leave a note in his mailbox or something—"Go look in the creek by the south park entrance, fucker."

Hmm, that's not bad...

"This is what happens when you cheat the workingman, fucker."

"Your lawn mower gets thrown in the creek, fucker."

I look around to tell Kyle our plan and find him behind us, turning in a circle, swinging the mower at the end of his extended arms faster and faster and faster, taking tiny delicate steps with the grace of an Olympic shot-putter as he picks up speed. It's silent except for the whirring of the blades cutting through the air, and then bending his knees and surging upward, he releases the mower. It arcs through the night and to a man we look on with wide eyes and various expressions of delight as we think of all our own unavenged grievances against "the Man" and that this one smallish gesture would go a long ways toward making things, if not right, then better at least. I can say unironically that I prayed for a higher power to guide that mower to its reward, and I don't think I was the only one, and just like they told us when we were kids, *ask and ye shall receive*, that mower went no place but where it had been aimed, and just before it breaches that gleaming pane of glass in which we could just then see our own awestruck countenances returned back to us in silvery magnesium-stricken tones, we turn and run down the street, where very shortly we look as if we are being propelled forward by the wonderful horrible rending of the night that we'd unleashed...

We scatter through alleys and backyards and vacant lots and reconvene at Kyle's house, one by one trotting up the front steps breathing hard and grinning sheepishly. Last of all comes Kyle, the man of action himself. He walks up to ironic applause, still caped with the stolen flag, which he unties as he walks and lets flutter to the ground, and we all go inside and drink for a while longer and agree that we'd made the world a better place that night. And this warm feeling of action and righteousness stuck with us all night and into the next day, when we walked over to Fourteenth Street for coffee, and by silent assent took a route past the scene of the non-crime. As we passed the house, at that moment being assessed and measured and prepared by various tradesmen as a fretting Asian family stood by watching, Kyle looked over and said, Oh shit, that's not my boss's house! This isn't even the right street!

CHAPTER 2

Portrait of the Artist as a Young Field Laborer

or, Gateway Drugs

I grew up in Burlington, Iowa, a small town on the Mississippi River with all the dynamism of a car on blocks. It was a great place to raise kids but not necessarily to grow up. By the time I was thirteen, my friends and I, our minds blown out by Nintendo games and Stallone movies, had taken to wandering the fractured streets, beset by vague unarticulable longings. Escape was our only thought, but from what, and to where? Parents locked their daughters away when we came around; we fairly bristled with blind priapic determination. Younger boys ran from us and older boys beat us senseless. Bored and, if not as smart as we thought, still not stupid. Was it any surprise we turned to petty crime?

We went to the mall, put on anything that caught our eye, and walked out past the oblivious clerks, sweltering and stiff legged under so many layers of clothing. We shoved comic books and candy into the front of our pants and ran, but often as not threw our booty unread and uneaten into a Dumpster the moment our getaway was secure. We stole our rivals' bikes, pedaled them furiously toward the edge of a bluff overlooking the river, and jumped off at the last minute to watch them plunge silently into emptiness. We did it because we were bored and because they told us not to do it. Our mischief climaxed in a burglary on Christmas Day. (One must grudgingly admire the sheer audacity of youth. In a way it was a stroke of genius, as there were no witnesses around to see us dragging garbage bags of stolen merchandise home through the snow. Our downfall was an accomplice who got nabbed while pawning his share of the spoils and sold us out to save himself.)

The only problem was that we were laughably incompetent criminals and almost always got caught, and our parents got stuck with the damages. Several weekends picking up used condoms and cigarette butts in city parks with other teenage felons (a crowd in which it was quickly apparent I didn't belong) finally chastened me. Like all failed criminals, I decided to try going straight.

What does the straight-and-narrow life entail? The thoughts of the powerless tend to turn toward money, as the life solutions we're presented with are generally in the form of products. Unfortunately, the few summer jobs available to teenagers in my town were as a rule filled by my female counterparts, males my age being too uncivilized to interact with the public. The only real job available to someone of my station in life was detasseling.

Detasseling is a peculiarly Midwestern tradition, maybe the last corner of agriculture that still requires human hands. To ensure the proper hybridization of a cornfield, 99.5 percent of all undesirable pollen tassels had to be removed from a field, a percentage unattainable by machine. Enter the detasselers. Our job was to trudge down mile-long rows of corn in the dead of summer, removing the offending tassels; essentially, we were primitive eugenicists and our job was to preclude agricultural miscegenation by castrating inferior plants. And it was just as depressing as it sounds...

Corporate agribarons subcontracted the detasseling out to local brokers, who set up folding tables at the local minor-league ballpark to recruit during games. Application entailed writing your name on an index card, and the evaluation process was they took everyone. Despite the wretched field conditions, they paid little more than minimum wage, and so the only people who signed up were those who had no other choice—kids, mostly. This being midsummer, work started at the ungodly hour of 5 a.m. and ended before the afternoon heat intensified to a murderous level. My parents readily agreed to drive me to the pickup point each morning, glad that I was finally making an effort at legitimacy and also because frankly they looked forward to seeing me suffer.

It'll teach you the value of a dollar, and build character, my father said curtly. He'd held the same blue-collar job in town for decades. I had no idea what he was talking about, but I was willing to give it a try. Like most adolescents, I had a strong interest in self-improvement, though only to the degree that it would enhance my chances of someday having sexual intercourse.

I joined on with my neighborhood friend Jimmy, a pudgy taciturn boy my age who seemed to already have accepted that his lot in life would be rote labor. He had a luxuriously curly blond mullet, like some kind of Swedish pirate, or an ABBA roadie, the back of his T-shirts perpetually striped with sweat stains even in midwinter. I can still see him, trudging through the fields wearing his homemade trashbag poncho, talking compulsively of nothing but the Air Jordans he was going to purchase with his summer's wages, those goddamn fucking Air Jordans that even today still make me roll my eyes. Even at that marketing-susceptible age, I was mystified as to why an overweight thirteen-year-old with the vertical leap of a quadriplegic needed hundred-fifty-dollar butt-ass-ugly basketball shoes. When I pressed him on it, Jimmy simply shook his head and said I wouldn't understand. I took this to mean that he didn't know himself why he wanted them, and pronounced him a fool, even as I nursed my own dreams of brand-name jeans and imported Japanese role-playing video games.

The Mississippi River had flooded that year to catastrophic levels, as it does every few decades or so. The lower half of my hometown was completely under water, and every day the front page of the newspaper featured another photo of local kids doggy-paddling past the ruins of a post office or department store, ebulliently spitting jets of brown atrazine-tainted bilge at each other. The detasseling crew had to pass over several bridges on the way to the fields, and there were worries about the stability of the flood-battered supports. We were aghast when the crew leaders showed up on the first morning piloting a caravan of the short buses of playground legend. (The logic apparently being that in case of a bridge collapse it was better to have us drown in batches instead of all at once.)

There was some muttering in the ranks of quitting on the spot, that this was an unacceptable indignity, but in the end everyone climbed aboard. We were spurred on by visions of the massive sums our labors would bring, four, five, perhaps even six hundred dollars, surely enough in our estimation to purchase whatever our hearts desired. Besides, the sun wasn't quite up and the girls whose contempt we risked by riding through town in short buses were still fast asleep between clean pastel-colored sheets, not to rise for hours yet for their cushy jobs in the air-conditioned Dairy Queen or lightly trafficked mall stores, and even if by some staggering coincidence they'd happened upon us there in the dawn, let's be honest, they didn't know who the hell we were anyway.

This was the first job for almost everyone there, and we had the sensation of being carried out of childhood and into the foyer of adulthood. Most of us were between thirteen and fifteen, old enough to work but not to drive, but there were also a few adults on the crew, leather-faced veterans decked out in ponchos and work gloves and pollen-proof safety goggles. They kept up a poker face, but it was clear they were crestfallen to find themselves in our company. For our part, we couldn't imagine what misfortune could possibly have befallen them that had consigned them to the same labor hell as us, but we steered well clear of them, just in case it was contagious.

Our first field was adjacent to a massive hog lot. Floodwaters had completely overrun the land. The field, which lay downhill from the hog lot, was swamped with a knee-deep mélange of pesticides, topsoil, and hog shit. As dark as crude oil, it rebated no light and in the ninety-five-degree humidity the smell was truly staggering. We all stood in the grainy dawn regarding this stinking lagoon. We weren't actually expected to wade into this, were we? We were. The supervisors all but shoved us in, circulating behind and bellowing for us to go on now, time was money and what were we afraid of, a little mud? This was all relayed of course from high ground. One detasseler dipped a toe into the mess and then jumped in. His entry made no ripple and almost no sound, just the barest muffled flump. He was short and the filth came up past his waist. We held our collective breath, but thirty seconds passed and when he neither went into convulsions nor dropped dead we figured what the hell.

The corn was six feet tall, and we made excruciatingly slow progress wading through the muck with our arms extended overhead, our shoulders cramping and hands tingling. When the corn grew taller we had to bend each stalk downward to reach the tassel, which slowed our progress almost entirely. By my estimation my row was a little over a mile long, and it was several hours before I emerged on the other side. The supervisors were sitting on the rear bumper of the bus playing cards in their pristine work clothes, and when we filed past to the water cooler, they pulled their bandannas up over their noses and shot us dirty looks.

At lunch we sat in the bus eating our baloney sandwiches with brown-flecked hands. Some people complained about the conditions, but Jimmy opined that it wasn't so bad and even had its advantages.

Like what, I asked.

Well, he said, for example...if you had to go to the bathroom, you could just go. No more tromping the length of the row back to the porta potty or finding a secluded spot and squatting and fumbling with wetnaps or folded napkins for wiping. Why bother dropping your pants when they were already soaked through with pig diarrhea? From his tone it was clear he was speaking not theoretically but from direct and recent experience.

I shook my head in disgust. You're fucked up, man, I said.

But the logic of his words was indisputable and later that afternoon after pondering the half-mile-walk back to the porta potty I found that he was right. It was almost pleasant, the warmth spreading secretly across the front and back of your pants like a diaper made of sunlight. Riding home that afternoon after a long day, the bus was filled with a ghastly odor, and my mother made me strip down and hose off in the yard, neighbors be damned. By the end of the week most of us were weepy with pinkeye, racked with dysentery, our arms and hands covered with angry red infected scrapes...

On the bus ride back to town at the end of the first Friday, I wondered aloud if there was a worse job to be had on earth. Jimmy shrugged and said it didn't matter if there were worse jobs or better jobs because this was the job that we had and besides, all jobs were bad jobs, just ask his dad who we both had seen come home in the evening and go straight to work on the heavy bag hung in their screened-in back porch as we retreated meek and inconspicuous out the side door. It was plain from Jimmy's tone that he'd accepted this future as his own, but I had other thoughts. As Jimmy launched into his usual monologue on the transformative and aphrodisiacal virtues of Air Jordans, I comforted myself with thoughts of my future adult job, a fairly compensated, fulfilling position free of pointless drudgery and with no bosses or supervisors of inferior character hovering over my shoulder, making twice the money for half the work, and so forth.

It's fortunate that children have no idea what life holds for them, because if they did they'd have no will at all to go on.

The next field had been flooded, too, but the waters had since receded. Unfortunately, the ankle-deep mud left behind was in some ways even worse than the bog we'd just left. The mud was thick and puttylike, and after just a few strides we had to totter along, dragging our feet monstrously swollen with mud. A few of us tried to fashion crude pampooties out of plastic grocery bags, but the ground sucked them off almost straightaway. Jimmy and I were put into adjacent rows, but after just a few dozen feet we had to rest from the strain of dragging our clotted feet along.

Just keep thinking about those Jordans, I said sarcastically. Jimmy showed me his middle finger.

On the right, one of our fellow detasselers cruised by at a fast walk, barefoot in the mud with his shoes tied together by their laces and slung around his neck. When he saw us crouching there in our rows, he stopped and waggled one shoeless foot at us.

You should try it, he said. You can walk much faster and the mud doesn't stick like it does to your shoes. Receiving no answer, he shrugged and continued on his way and had soon disappeared into the field.

Fuckin' hippie, said Jimmy.

The rows were so long, the work so tedious, especially on days like this, that it became a matter of psychological survival to resign yourself to walking forever. (Put another way, this was when I first grasped the key to adult life—abandon all hope!) When you did emerge from the other end of the field after having maintained this present-tense trance state for the previous hour or two, you were too surprised to know whether to be surprised or angry or relieved. And then came the real work of recommitting yourself to the next row, now once again conscious of your lot. It was impossible not to feel a little resentment that this was what we were forced to—and for what? The fields we worked were tasked for industrial use—the corn earmarked to make pseudo-green government-subsidized ethanol or high fructose corn syrup for the legions of wheezing American sofa manatees or cheap feed for the huddled millions of animals in corporate megafarms, whose existences were come to think of it not so different in outline than our own, born into involuntary understimulated servitude, housed, yes, fed, yes, but only nominally alive and only as valuable as what they produced.

Later that day we were eating lunch, engulfed in clouds of marble-sized horseflies, when I noticed the industrious barefoot fellow sitting next to us. I elbowed Jimmy and winked.

I just hope there's no cockworm in this field, I said.

Jimmy shuddered theatrically.

Our friend looked over. What's that, he asked.

Cockworm? I shrugged. It's just what it sounds like. It's a little worm that lives in the mud out here. It can get in through a cut or your eyes or mouth or even your feet. It just wriggles right under the toenail, up into your arteries and stuff, and goes and sets up camp in your peehole.

What does it do then?

What does it do? Jimmy and I exchanged incredulous glances. Whatever it wants, that's what it does. Sometimes it lays eggs in your scrotum, and then when the larva hatch they eat their way out. Sometimes it just stays in the peehole and gets bigger and bigger until it's totally blocked and you have to get this surgery where they put a little spout on your lower back and then your mom has to drain out the excess pee and cum for you every few hours for the rest of your life. And then other times it'll just kind of wind its way around and around the inside of the your cock until all the blood flow is pinched off, and then your cock turns black and shrivels up and finally falls off.

Happened to half the crew last summer, said Jimmy. That's why I wear a cup.

We spent the rest of our lunch eating in silence, Jimmy and I exchanging mirthful half-smiles at the expense of our companion. Later that afternoon we saw him laboring along at a snail's pace in his heavy mudcaked boots, and the next morning he wasn't at the pickup point when the bus arrived. When it became clear he'd quit, Jimmy and I shared a hearty laugh at this small victory, and kept laughing the whole bus ride there, until we arrived at the field and realized we'd have to work faster and longer to make up for his absence.

One of the girls on the detasseling crew was discomfitingly beautiful, tall and dark haired and striking even in a baggy flannel shirt and hip waders. We all wondered why she didn't get an easy job in town, and we would've asked her except that her presence rendered us mute with terror. One night on the way home, Jimmy and I decided that one of us would approach her. I was chosen because I was slightly less cowardly and knew a few big words from books, which, as we all know, beautiful women find highly arousing. ("Long words, long _____.")

Just butter her up, Jimmy instructed me, and then arrange some sort of double date. And make sure the friend she brings for me is good looking.

The next morning as the whole crew of us walked from bus to field, Jimmy elbowed me as he consumed his standard breakfast of Ecto-Cooler juice box and two Hostess cupcakes.

The girl—I think her name was Monica—was as usual walking all alone in front. (All the males lagged behind to ogle her.)

Here's our chance, said Jimmy.

I had no idea what to do. I was very good at talking about talking to girls, but horrible at actually talking to them. But I didn't want to seem cowardly in front of Jimmy, so I jogged up past the incredulous mass of boys and fell into step beside the girl.

Hey, I said.

She looked at me without curiosity. Hey, she said.

A long uninflected silence elapsed between us, and I heard a few derisive chuckles from behind.

Those are nice gloves, I said, pointing to the work gloves tucked into the front pocket of her overalls. Those are the good kind, they got that sticky stuff on the palms so it's easier to pull the tassels.

She looked down at her gloves and then at me. Yes, that's true, she said.

I used to have a pair like that, I said. I could feel thirty pairs of eyes on me as I spoke, and my entire body began to prickle with heat. But I left them on the bus and someone stole them.

Huh, she said. Another interminable silence. And then she said, are you accusing me of stealing your gloves?

No, I said. And I wasn't. It had never occurred to me at all, but now that she mentioned it, they did bear more than a passing resemblance to my missing pair. Why, did you steal them?

What?! She laughed incredulously.

They do look like my gloves, I said. Can I see them? My initials were on the cuffs. My mom wrote them there with a marker.

Fuck off, she said, and quickened her pace.

When I fell back beside Jimmy, he was wide eyed with admiration.

So what'd you say to her?!

Well, I said, I said I'd noticed her and that I think she'd noticed me noticing her.

Oh man, that's awesome. And what'd she say?

She said yes she had...

And what'd you say?

I said that maybe we should get together, go to a movie or something.

And then what'd she say? Jimmy asked.

Then she said that her parents were going out of town this weekend and that I should come over and we could drink some beers and talk and stuff and maybe I could sleep over, too.

Jimmy nearly choked on his Ecto-Cooler. And then what'd you say?!

I asked if she had a friend she could invite along so I could bring you, since you were my right-hand man and best pal.

Yes, and?

She said no, she wanted it to be just me and her, so I said just forget the whole thing, me and Jimmy are a package deal. Then she got mad and was like, fuck off, and then she stormed off. You saw her.

Shit, exclaimed Jimmy. His juice box emitted a wheeze as he crumpled it in one hand. That fucking bitch, he said. He turned to stare balefully out at the cornfield, as if to locate the source of the forces which seemed to frustrate him at every turn. He clutched his remaining cupcake in one hand, now forgotten...

You going to finish that cupcake? I asked. Jimmy made a dismissive noise and tossed it to me. I took it and swallowed it in two bites.

Thanks, pal, I said.

When we started our day's work at dawn, the corn was heavy with dew and five feet into the first row I was soaked through to the bone. I would spend the next few hours shivering, but as the sun climbed higher I was gradually steamed dry, and at noon we convened at the bus for lunch all smelling like infected feet. In the early afternoon, the humidity thickened and the heat became almost liquid. Many days it was hard to breathe and hard to even move, the heavy air pressing down on us like an embarrassing memory. One day deep into a row I came upon a girl about my age, bent over at the waist and desperately hyperventilating.

Are you all right?

I think I've got heatstroke, she wheezed, looking at me with eyes rolling, her face blotchy red.

You're all right, I said with extravagant assurance.

No, I'm not, she said, her voice trembling. I could see tears streaming down her face. I think I'm going to pass out.

You're not going to pass out, I said dismissively. No one ever really passes out except on TV.

This was (and to this day remains) my strategy when confronted with someone else's distress, to deny its existence in the hopes that doing so will actually make it so. (No wonder all my girlfriends end up hating me.)

A fellow detasseler emerged from an adjacent row, took one look at the sick girl, and sprinted back in the direction of the bus and the crew leaders. Eventually the heat-stricken girl was carried back to the bus on a trash bag stretcher, tucked in a shady corner, and swaddled in ice. For a while we all thought our day might end early, but unfortunately she didn't require hospitalization.

When I boarded the bus at the end of the day, I found the girl lying on her back on Jimmy's and my customary seat. She looked wan and exhausted, all but her face encased by cold packs, but her eyes followed me as I approached, sharp with recognition.

I told you it was nothing! I said cheerfully, showing her a thumbs-up.

* * *

One late morning as I shuffled mindlessly along, my arms working of their own volition, I heard cries from up ahead. Emerging into a large clearing I found a dozen of my fellow detasselers huddled around a plot of vaguely familiar non-corn plants.

One of them turned to me and squeezed my arm. Can you fucking believe this, he exclaimed.

I said that no, I couldn't believe it, though I had no idea what he was talking about. All of them were wild eyed as they denuded the plants, stuffing handfuls of greenery into their pockets and hats and socks and lunch boxes. Other detasselers were trickling into the clearing and, once they'd assessed the situation, quickly got in on the frantic harvest. One of them was a boy from my junior high school who did a little jig and waved me over.

Look at all this pot, man! He was shaking. This is worth, like, millions of dollars!

Pot! *Marah-wanner*, pronounced in the flat nasal tones of our elementary school gym teacher, who doubled as instructor of the drug prevention class. Vile demon weed, catalyst of nymphomania and thrill-killings, gateway drug (?!) to baser evils, a single puff leading incontrovertibly to a life of dirty needles, suburban home invasions, and scabby-lipped fellatio in train station restrooms. All I knew was that anything that our authority figures so firmly admonished us against had to be downright spectacular. I also knew from television (my father never missed an episode of *Miami Vice*) that drugs were worth their weight in gold. I joined in the picking frenzy, plucking plant after plant until my shorts were bulging with contraband. As my bounty grew I mentally tabulated my take; a new bike, no, a new moped, a fleet of mopeds, my college education, Ivy League no less, a Corvette for when I turned sixteen, perhaps even a Lamborghini, a yellow Countach just like the one on my Trapper Keeper. Fuck Jimmy and his stupid Air Jordans, I'd hire Michael Jordan himself to come to my fifteenth birthday party, to dunk successively on each of my teenage rivals, first with basketballs and then with balloons filled with urine (why not?), all in full sight of the girls in my class, the hottest of whom would at this point be writhing with lust on top of my aforementioned yellow Lamborghini Countach, the hood of which was airbrushed with various tasteful graphics; naked buxom harlots, flames, Wolverine.

After a few minutes there was nothing left but a crater of churned topsoil. The latecomers had even taken the stalks and clots of roots, on the off chance that these too might be valuable. One by one we slunk back into the rows, to continue our labors but now halfheartedly, as we were all in our own minds now rich men.

The news got out, as news tends to get out, and at the end of the day when we boarded the bus, the crew leader stood up front eyeing us coldly.

This bus will not move until every last bit of contraband has been removed, he said.

No one moved.

Right now! I want those drugs off this bus now, or I'll search every one of you! He and his two lackeys stood with hands on hips, trying to exude resolve, but we weren't moved. If there's one thing children are good at, it's reading intent, and we could tell he was unprepared to carry out his threat.

You can't search us, someone in back yelled. We've got rights!

Yeah, I saw it on television, said another kid. It's illegal to search us, even if we have a seizure!

The foreman regarded us with disgust. Illegal?! Drugs are illegal!

He had us there. But we didn't care. If we'd been willing to labor under a molten sun for ten hours a day wrenching cornstalks, we'd endure much worse for the presumptive bonanza secreted away in our underpants. Just as my father had predicted, my summer of detasseling had taught me the value of a dollar. I had learned that while corporate agribarons made millions, and card-playing supervisors pulled in low five figures for laissez-faire babysitting, we at the bottom had to slog through a literal ocean of shit for the smallest legally allowable pittance, that each penny we earned was bought not only with our labors but with our dignity, the knowledge that we were being taken advantage of and that there was nothing we could do about it except grind forward until we ourselves moved up the ladder, at which point we would be granted the privilege of exploiting our underlings. *Of course* our underpants bonanza was illegal, for what was legality except the means by which power maintained its privileges? As kids subject to the slightest whims of adults, we understood this instinctively.

Unfortunately, as generations of would-be revolutionaries will tell you, solidarity is easier in principle than in practice. The supervisors retired to a shady spot twenty feet from the bus and let us bake in our aluminum bread box. We opened all the windows but the air was completely inert. The odor of thirty sweltering adolescents not yet acquainted with the wonders of deodorant, wearing mildewed fertilizer-soaked rags not laundered for a week and perhaps never at all, in a confined space. I don't think it even took five minutes for the first boy to cave. One by one we all slunk outside and turned our pockets out, and as the ranks of the repenters grew so did the pressure on the holdouts. Jimmy and I weren't in the first wave but we weren't in the last, either. We were still on probation for various petty crimes and as we sat in the bus it slowly dawned on us what it might mean if the supervisors just turned us over to the authorities. At best we'd get stuck with another fifty hours of garbage duty, and at worst we'd be shipped off to the state home for troubled boys and left to hold our own against peers who shaved daily and made knives out of toothbrush handles.

At the end of an hour there was an impressive pile of marijuana beside the bus, tattered wilted leaves intermingled with pocket lint and gum wrappers. The head man strolled over and stood looking at it, shaking his head. Finally he climbed aboard the bus and started the engine.

All right, let's get back to town, he said, adjusting the mirrors. By the way—you're all fired.

The bus stopped just long enough in town to disgorge us all and then sped back toward the city limits. (It wasn't until years later that I realized the bosses had probably kept the pot for themselves.) A few of us exchanged dazed insincere goodbyes and then trickled off in various directions. Jimmy and I walked to a nearby convenience store to call our parents for a ride home.

We were known in town as devious little kleptos and at our approach most shopkeepers either barred the entrance or openly followed us from aisle to aisle like we were gypsies. But since we'd joined the ranks of the proletariat, we'd noticed that we were treated differently. Our soiled boots and grass-stained jeans and sun-darkened necks marked us as decent working folk and the shopkeepers who'd previously shunned us now greeted us with deferential nods of recognition. We immediately exploited our newfound respectability by ransacking the shit out of these places. On this day, while I conspicuously examined a rack of work gloves in the front of the store (I go through about three pairs of these a week! I told the clerk), Jimmy moved through the aisles and filled his cooler with all our favorite cakes and candies.

While we sat on the curb waiting for my mom to pick us up, we gorged ourselves on cheap snack cakes with the consistency of wet Styrofoam and epoxylike fluorescent taffies and other miscellaneous junk nonfoods, all of which had been sweetened with corn syrup derived from our very labors, though we took little pride in our hand in their origins, as we generally discarded each item after only a bite or two.

I'm going to kind of miss this job, Jimmy said, his mouth ringed with pink-dyed coconut flakes.

But of course there appeared in my mailbox one day soon after the largest paycheck of my life. Each time I recounted the sheaf of bills in the cigar box under my bed, a little more of my bitterness over my summer of labor evaporated. *Over six hundred dollars!* I literally couldn't think of a single thing I desired that wasn't now within my grasp.

The week before school started, my family went on a shopping trip to the Mall of America. Eight hours in the family car hot-boxed in bodily odors, shooting like a bottle rocket up through the Iowa hill country, one-stoplight towns of almost cruel modesty, sprung up around meatpacking plants and gypsum mines. I tried to read comic books but I was too restless. Hailing as we did from small-town Iowa, we'd had little access to the upper echelons of name-brand consumer goods. Most of the brands we'd seen on television and in magazines were completely inaccessible to us. This trip was our chance to take part in the cultural discourse carried out through the careful selection of consumer signifiers. My sister and I passed the time parsing the connotations of various name brands: what did a Ralph Lauren–striped rugby say about who you were as a person as opposed to, say, layered pastel-colored Gap T-shirts? Were our personalities better advertised by the urban dynamism of Nike Air running shoes or the counterintuitive drabness of British Knights? The reactionary traditionalism of a brown Chess King leather bomber jacket or the rebel cachet of a black leather Banana Republic jacket? The hypermodernity of the acid-washed cargo jeans (with elastic ankle bands!) or the retro-wholesomeness of Levi's 501s?

The Mall of America! The name was almost redundant, for what could be more American than a mall? It was the mall to end all malls, just as America, in that period between the collapse of the Soviet Union and 9/11, truly seemed to be the nation to end all nations. In the center of the Mall of America, where other more modestly proportioned shopping centers had an Orange Julius or an old-timey gag photo booth, there was a full-size indoor roller coaster. Why? Because they could, of course. (Again, what could be more American?) Why build the world's largest mall around an indoor amusement park? Why a store that sold only silk T-shirts, another that sold only Elvis memorabilia, another that sold only commemorative plates? Well, why not? To argue the point of fundamental superfluity was, I had learned, to devalue in a single stroke the majority of what might be described as modern life in America. And where did that leave a naïve understimulated Midwestern teenager to turn? Like most people, I had learned to avoid questions whose answers complicated my immediate existence...

I must have walked ten miles that day, crisscrossing that indoor city in search of just the right items. During the long ride home I slept better, it seemed, than I had in years.

The next day I laid my purchases out on my bed, all in a row like corpses at a crash site. I tried on various outfits I'd purchased; the "limited edition" Ralph Lauren T-shirt emblazoned with little multicolored fish, the violet-and-turquoise officially licensed Charlotte Hornets hooded sweatshirt, the billowy Levi's ornamented with a profusion of pointless loops and pockets. But as I modeled them in the full-length mirror in my room, something was clearly wrong. I had, finally and decisively, acquired the coveted clothes. They were "cool"; that was beyond debate, but though I was wearing them, it was obvious even to the casual observer that I myself was still not cool. What I was seeing in the mirror was the same slump-shouldered bowlegged sour-faced half-Asian crustached uber-poseur as before, now draped in low-end designer clothes but still unmistakably not…cool…*at all*. Clearly, something was wrong here. Perhaps the clothes were in some way defective. Perhaps they had to be washed first to achieve maximum effect. I turned this way and that, made various facial expressions, parted my hair on the opposite side, put on some music, but no, no matter what I did, I was still definitely a loser. How could this be? Was coolness not something that could be bought off the rack, or conjured up at will by the simple donning of the "right" products? My God, I thought as I stood there in my gaudily colored patchwork, if you can't trust television commercials, what *can* you trust?!

Jimmy came over the night before school started, shuffling heavy-footed up into my yard in his bulbous Air Jordans. At the end of his spindly legs they looked like the cement shoes of a mafia snitch. We sat on my front porch talking of anything but our summer of labor and its questionable fruit. As we regarded each other in our clownish finery, I was thankful and I think Jimmy was, too, that our skin had been broiled deep brown from the field work, as it concealed the flush that now spread itself across our faces as we realized what fools we were. I never wore any of the clothes I bought, and when my mom donated them to charity the next summer most of them still had their tags attached.

It was a sordid chapter in my development, and one that I'd like to put behind me, but I'm reminded of it every time I visit my parents' house. On their living room wall hangs a school portrait taken days after the close of detasseling season that year. My face in this picture is a deep bronze, but my forehead is blindingly white except for a small brown trapezoid in the center, the result of having worn a backwards baseball cap all summer in the sunny fields. I've asked my parents several times to take it down, but they just laugh and refuse. They like to point it out to guests.

CHAPTER 3

Shoplifting Interlude

or, How to Lose Ten Pounds in One Week (Starve)

This morning when I brushed my teeth I had to suppress an urge to swallow my toothpaste. My stomach kept trying to convince my mouth it was ice cream. It's about six months before I would sell this book, and I'm broke. I've eaten every last edible item in the cupboards, for the past week consuming makeshift dinners of anchovies and plain spaghetti, dusty dented cans of soup I ate with my fingers crossed against botulism, an enormous pot of unspiced quinoa I picked at for days and finally, as a last resort, reconstituted bowls of brothless kelp from an enormous bag I found under the sink, left by a health-conscious ex-girlfriend, having to piece together the cooking instructions from the pidgin English on the label (STIRRING 120CC OF "WATHR" AND FOR A KING LONG HARD BROTH 30–45 YES!!!). I'd never looked better (is it possible to get down to zero percent body fat? If it is, I was) but I guess that as of today I'd officially commenced starving...

How did this happen? Too many bar tabs, too many cab rides, too many deluxe hangover breakfasts. The next unemployment check is still days away and my savings amount to a stocking cap full of change, and not a lot of silver among the copper, either. Rifling through the sofa brings a half-handful more, but total I've got just a few dollars. There's always someone who'll pick up a bar tab, so I've got the really important thing covered (one must keep one's priorities straight!), but what about food?

I was usually driven by more abstract imperatives, so, with apologies to all the doe-eyed famine-stricken African kids in those commercials, I found starving to be a somewhat novel experience. Here now was an unambiguous physical imperative! Sex was rooted in the corporeal, too, but even it could be easily spoiled by all kinds of mushily aesthetic considerations: *What's with her stupid Aniston hair? What does a fake tan say about someone? Nothing good. Doesn't all this moaning seem a little over the top? Am I obligated to match her enthusiasm? OH GOSH, YES, THIS IS SOMEWHAT BETTER THAN ADEQUATE! Oh man, I hate myself.*

But now that I was starving, I had finally gone past any kind of subtler considerations. I had a sense that the body was really just a machine like any other, and that it required fuel, and that I was rapidly approaching the point where I didn't care what form that fuel took. Forget organic or free-range or fair trade or no trans-fat or whole grain or fat-free; another twelve hours with no food and I'd eat the contents of disposable diapers, and happy to do so.

And it was too bad I'd gotten to this point, where food was once again an adversary to be stared down and bested, because since I'd gone on unemployment I really felt I'd recovered some kind of purity of motive when it came to eating. Long gone were the days of bored cubicle grazing, hourly coffees with whole milk and four sugars, three-thousand-calorie lunches at sushi buffets, what we used to call "office ass" at my last job, where you expanded at a rate of about 5 percent a month the entire time you worked there, until you either got fired or laid off or died from congestive heart failure. Now that

I was broke, from necessity I ate brown rice and vegetables and black coffee and only occasionally meat or sweets, and since I was no longer chronically understimulated and over-stressed this struck my palate as perfectly adequate. I'd lost all the excess weight I'd put on and I felt better than I had in years. And I thought back to my last job, where the CEO regu-larly missed board meetings because the sad fat fucker had gout from eating too much pâté and veal and sweetbreads and wine, and even when he came in he tottered down the halls obese and wincing at the stabbing pains in his joints, and if there's a better metaphor for the ravages of office life, well, I don't feel like coming up with it right now...

I took up my stocking cap of change and walked to the grocery store. In most cities there are three tiers of grocery stores; bourgeois emporiums hawking organic locally grown fare aimed at progressives with money to burn; midrange stores offering sensible bargains and traditional fare for middle-class families; and then at the bottom there's the inner-city grocery store where all the carts have three working wheels and there are brawls in the aisles hourly. The place I went to had a policeman posted there full-time, and the week before I'd seen a sparrow flitting down the bread aisle suddenly felled by a broom swung by a stockboy and cursorily stomped.

What to buy with only a hatful of pennies? First and fore-most I had to consider the dollar-to-calorie ratio. Nothing fresh, certainly nothing green. Nothing very perishable. I perused bags of dried beans, rice, pasta. Four pounds of chick-en for four dollars! Plain oatmeal—hadn't there been an eccentric nobleman who'd lived to a hundred and ten on nothing but plain oatmeal?

I was making these value calculations when I saw my friend Kyle wheeling his cart down the aisle. It had been several weeks since the lawn-mower incident, and we hadn't seen each other since. We greeted each other with a sly complicity, as if we were afraid to let on to our fellow shoppers that we'd hit the antisocial's jackpot.

How's it going, he asked with a twinkle in his eye. You still on unemployment?

Of course. You?

Oh yes. Almost a year now. A year next month.

I just hit two years, I said with extravagantly false modesty.

Kyle grinned. Allow me to shake your hand, sir.

We shook hands, snickering.

I saw some politician on television the other day pontificating about the latest unemployment extension, Kyle said. He was saying how people on unemployment want to work, they want nothing more than to work, but there just aren't any jobs and so they have to stay on unemployment.

I laughed. Oh yeah, I want nothing more than to rise at dawn and take a packed cattle car to some horrible fucking office eight hours a day. That sounds way better than just cashing free checks!

Please, no more leisure, said Kyle. I want to take orders from inferior people and make rich people richer. That's what I really want in life!

How may I contribute to society? I asked, rubbing my chin. Because if every man, woman, and child in America isn't miserable, the terrorists will have won!

Is there data I can enter? Kyle asked. I'll work for free; I just want to be part of something! A cash register I could man? A broom to push?

We paused and then burst into laughter, bent over our carts.

Something about his cart caught my eye, and I scrutinized its contents. Crab legs, Amish fruit preserves, French bread, a stack of pies from the bakery. I rifled through these goods in open disbelief. How can you afford all this?

Kyle looked left and then right and then gestured for me to

lean in closer. There's a crackhead in my neighborhood who sells me his food stamps, he said. Pennies on the dollar. Pennies. All this stuff is costing me less than ten dollars.

My God, I said. Does he have more to sell?

Nah, said Kyle. This is it for the month. Come by next week, though, and he should have more. I'll introduce you, he's got this whole network.

Kyle and I made plans to go on a drinking spree later in the week, and then he went to the front of the store to signal his accomplice to come in and swipe his food stamp card. I wandered down the aisle dazed at the plenty I'd seen in his cart. I regarded my dried navy beans and plain oatmeal with resentment. I had to give it to Kyle, he was resourceful. Black market food stamps! You had to make your own luck, that was clear.

And really, why should I settle for a week of subsistence on whole grains? Let's say that I stole some food—who'd suffer? Taking food from another man's cupboard would ensure that he'd starve, and therein lay the crime. But let's say I took something from a grocery store shelf. Who suffered? No one. How much would I have to shoplift to move the store's stock price even a cent, or to raise the retail price by the same amount? Truckloads at a minimum. Sure, stealing was illegal, technically, but so was jaywalking. So was sodomy in some precincts! So was milking unemployment, and that certainly didn't hurt anyone! I was starving—should my own welfare really take a backseat to some amorphous highly specious conception of the general welfare? Really? If you wanted to make that argument, I'd gladly listen to you and then laugh in your face. Once again I was up against that particularly modern invention, the most absurd of oxymorons, the victimless crime.

So then to practical considerations. How to do the deed? I thought back to my days of juvenile delinquency, all the little tricks I'd learned. Act friendly and natural, attract no attention, monitor all lanes of visibility, be patient, but when the moment of opportunity arrived, one had to act decisively and swiftly. Ironic that then I'd stolen to alleviate boredom and now I did it out of necessity.

I carried no bag, so my loot would have to be secreted under my coat. Unfortunately I was wearing a snug jacket. Very little room to spare between chest and coat. Going down my mental list of favored foods, I realized that none of them would be shopliftable in current circumstances. There's nothing I like more in the morning than a bowl of Raisin Bran, but I had no hope of concealing a box of cereal under my coat, let alone a quart of milk. If only I was obese; I'd be able to hide a month's worth of groceries in my billowy garments. Curse my ectomorphic Asian genes!

I perused the shelves for flat, shopliftable goods. Slowly I accumulated a nice flat assortment of edibles; a bulk pack of Reese's peanut butter cups, Indian flatbread (seemingly made for shoplifting), and a couple pounds of New York strip, the shrink-wrapped family pack. I found a deserted aisle, checked for cameras and stockboys, and shoved the three flats under the waistband of my pants. I pulled my shirt down over the pilfered goods and fluffed it to look inconspicuous. The items were five or six inches thick and I had to suck my stomach in to prevent them from protruding noticeably. I could inhale perhaps a quarter-breath at a time. As I sauntered toward the checkout registers, whistling jauntily and greeting every clerk and fellow customer with cartoonish good cheer—*nothin' suspicious 'bout me!*—I became increasingly light-headed from oxygen deprivation.

I found the surliest clerk and placed my single bag of dried beans on the conveyor belt. She didn't even look at me as she recited her spiel with an indifference I knew firsthand. *Couponscreditordebitpushthegreenbutton.* I thought I was going to make it, but she just had to count the change I gave her twice! When I was just on the point of passing out I chanced a deep breath, and as my torso expanded and then snapped back I felt cellophane tearing. Cold beef drippings trickled down my legs and a dozen loose peanut butter cups fell down into my long underwear, settling around my sockline. My posture of affected casualness took on a deranged aspect, but I otherwise maintained the façade. As I walked past the security guard and exited the store, with military posture and striding along with utmost delicacy, I appeared at this, arguably my lowest moment, as dignified as I ever had in my life.

CHAPTER 4

The Sweet Smell of Futility

or, Unplanned Obsolescence

One summer during college I got sick of drinking twenty-five-cent beers at sports bars and smoking ditchweed out of gouged apples and dropping shitty LSD that made your stomach hurt for days afterward, sitting in dilapidated houses with no functional plumbing, talking up art films you'd never shoot and books you'd never write and bands you'd never start, ordering pizza from several different places when you were broke and then telling the delivery guy that nah, you didn't order no pizza, it's your goddamn ex-girlfriend trying to get your goat—she orders pizzas and taxis and cleaning crews to your apartment morning, noon, and night just to make you miserable, but hey, why don't you just leave the pizza here, you're going to throw it out anyway, right?

So I went home. I figured I'd enjoy some peace and quiet and get some reading done and sleep in a bed instead of on someone's imploded burlap-upholstered sofa. Free meals, free laundry, what could be better? My parents, however, had other ideas. They'd gotten used to having the house to themselves and my goody-two-shoes sister, a straight-A high school student, and here I was suddenly slouching unkempt around the house contaminated with dangerous university ideas, sleeping late and giving my sister subversive books like Henry Miller's "Tropical Unicorn," whatever the hell that is.

Worse yet, I'd announced that I wanted to be a writer. Before their eyes they were witnessing the slow dissolution of their most precious dream, the dream of the first-generation immigrant son making good. My mother was more progressive in her ambitions for me than most immigrant parents—I could become a doctor *or* a lawyer. She'd graciously let me decide which one, as long as I kept the real goal in mind, that of the highest office in the land. After all, I'd been named after FDR; while pregnant my mother had seen a television program about "the greatest president," and Koreans believe that if you name a child after a great man, that child takes on the great man's characteristics. And now here the culmination of two decades of hopes, a child they'd very literally hoped would become the greatest president in American history, was announcing he wanted to be a writer, which is like saying he's majoring in rejection and dope-smoking and repeatedly borrowing money, which he has every intention of paying back but never quite does...

My father sat me down and told me that if I was going to turn my back on guaranteed white-collar job security, I would have to get a job to see what my future might hold. Just so I understood what I was doing. I told him that I'd be happy to get a job, that in fact I'd love to get a job (hee!), but that as he knew full well, jobs in Burlington, Iowa, were few and far between, and even the detasseling crews had already met their quotas.

Well, he said, taking out a folded newspaper, I looked in the Help Wanted ads today, and I think I found something for you.

Knowing in retrospect what was to come, I'm ashamed to say that when I saw what he'd circled, I felt not dread or disappointment, but relief. *Workers needed, Vista Cookie Factory, all shifts.* A cookie factory? What could be more pleasant than light work amid the pleasant aromas of warm pastry? I almost laughed out loud. Perhaps I could be a taster, flitting deliriously from batter vat to frosting vat, dipping a pinky into each one, more sugar here, less vanilla there, arm in arm and laughing with my fellow elves, yes, elves, I'd seen the commercials. We'd be singing all day in unison, merry undirge-like tunes with choruses of yum-yum-yum, and would they provide me with a pair of those shoes with pointy toes that curled up at the ends, or would I have to bring my own? Even the name—Vista—sounded appealing, with its intimations of floor-to-ceiling windows overlooking green horizons. *I hope my spot on the line has a good view*, I remember thinking.

You may be surprised to hear that the reality of working at a cookie factory was not like that at all. No songs, and no elves, either. (I do recall a single midget, though she was not the least bit merry.) Mornings began with a trudge through a massive parking lot enclosed with a chain-link fence topped with barbed wire. Before the first whistle people sat in their cars taking little slugs from pint bottles or smoking various substances, fortifying themselves for what was to come and ruing whatever misfortunes had led them to this. Work took place in a Soviet-style concrete bunker of alienating proportions, sooty cement floors, walls latticed everywhere with exposed pipes and cables, rickety scaffolding and smoking conveyor belts and grinding gears all glistening with black grease like the bastard nightmare of Charles Dickens and H. R. Giger.

I found my way to the office, and the floor manager gave me a quick tour.

Here are the forklifts, here's the break room, here's the packaging line, where you'll be working. He made a quick flapping motion with one hand that said it was all the same anyway. After a few minutes, we came to a long row of huge aluminum vats into which cranelike steel robot arms plunged downward. When I realized what I was looking at, I perked up.

Oh, is this where you make the batter and the frosting?

That's right, said the manager, picking at a scab on the back of his hand.

Maybe I could work in this section for the first week, I said, tasting the batter and frosting and making suggestions about ingredients. I have a very good sense of taste. I could just, like, dip a pinky in each vat once an hour and make sure it was, you know...yummy enough.

The manager regarded me distastefully. I think the mixing arms would rip your arm clean out of the socket if you tried to reach in there, he said. But go ahead and give it a try if you want.

The tour ended in the employee locker room. All personnel were required to wear a makeshift biohazard suit of hairnet and surgical cap, elbow-length gloves, smock, and floor-length apron while working. God forbid a stray hair contaminated a package of ninety-nine-cent zero-nutritional-value artery-clogging cookies. As the manager stood by watching, I assembled the many layers of my barrier suit. It was hot, laborious to put on and take off, and looked utterly foolish. I stood in front of the mirror and regarded myself. I looked vaguely like a white Druid.

How do you feel, kid? The manager asked. You comfortable?

No, I said.

Okay, good. Now get out there. If you're more than five minutes late to your station, you get docked the whole hour.

The section to which I had been assigned consisted of three stations—two slingers and a boxer. The slingers stood alongside a conveyor belt and made sure each tray of cookies contained sixteen units, four rows of four. They had a huge bin of loose cookies to make up any differences, and depending on the temperament of the ancient machine, many packages came out with half the allotted amount or sometimes less, sometimes one or two or no cookies in each row. During these spells we had to shuffle laterally at high speed, frantically slinging pairs or threes of cookies into the trays. If too many underfilled and underweight packages made it to the scaled platform at the end, a deafening klaxon sounded, the conveyor belt ground to a stop, and everyone looked at us like we were fucking idiots. Then the forewoman came over and restarted the equipment at a slightly slower pace. Some days when the cookie loader was particularly out of sorts she just stood at the controls, keyed it to roll out a dozen or so empty trays for us to fill entirely by hand, and then repeated.

Everyone hated this job except for the meth freaks, who didn't care what job they did. One gaunt fellow who filled in on our section when somebody called in sick would stand completely immobile, head down and mouth hanging slack, shuffling cookies into trays at incredible speed for hours straight. During the coffee breaks he scrubbed the counters with equal fervor or stood in the corner drinking a cup of coffee from shaking hands, intermittently breaking out into a little aphasic jig. I saw him one day doing lines in his car and thought about trying to cadge a few from him but decided against it. I was too skinny already, but more than that I begrudged the bosses the benefit of any drug-fueled hyperefficiency.

The other station, the boxer, was at the end of the line. As the packages of cookies emerged warm and hermetically sealed in plastic, the boxer had to stack them in a cardboard box, four rows of eight, lift the box, pivot to the left, and place it on a wooden pallet that would be forklifted away once it was filled. This job was less frantic than tray filling, but by the end of the day half your lower back was shot from the repeated lifting and pivoting. By the end of my first week it was clear that while working at this station for any significant length of time would entirely wreck your body, slinging would entirely wreck your mind, and the schedule of rotation between line stations insured that these twin deteriorations would take place at the same approximate pace. On the other hand, we got free cookies in the break room, so that's something.

I don't know how many people got high or drunk or stoned to get through the day, but it was a significant percentage. At lunch it seemed that ambiguous vapors wafted from every other car, and when the parking lot emptied after my shift there remained an approximate grid of brown-bagged empties. It just wasn't a job that could be done with a clear mind. The Buddhists say that the mind is a monkey. It rebels at this degree of tedium and has to be deadened, if not chemically now then eventually by despair. Each day seemed to last a week and each week a month. By the end of my second week I was barely hanging on. I stopped going outside for smoke breaks because I was afraid that upon seeing a glimpse of sunlight I'd start running and never stop. And yet a lot of my coworkers seemed to deal with it just fine, even without any chemical assistance. Not quite happy, perhaps, but not chafed, either. How did they do it?

And then I realized their secret. A cursory poll of my coworkers revealed that they were almost all single mothers with kids at home and no help from the fathers. This was the source of their endurance; if you have no choice, you're capable of anything, indefinitely. This was a summer job for me—I was just a tourist, and it was no wonder so many of them gave me cold looks in the break room and let me sling on my own while they went out for smokes.

That was the dreadful truth about the factory; no one would ever choose to work there if they had any choice whatsoever. I'd finally arrived at the proverbial margin between rock and hard place. I had always been leery about the idea of having kids, but I'd never quite formulated why until seeing the aftereffects up close. And now it was terrifying! The miracle of conception took on an entirely sinister new aspect, two little zygotes in an instant creating one life and destroying two others. After all, existence is a zero-sum game; life lives on death and vice versa, and while you're taking adorable snapshots of your toddler in his Tigger jammies, does it ever occur to you that his future used to be yours? That you have produced your own replacement? And come to think of it, my friends who had kids really only existed anymore to supply resources to their genetic continuation; that was the subtext to all their complaints that they never got out anymore, couldn't afford to go on vacations anymore, couldn't stay up late anymore, and so forth. On a fundamental level they no longer mattered, they hadn't mattered from the moment that prune-faced slimy little extraterrestrial had slid out of the womb. They were obsolete; the future belonged to someone else! And of course sex is so great, it takes the greatest pleasure to entice you to sign your own death warrant!

And this was the final insult—this job had ruined my lower back, my attention span, my stomach, my confidence in my recently chosen life path, and now it had ruined sex for me.

But on the other hand, we got free cookies.

We were allowed three breaks a day, thirty minutes for lunch and two fifteen-minute breaks at midmorning and midafternoon, all of which we spent in the cavernous windowless break room. We sat around letting time pass while drinking out of Styrofoam cups filled with brown-tinged water dispensed by the coffee machines. Along one wall were massive tubs of broken cookie shards, the one perk of working at the cookie gulag. Everyone ignored them, and I asked the forewoman Simone why no one ate them, were they contaminated or something?

No, they're perfectly all right. Go ahead eat as much as you want, she told me with a shrug. You'll see.

Upon close examination they indeed looked and smelled normal. I ate a handful and then another handful and then began to earnestly gorge myself. Free cookies are free cookies, after all. A few of my coworkers were watching me bemusedly, and I gave them a crumb-speckled smile. The whole rest of the afternoon while I worked I craved more cookies, and during the afternoon break I ate until I almost vomited.

This was on a Monday. By Wednesday I was nibbling one or two with my beige coffee-tinged water and by Friday I couldn't even look at the remaindered cookie tubs. Just the sight of them made my stomach turn. You could've locked me in a warehouse full of the cookies and I would've starved to death inside of a week. The next Monday I was sitting on a bench trying not to think when a new guy sat across from me with a paper plate piled high with cookies.

Can you believe this shit?! he asked me as he shoveled the cookie shards back with both hands. What's wrong with you? Get some!

I'd begun to notice, as I sat in the break room three times a day, sidelong glances cut my way by a bashful red-haired girl who also sat alone. One afternoon she walked over with her coffee cup and sat across from me.

Hello, Franklin, she said.

I looked down at my robe to check if I was wearing a name tag; I wasn't.

How do you know my name?

It turns out that we'd gone to high school together. The fact that I didn't recognize her didn't surprise either of us; I'd drifted through those years in a haze of confused delinquency, doing the minimum (or less) and generally just killing time. I had in fact done more than enough to get expelled many times over, but I'd always performed prodigiously well on the standardized tests the state administered once a year to assess the public school system, and of course the administrators couldn't kick out living proof of their own instructional excellence. Whenever my number of demerits approached a critical level, I'd be assigned a "special" all-day Saturday detention, during which I'd sit around the school offices with my feet up, reading comics and playing cards with the vice principal. (And this was when I learned that second rule of adulthood—the Rules/the Law/the Word are just something that some guy said, and that he or anyone else can just as easily unsay.)

Her name was Annie and she was also working there for the summer. We began to spend our breaks together, talking at the long tables and nibbling on cookie fragments. At first our conversations were intense, like two prisoners on death row, and yet as the days progressed and we should've become closer, we seemed to stray further apart. Working in the massive vaulted atrium of the work floor made us feel tiny, literally physically tiny, and our precisely directed movements, signaled by a constant bombardment of bells and klaxons, had shorn us of any feelings of agency. Even our uniforms, while primarily functional, had rendered us all identical in our white robes and masks and goggles, and on break it sometimes seemed that my hands were working of their own volition and my voice was some kind of queer instrument being played by someone else. We never talked about this—how could you, without sounding insane?—but after a couple of weeks we stopped sitting together, not avoiding each other exactly but just taking the first open seats in the break room, because what did it matter where we sat, what did any of it matter? And as we sat at our separate tables nibbling mechanically on free cookies, I think we were both embarrassed and puzzled at our recently felt anachronistic desire for human contact.

It became clear by August that I wouldn't last the summer. My situation was not desperate and so I hadn't been gifted with the endurance of the desperate. I resented my mother for making me work there, especially since she'd worked in a factory when she was about my age and knew how horrible it was. (This was back in Korea, when she was supporting five siblings and working the line in a candy factory where she smuggled candy out in her upswept hair to feed her starving brothers and sisters while her parents got drunk and lost the family fortune playing cards.) But I knew how miserable my parents were prepared to make me if I quit the job, so I decided to do what I had to do to hang on.

One day at lunch I found the meth zombie coming back from the parking lot and asked him if I could have a moment of his time.

He stopped in his tracks as if jerked on a leash and looked at me with crazed red-rimmed eyes.

What?

I was wondering, I said, and trailed off. Up close I saw how sick and vampiric he looked, and suddenly I wasn't sure if this was such a good idea. I wanted to buy a certain something from you, I said. Some white magic, if you know what I mean.

He recoiled incredulously, tilting his head to the side as if he'd just recognized me.

You want to what?

I want to buy some meth from you. How much is it going to cost me?

Meth? Meth?! He jabbed a finger in my face, first at one eye and then the other and then down at my feet. I knew it! I could tell by your shoes!

What? I looked down at my shoes, soiled gray Nikes. What are you talking about?

Cop shoes! He crowed triumphantly. You're a cop, aren't you? You think it's going to be that easy? You gotta get up earlier in the morning than that, you fucking pig! Fuck you, pig!

He skipped into the warehouse, looking over his shoulder deliriously and screaming, rat, pig, cop, I smell bacon, as a few smokers looked on with amusement.

During the afternoon break I told Simone about what had happened, and she laughed. That's what that shit does, she said. It rots your brain and makes you paranoid.

If he's so far gone, why don't they fire him? I asked.

He's the last guy they'd fire, she said. Haven't you seen him in action? He's the best worker here by a mile.

There was no whimsical firing this time, no wacky scene. I just didn't get out of bed for a week, and then one day my mother shouted from the top of the stairs that the factory had called and I was fired. I thought this was a bit disingenuous, as technically I'd initiated the separation by not going to work for several consecutive days, but I decided it was too much trouble to argue the point. For the next few weeks, every time I closed my eyes I saw a conveyor belt filled with plastic cookie trays, always going just a bit too fast to keep up, and to this day the smell of oatmeal cookies provokes a little twinge of despair.

Years later I ran into one of the women from the packaging line on the street, and we chatted for several minutes. But when the subject of the factory came up, the mood darkened and she said curtly, I don't want to talk about that. We had both been scarred by the petit mal of the assembly line, where each person was really no different than a cog or a gear, only valuable as a tiny component of the whole, and it seemed even worse when you considered the absurd ends toward which we labored. And to think that you can turn on the television any hour of any day and find a politician railing against the outsourcing of these manufacturing jobs, as if this is any great loss or any loss at all. The outsourcing hasn't gone nearly far enough if you ask me; parking these misery complexes in the third world is akin to cultural warfare. We should be outsourcing these factories to the ninth circle of hell, outsourcing them into oblivion! It's not work fit for a human being, and if we can't devise some kind of robot-manned factory to manufacture our crap, perhaps we should consider life without ninety-nine-cent oatmeal cookies and pet rocks and cheap scuba flippers. (Crazy, I know.)

Ever since my factory stint, when I pass a homeless person huddled in a doorway or on the sidewalk and someone says, why don't they just get a job, anyone can get some kind of job, I have to bite my tongue, because I know that there's a life worse than sleeping under bridges and subsisting on Dumpster food.

Unemployed I wasn't welcome at home, so I decided to lay low for the rest of the summer. My pal Uzodinma had sublet a sad basement apartment in Iowa City and said I was welcome to crash there, if I didn't mind sleeping on the carpet with no blanket or pillow. I didn't mind.

My first night there, there was a knock at the door, and it was two high school girls who'd known the previous tenant. Well come on in, said my pal, and I'll get you his new address; it's around here somewhere, though he knew full well that he didn't have it. I chatted them up, and before long they'd confessed that the previous tenant had been the only adult they knew who'd buy them beer and would we help out two ladies in distress? Uzodinma, better versed in these matters, agreed that we'd gladly do so if they bought us a bottle, too. They agreed and we drove off to the liquor store in their convertible.

Hours later I was lying on the filthy carpet with one of the high schoolers as she tried to dandle my cock to life, whispering in my ear that she was a virgin but not for much longer. I was thinking, how many times have bored men with no prospects sitting in shitty apartments dreamed of two high school girls in a convertible coming to the door, buying them whiskey, and then offering up their hymens? But all I could think about was what if the condom broke and I had to be like the glum resigned sad sacks on the assembly line, yoked to a shitting screaming primate and forced to work at whatever I could get, no freedom, no relevance and no place in the future? I might even have to return hat in hand to the cookie factory in nine months' time, and I'd rather die, literally die, than do that. After a while the girl asked me what was wrong and I said it was the whiskey, because let's be honest, how do you explain that you couldn't have intercourse because you were scared of a cookie factory?

I was terrified after that night that my assembly-line summer had ruined me, but after several weeks of systematic disordering of the senses, I'd erased all effects of those horrible months and I was back, carefree and confident and psychologically delineated like the rest of my college town peers, the ghastly underbelly of our economy once again banished from my consciousness. Though from then on I did make a point of keeping five hundred dollars on hand at all times, just in case anything needed "taking care of."

By which I mean, an abortion.

CHAPTER 5

Zoo Interlude

or, I Know Why the Caged Monkey Flings (Poo)

I never had another job quite as dehumanizing as the cookie factory, but every job seems to reduce you on some level to just another rat in a maze, what with the dress codes and the cubicles and the three-hundred-page employee handbook that you have to read and sign (all those rules for your own benefit, they always stress). Years later, I'd often be sitting in a meeting and feel a sudden stab of that chilling anomie from years past, as some alien voice came out of my mouth blathering on about *added value* or *target demos,* sitting across from nine other people who like me were all wearing variations on the same tasteful biz-cazsh ensemble, and I'd have to excuse myself. I'd find the boss and tell him/her I was sick and it wasn't even a lie, as I was at this point trembling and pale, and I'd flee mindlessly out into the afternoon.

On one of these occasions I was meandering around the city, stopping on benches to drowse an hour away before moving on, petting stray cats, giving tourists intentionally wrong directions, when I found myself at the entrance to the National Zoo. I still had a few hours before I could go home without my girlfriend Sadie suspecting I'd cut work again, so I decided to stop in.

I wandered through the exhibits, craning my neck to see over the families hunched at the front. The pandas that had gorged themselves on bamboo and then passed out where they sat, draped awkwardly over plastic rock arrangements like half-finished taxidermy projects, the lynxes and antelope and zebras that endlessly circled their cages looking for the exit, their tiny reptile brains repeating the same imperative like a knell; escape, escape, escape.

The comical emus strutting across their terraces, and I remembered an older friend who lives down south telling me years ago about his own encounter with an emu. He'd also tried the clock-punching life, first as a real estate agent and then as a sort of clerk, before deciding that he couldn't take any more. After investigating various ways of making money, he'd settled on the sale of psychedelic mushrooms. These were widely available, if you knew where to look, and since they're free it's all profit. Each night he set out on midnight expeditions across outlying farmland, clipping and then retwisting fence wires to wander across pastures with a hooded flashlight, comparing specimens he found to blurry pictures he'd printed out off the Internet. One night he was stumbling about in the dark when suddenly he heard a bizarre cry, very near, and whirled to find a six-foot-tall carnivorous bird rearing up in the bore of his flashlight. He'd accidentally wandered onto an emu farm. The emu looks fluffy and unthreatening but in fact possesses fearsome talons, and kicks like a thoroughbred; with very little effort it could lay a man open from crotch to throat. Screaming like a five-year-old girl, my friend threw his flashlight at this gaping avian demon and sprinted in the opposite direction, head-on into a barbed-wire fence. Catapulted backward by the bowing of the wire, he leaped back up amid a cacophony of prehistoric screeching and, anaesthetized by terror, grasped the top wire in both hands and vaulted over the fence. He sprinted to his car and sped back to town, leaking blood from a hundred different perforations, alternately laughing and crying all the way home.

Still, he'd said at the conclusion of this anecdote. It beat working.

At the time I'd laughed, but now, a workingman myself, I realized he'd been serious.

I sauntered in a general downhill direction and sat on a low wall overlooking the tigers. They roamed a small island indifferently scattered with driftwood and pinecones, surrounded by a moat of brown water. On the shore of this underwhelming atoll paced a paunchy greasy-coated tiger. He stalked from one end of the enclosure to the other and then back again, looking out at the onlookers with dead puzzled eyes. Every few minutes he tried to go back inside, but the door was locked; it wasn't closing time yet. Then he'd recommence his pacing, looking like one of those old women you see speed walking in shopping malls, trudging mindlessly forward because, well... just because.

It seemed a rather bloodless spectacle, figuratively and literally, and I wondered how much trouble it would be to somehow bring an antelope over from the savannah exhibit and drop it into the tiger enclosure, perhaps through a midnight crane hijacking, steering it over the deserted roads and through the front gates. But then there wouldn't be an audience for what happened next, and that was the whole point, all these delighted gawkers weren't really seeing a tiger, any more than going to a strip club teaches you about sex. Nature made the tiger to run and kill, but nothing of that essence was on display in this neurotic glassy-eyed automaton...

And of course I knew it irritated me so much because I saw myself in that neutered half-life, the compulsive pacing like my smoke breaks and hourly sojourns to Starbucks for coffee I barely sipped, the sagging piebald hide and atrophied muscles like my own razor burn and chair ass, and all for what? And when the occasional tiger turns on his keeper, even that was understandable. I thought back on all the fellows I knew who cheated on their wonderful girlfriends and wives with orange-faced PR bimbos they'd met at happy hours because they couldn't quite explain it, they just needed *something*. The apoplectic foaming-at-the-mouth break room rants about who the fuck ate my yogurt, the usually meek bow-tied IT guy all of a sudden purple faced and screaming. *It was clearly initialed right there on the lid!* The time a coworker actually rammed another coworker's car in the parking garage over a disputed attribution in some already-forgotten presentation, the fist-fights and wrestling matches in the cubicle maze, the time I slammed an uncooperative graphic designer to the floor and sat astride him squirting a nearby bottle of ketchup (long story) into his mouth and nose until he nearly drowned. And at no time did anyone involved, not myself or any of the participants or the bystanders or the managers and HR people in the post-incident meetings ever ask why it had happened. Because we just knew why.

And it was the same when we were having lunch at our desks in the weeks before a product launch, no time to go out, and we were all watching CNN and a report came on about some fellow who'd gone to work that morning with an assault rifle and gone from office to office firing off clips until he'd been taken down in a fusillade of SWAT team fire. No one said a word—not why, or that's too bad, or oh God, we just sat and watched and perhaps a few of us even almost imperceptibly, perhaps unconsciously, nodded our heads. Because, again— we knew why. And I guess we should count ourselves lucky that zoo animals have neither opposable thumbs nor access to gun shows.

I moved on to the ape house, hoping to have my mood lightened by some poo-flinging or public simian masturbation. I sat in a small gallery of chairs, and for a few minutes I watched an orangutan sifting through piles of straw like a woman looking for a lost ring, shambling to and fro looking eerily human with its sharp eyes and finely articulated hands. Across the way was a warren of gorilla rooms, what looked like a series of repurposed middle-school classrooms behind Plexiglas. There were a few families gathered around a window, and I sauntered over to see what they were watching.

It was a large potbellied slope-browed gorilla sitting with his back to the glass wall, plucking leaves off a branch and eating them one by one. He seemed conscious of what he was doing, and the more animated his audience became, waving their arms and squealing to attract his attention, the more stoic and indifferent he was.

Next to me, a dark-haired kid, maybe six or seven years old, had his face pressed against the glass as his father hovered indulgently over his shoulder.

How'd the gorilla get here?

They brought him here, said the father.

Does he like it here?

Of course he does.

The kid looked up at his father to see if he was serious, and found that he was. Are you sure, he asked after a moment.

Of course! Look at him, he gets to live in this big house and gets all the food he wants, and if he gets sick a doctor comes and fixes him right up. What could be better?

What, indeed? I could tell that the father meant every word he was saying. What could be better than a big house and tons of food to eat and health insurance? And at such a small price! Sure, take my freedom, I wasn't using it anyway. We may be higher primates, but at least the gorilla had the decency to resent his cage.

I could see the kid was troubled by what he saw, and I tried to give the boy some kind of sign, some confirmation to trust his eyes, but he was transfixed by the gorilla. And considering

my haggard pale tight-pantsed long-haired bestubbled appearance I couldn't risk any questionable glances toward children
as I could all too easily imagine these upstanding citizen parents
denouncing me as a child molester or some general deviant
("He's different! Get him!") and falling upon me swinging Nal-
genes filled with apple juice and folded Danish strollers and
then dumping my broken body over the wall of the tiger
enclosure, where I would be gleefully dismembered as the first
live meat in years and perhaps ever.

I felt ill and immensely discouraged by what I'd seen and
shuffled home thinking about the gulf between what people
say they want (freedom, happiness) and what they actually
want (security at all costs, absence of unhappiness). Something familiar about the child in the ape house—his cowlick at
the back of his head, on the left side, his wide old-man forehead and melancholy demeanor—nagged at me until several
days later it came to me in a moment. The child was my
younger self! And I felt immediately ashamed, because I'd
shirked my responsibility to myself, bought in and sold out in
defiance of that first essential insight, and I vowed that the
very next day I'd start laying the groundwork for getting fired.
And within a half-year I'd gotten my wish...

CHAPTER 6

Arcaged!

or, Attendants Have No Access to Safe, or Dignity

A few years after the cookie factory debacle, I found myself in Iowa City, Iowa, again, with no particular plans or ambition. I'd murdered four years as an unenthusiastic college student and then another year crashing in a friend's East Village walk-up. Now I was back in town, flat broke and desperate. My worldly holdings consisted of a scratch-off lottery ticket redeemable for a five-dollar prize; I'd found it in a coat pocket. There were only two places in town where they'd hire you on the spot: the mall and the telemarketing call center. I wasn't quite desperate enough yet to bilk semisenile retirees out of their Social Security checks over the phone, so I took the bus to the mall.

Coral Ridge Mall, the largest in Iowa, was the size of a military installation, a massive coliseum-like monument to disposable income and disposable merchandise, a repository of hyperspecialized consumer ephemera. It may not have had a roller coaster in the middle, but it did have an ice rink. The mall was always crowded. A steady stream of organized bus tours trickled in from the big nothing states to the west, Kansas and the Dakotas and the hinterlands of Iowa, bringing armies of countryfolk who'd heard rumors of a place where cargo shorts and scented candles were as plentiful as meth sores at a truck stop. The first time I entered the swooshing airlock-like double doors of the mall I was overcome with déjà vu, at the sight of all those gawky young teenagers, eyes aglitter with logos and insignia, weighed down like pack mules with shopping bags.

My only inflexibilities were that I wouldn't wear a uniform, I wanted to work with a minimum of coworkers, and I didn't want a supervisor breathing down my neck all day. (The only thing worse than working with a spiky-haired acne-bearded community college student is taking orders from one.) The food court was also out of the question; the commingled odors of fried grade E meat, synthetic chili, bubblegum-flavored frogurt, and corn-syrupy "Chinese" food made me nauseous even at a distance of fifty feet.

This didn't leave much. I asked the attendant at the ice-skate rental counter if they were hiring. They weren't. There was a small nail salon that may as well have had spiderwebs in the entrance, but when I asked for an application, the receptionist said something over her shoulder in a foreign language and everyone in the place burst into laughter. I left.

I was about to give up when I spotted a small, dark, recessed storefront by the exit. Upon closer inspection I saw that it was an arcade, and there was a Help Wanted sign hung in the window...

Inside, it was deserted. A surly attendant reclined behind the counter reading a hot rod magazine. I asked him if the manager was in.

No.

I'm interested in the job. Do you know when he might be in?

He comes in for an hour in the mornings.

That's it? The rest of the time, it's just you?

He'd already gone back to his magazine. Why, you robbing the place? Don't bother, I don't have access to the safe.

I returned to the arcade several mornings in a row before I finally encountered the manager. Ike was a pasty, bull-necked man, wearing a reeking Harley T-shirt and pajama pants with little sheep and obvious semen stains on them. The arcade had only been open for half an hour, but he was already heading home. When I told him I'd come to see about the job, he told me that it paid five fifteen an hour, the federal minimum wage, and the only benefits were five dollars in free tokens a week. I said that would be fine.

Can you start today?

I spent that day learning the ropes from Lester, the surly attendant I'd met before. He'd been working doubles six or seven days a week for months and was thrilled that they'd finally found someone to share the load. Lester was a hulking snake-eyed high school dropout with a ZZ Top beard and several missing teeth. He had several spectacularly antisocial tattoos, including a bar code on the back of his neck, a goat's-head pentagram, and, on his inner forearm, a large photorealistic rendering of a bug-eyed Jesus Christ hanging from a noose. Like most people of such sinister appearance, he was extremely personable once he warmed up to you. He didn't particularly like his job, but he'd been there for years, mainly because no one else would hire someone who looked like he did.

The job was everything I hoped it would (not) be. The arcade was entirely automated; the attendant's only responsibilities were to ensure that the machines functioned smoothly. While we sometimes had to break up a preadolescent shoving match, change a twenty, or throw out obvious pedophiles, the job consisted mainly of sitting around and doing nothing. It was quite futuristic in that respect—the human element was secondary, a mere contingency. Only the store manager had access to any real cash or tokens; Ike shuffled in every morning, unlocked the place, restocked the token machines with tokens from the safe, and then immediately went home, presumably back to bed. The rest of the time we were on our own. If any problems came up, we were to use the master key to give the complainant free games until he was mollified. In the event of something serious, we were to call Ike at home, who would neither pick up nor return the call.

Lester showed me how to use the master key. The rest of my training period was spent using the master key to play free games until the nail on my button-mashing finger turned purple. Lester had long ago mastered every game in the place and spent most of his shifts just staring off into space. This was shortly after 9/11, and there were persistent rumors that "Osamer" was going to strike small towns and malls. Lester would often stand at the threshold of the store, which faced the huge glass façade of the mall, his eyes trained on the horizon. He was convinced that one day very soon a tractor trailer loaded with explosives was going to roar up, ram through the front of the mall, and vaporize the entire wing.

We're set back from the main plaza and shielded by that support pillar, he told me when I sauntered up to ask if he'd spotted any parking lot jihadis. There's a good chance we'd survive the initial blast, assuming they don't get past the skating rink. But those kids at the movie theater across the way— they're totally exposed. They wouldn't stand a chance. One of us should go over and warn them.

You go ahead, I said.

Only a year out of college and I'd already found my dream job! The fact that it paid minimum wage was irrelevant. I'd seen already that in adulthood, you became your job. I had no desire to be anything other than what I was. I had been appalled to witness, upon graduation, the willing and eager capitulation of my peers as they shed the iconography of youth, married up, and plunged jubilantly into business-casual mainstream anomie. Behind their token gestures toward reluctance there was a palpable relief; it wasn't youth they were eager to leave behind so much as the burden of individuality.

Not me. I wanted a job where they would pay little but expect little, where my physical presence would be the extent of my contribution. I didn't want to join a family or a team or a tradition of excellence, I just wanted to not starve. The most horrifying aspect of the professional world was how I would be expected to care about things—quarterly stats, product launches, my coworker's daughter's soccer games—to which I was not only indifferent but in many cases actually contemptuous. When I asked friends who'd transitioned into the professional sphere how they handled it, they replied, *I don't actually care about my work or my coworkers—I just pretend.* Somehow this seemed to me an even worse compromise of integrity.

I got a shitty apartment with a dead-ender I knew, a white guy with cornrows who worked at a car wash and occasionally sold drugs. My room was so small that with a twin mattress in the room you could only open the door about nine inches. Every surface in the apartment—carpet, floors, walls—was brown. (Why is it that poor people always live in brown places?)

Thus began my journey into adulthood.

It was September, so during the day most of the arcade's target demographic were off in overcrowded classrooms moving their lips while reading out of remedial textbooks. Entire shifts passed without a single customer. Ike came in each morning, did what was required of him, and left. The rest of the day was mine to kill.

When I was hungover I went back to the storeroom and napped in a nest of trashbags filled with Styrofoam shipping peanuts or did push-ups behind the counter or burned through a list of classics. (I'd just read a Joseph Campbell biography and had some vague ambition to reproduce his year of reading in the wilderness.) Sometimes I spent hours gazing into space, reveling in the total absence of upward mobility in my new job, or organized huge video game tournaments, courtesy of the master key, between the hangdog fatherless fat kids and trench-coated longhairs who haunted the arcade. First to fifty wins; last place has to hump the statue in the middle of the food court for a full minute! If a customer wandered in during these pursuits, looking for change or a clerk, I quickly removed my nametag until they gave up and stomped out.

I was dozing off with my feet up one afternoon when a large man in shirt sleeves came up to the counter and, banging one hand down on the counter, asked, Who are you?

Who am I, I said. Who the hell are you?

I'm Chuck. The district manager.

Whoops. No one had mentioned anything about a district manager. I could see from his glowering expression and alpha-male body language that he didn't share Ike's and Lester's disdains for protocol. I took my feet down from the counter and sat up.

I was just resting my eyes, sir, I said. I was up all night optimizing the joysticks.

Chuck the district manager was a potato-faced martinet with a tumorous potbelly and brown teeth—the result of constantly chewing tobacco. Like many fat men, he carried himself as if he were big and tough rather than merely large and soft. His job was to monitor ten arcades in the tristate area, which meant he spent fifty weeks a year on the road. All that driving had ruined his hips, and he walked with the stiff-legged, hyperextended gait of a toddler. He blew into town once every week or two to check the latest numbers and degrade our morale with his pep talks.

Chuck set up camp in the office while I remained at my post. I refrained from putting my feet back up on the counter, but otherwise continued to do nothing, as there was literally nothing to do. I was halfway through a crossword puzzle by the time Chuck left. On his way out, he stopped at the counter.

This month's take is dramatically lower than last month's,

he said. When revenue stagnates, it's standard industry proce-
dure to change up the floor plan. I want you to rotate all the
machines; put some new ones facing the entrance and shift all
the ones on the west wall to the east wall. It'll lure in new customers.

The take probably went down because school started, I
pointed out. Besides, even if you lure them in, they'll just leave
when they see they're the same old machines rearranged.

Just rearrange the freakin' machines or you're fired, Chuck
said, and then he was gone.

There were almost a hundred machines in the arcade, and
even the lightest ones weighed several hundred pounds. The
heaviest, a two-player racing game engineered to look like a
car, weighed as much as an actual car. I went to the storeroom
and wheeled out the extra-wide industrial-grade dolly. It was
solid steel and because of its width had to be shimmied sideways through the doors. By the time I wheeled up to Ms. Pac-
Man, a relatively light three-hundred-pounder, I was already
sweating. I inserted the steel forks under the machine, strapped
it in, and, grasping the dolly handles, tried to tip the machine
backward so it could be wheeled about. It wouldn't budge. I
weighed less than half as much as the machine and couldn't
generate any leverage. Clearly, I needed a new strategy.

I wedged two doorstops behind the wheels of the dolly so it
wouldn't move backward, and placed a folding chair behind
the machine. My plan was to go around to the front of the
machine, slowly tip it backward from a squatting position,
using my leg strength, until it came to rest on the chair, at
which point I would scoot around back to the rear, lift the
dolly by the handles off the chair, and wheel the machine to
its new home in the front of the store.

Physics enthusiasts will see where this is going. I tipped the
machine backward: as soon as the center of gravity shifted,
the dolly wheeled forward at tremendous speed, bashing my
shins, and the game missed the chair by a good two feet. It

struck the floor with a sound I can only describe as pure crystalline destruction. If you'd like to reproduce the sound (and I highly recommend that you do), place a television and a computer in a plywood cabinet and throw it out of a second-story window.

With the last of my strength I got the game back upright, unstrapped it, and returned it to its original spot. Outwardly it appeared to be unharmed, and I allowed myself a moment's hope. But when I plugged it in, nothing happened, and when I shook the machine I could hear a profusion of small objects rattling freely about the insides. I went back to the office and noted in the log that Ms. Pac-Man wouldn't power on. In the Notes section, I wrote, "cause unknown!"

Okay then! I returned to the counter and rubbed my bruised shins while reading *Thus Spake Zarathustra*. I'd put in a modicum of effort and could now guiltlessly say, fuck it. If Chuck fired me for not rearranging the games, well, there were dozens of other underpaid jobs within a stone's throw of where I sat.

Chuck walked in a week later, looking homeless and pregnant as usual.

Did you rearrange the games like I told you?

I was about to deliver the meandering explanation I'd concocted when I saw in his face that he had no idea whether I had done the job or not. He visited ten arcades a week, I realized, and they probably all looked pretty much the same to him.

I sure did, I said, rubbing my lower back theatrically. Took me all day!

He glanced around. Looks good, he said.

A few hours later, he came out of the office. We did pretty well last weekend, he said. The new floor plan really blew them away. Very nice work.

Thanks, Chuck, I said. It's just nice to see all my hard work pay off.

* * *

After I received my first few paychecks, I realized why they hadn't been able to fill the position. For a full forty-hour week, I netted about a hundred fifty dollars. My total expenses for rent, utilities, and transportation each month were about five hundred dollars, give or take, which left me with twenty-five dollars a week for everything else. If I hadn't been friends with a crooked grocery store cashier (she only scanned every tenth item when I went through her lane), I would've starved.

It looked like I was going to have to get a real job or a second shitty job. This struck me as appallingly unjust: if a man is willing to give forty hours a week, he's at least entitled to a living, however meager. To ask a man for his time is to ask him for everything; in return, I was getting essentially nothing! The more I stared at my measly paychecks, the clearer I saw their implicit message: Fuck You. Indifference I expected, and could easily endure, but little by little I saw that the system was actively hostile toward me. I wasn't asking to get rich, I just wanted a living wage. What I was getting was a dying wage. A "living under a bridge, eating one baloney sandwich a day, dying slowly of malnutrition and exposure" wage. Essentially I was minding the shop for these corporate motherfuckers, overseeing the raking in of tens of thousands of dollars a week, and in return they were trying to kill me.

These are the thoughts I entertained as I lay at night on a bare mattress in my tiny brown room, listening to freight trains roar by at irregular intervals.

The next day as I was punching in, I mentioned to Lester that I was thinking about quitting. The job just wasn't paying the bills.

Even with selling tokens?

What do you mean, I asked.

Lester looked at me contemptuously. You don't sell tokens? What are you, religious or something?

Lester explained how to construct a small basket out of newspaper that was taped just inside a game's coin slot. This basket caught any inserted tokens before they hit the tiny "start" switch and triggered the token meter. When the customer complained, you used the master key to open the machine, palmed their token, and manually gave them a free game. If you rigged up the more popular machines, you could accumulate hundreds of tokens very quickly. (Now I realized why Lester was always so blasé about getting stuck with the hectic weekend shifts.) You spent the first half of the shift collecting tokens from rigged games, put Out of Order signs on the token machines, and spent the second half of the night selling your harvest for cash.

Four hours later I was striding purposefully across the arcade after opening the Dance Dance machine for the umpteenth time that shift, when my pants, weighted by two pockets bulging with tokens, dropped to my ankles. Luckily I was wearing underwear that day. Later, after I'd sold the last of my harvested tokens, I gave a pizza-faced Gap clerk thirty minutes of free play on Time Crisis in exchange for a new, tighter belt.

The arcade was an embezzler's dream come true; one person on shift at a time, indifferent management, and distant, faceless corporate ownership. (When I asked Lester who owned the arcade, he replied, Japan.) Any lingering moral qualms were rendered moot by the fact that they were making thousands of dollars a weekend but still paying us the lowest legal wage. To me, the choice was clear. I wasn't interested in being like the non-embezzling food-court employee who slept in his car in the far reaches of the parking lot because he couldn't afford rent. When Lester and I asked him why he didn't just skim fifty dollars off the five thousand they pulled in every day, he replied that "stealing was wrong." He didn't seem to understand that the virtue he so assiduously tried to embody was just a license for other people to exploit him. Which is to say, he may have occupied the moral high ground, but at the end of the day he took standing sponge baths in public restrooms.

I embezzled my way through the winter and spring, skimming just enough to maintain a manageable level of poverty. When school let out for the summer, the arcade went from ghost town to cattle car and my take quadrupled—but so did the aggravation.

In the summer, cheap-ass parents dropped their kids off at the mall in the morning and didn't pick them up until dinnertime. The mall boasted a large indoor playground, air-conditioning, a bookstore with dozens of couches, a multiplex, and a skating rink. It was like a free unsupervised day care center, albeit with pedophiles lurking in the public bathrooms.

All of these little crust-mouthed pants-shitters invariably ended up in the arcade, where the confluence of ear-shattering Japanese synth–pop and fluorescent strobe lights soon stimulated them into a Ritalin-enhanced fugue state of involuntary apelike shrieking and slack-jawed, dead-eyed insensibility. It took them about twenty minutes to blow their lunch money, and then they spent the rest of the day trying to hustle me for free games.

Shit Chickens ate my token, the kid would say, doing a little unconscious jig in place.

No, it didn't, I'd answer without looking up from my book. You didn't put any money in that machine.

Yes I did, mister! The kid would at this point play his trump card, crumpling his face into a pre-cry rictus.

Go ahead and cry, I'd say. I don't care. I'm not your parents. In fact, it'd be kind of funny if you cried. Crybaby.

At this point the boy would try a different tack. Okay, okay, he'd say. It ate my token all right—last week. I just remembered.

Look, if you just told me straight up that you blew all your money for the day and asked for a free game, I'd give you a free game. Shit, what do I care?

Okay, I blew all my money. Can I have a free game?

No, I'd say. You lied to me.

At this point, many of them really did cry. It wasn't as funny as I thought it would be.

Most of these preadolescent hellions gravitated toward the ticket games. In the back of the arcade there was a spread of analog games—skee-ball, Whack-a-Mole, free-throw shooting simulators—that dispensed tickets in proportion to your score, which could be redeemed for various worthless prizes at the counter. Management bought the prizes in massive quantities directly from factories in China; misthreaded yo-yos, stickers backed with carcinogenic glue, toy soldiers coated with lead paint, brittle radios powered by third world double-A's that probably exploded the first time you switched the radio on, spraying white-hot jets of battery acid in every direction. Though the prizes sucked, the tickets appealed to kids because it made them feel all grown up, like they were making and spending real currency. After enduring hours of a joyless, repetitive task (skee-ball, for example), they received little pieces of paper they could exchange for various novelties that weren't anywhere near as fun as they'd thought they'd be, then quickly discarded these to pursue some other shiny bauble, which of course required more little pieces of paper. I doubt they ever realized how precocious the whole exchange actually was.

On the wall behind the counter was a locked, glass-front cabinet containing the holy grails of ticket prizes: rotating disco balls, remote-control cars, toasters, and cameras that cost hundreds or thousands of tickets. Some arcade regulars had been saving tickets for years with an eye toward these big-ticket items. One day I was reading my book when a juice-box-swilling little nihilist chinned up to the counter and started heavy breathing while eye-raping a dusty remote-control car on the top shelf. He'd been saving for two years and had twenty-five hundred tickets—only a thousand to go!

Look, kid, I said. For all the money you've spent at this place, you could've gotten a whole fleet of really nice remote-control cars at the store. You could've gotten a remote-control plane!

Want that one, he said, not taking his eyes from the car.

I tried to go back to my book, but I couldn't concentrate with the kid standing right there. Finally I tore open the cabinet, pulled down the car, and tossed it on the counter.

Here, I said. Now go away.

The kid froze. B-but, I don't have my tickets with me...

That's fine. You can owe me.

Here now was the object of his most ardent desire, the goal he'd been working toward for years, being freely offered. I could see he wanted to take it, but he also understood that rules were being broken and that he'd always been told that when rules were broken, bad things happened. If only he knew that we had stacks of this crap ten feet high in the storeroom, massive weevil-infested crates of d-grade electronics and surplus candy, that it was almost completely worthless and that he'd already paid for the car ten times over anyway. I watched as his expression alternated between naked jubilation and God-fearing dread, the interval between the two steadily narrowing until his face vibrated with both simultaneously in a horrible frisson of self-reproaching exultation.

Just take the fucking car! I barked.

The kid snatched the car off the counter and made a bee-line for the exit, but as he turned the corner I saw him throw a resentful glance back at me. It was too late for that one. The damage had been done; his parents must have started in early with the whole "thou shalt not" routine. Already he'd made that fatal link between pleasure and transgression; anything enjoyable must be wrong, all pleasure must be paid for in suffering. He'd probably burst into tears the first time he got an erection! I'd inadvertently contributed to the creation of another killjoy asshole—the last thing the world needed. This kid would probably grow up to be another Chuck, a petty middle manager who devoted his life to nitpicking and anhedonia. I guess what they say about good intentions is true.

The next day Chuck walked in as I was reading the newspaper at the front counter. It was midmorning on a Wednesday, and the arcade was empty. He looked around and came over to the counter. I kept reading the newspaper as long as I could, but finally I had to look up.

Morning, Chuck, I said.

Isn't there something you should be doing?

I shrugged. There's no one here, Chuck.

Did you restock the token machines?

I don't have the key.

Did you vacuum?

Sure did, I said. This was not technically true, but Lester had worked the night before and he always vacuumed before he left. Chuck eyed me suspiciously and then began waddling around the arcade bent over at the waist, scrutinizing the carpet for detritus. I sat back, confident in Lester's marijuana-heightened obsessive-compulsiveness.

Chuck eventually circled back to the counter. I'd already gone back to my newspaper.

He cleared his throat. I notice that you did vacuum, he said. But you only vacuumed around the machines.

At first I didn't understand. What do you mean?

Chuck gave me a mirthless brown-stained chew-smile. I mean, did you vacuum under the machines? Kids kick all kinds of stuff underneath there, you know.

Numbly, I shook my head no.

Well, then, you better get to it, Chuck said, and then turned on his heel, strutting exuberantly back to the office.

I sat there stunned. From the recent game relocation debacle, I knew that to move even one machine was a herculean task. But more important, there was a principle at stake. Sweeping under the machines was pointless and we both knew it. This sort of make-work for its own sake is the delight of maliciously petty middle managers everywhere, a demonstration of authority meant to drive home the lesson that you aren't there to do a job so much as you're there to take orders. This kind of thing happens at every level, but never so much, and so demeaning, as at underpaid wage jobs. The very fact that you work for so little seems to incite in your superiors such contempt (partly because they feel guilty) that they make it informal policy to humiliate you at every turn. (I'm convinced that this is the real impetus behind the ridiculous uniforms at fast-food places and other employers of teenagers, immigrants, and dropouts. *If this person is foolish enough to work for a sub-living wage, then it's only appropriate for them to dress like a clown.*)

I just couldn't do it. Not only on principle, but also because I couldn't stand the thought of Chuck thinking he'd demonstrated anything to me. I went back to my paper. This job wasn't worth my time anyway, if I had to do actual work.

A while later, I heard the office door open and footsteps approach. I forced my eyes to stay on the newspaper though in my nervousness I was unable to make out any words.

I changed the daily checklist to reflect the new vacuuming policy, said Chuck, leaning over to speak into my ear. I merely looked at him, stone-faced. Sensing something amiss, Chuck surveyed the arcade floor and then turned back to me.

What are you doing? Shouldn't you get started?

Nah, I said.

Chuck recoiled. What?

I don't think I'll be vacuuming under the machines, I said. There's really no point.

No point?! Chuck asked with incredulous bemusement.

Clearly, such considerations were utterly irrelevant. He shook his head as if to clear it. Let me get this straight; you're refusing to vacuum under the machines?

That's right, I said.

Chuck's face darkened. He considered me with renewed sobriety. I maintained an inscrutable, vaguely benevolent expression as I continued to read my newspaper. He opened his mouth several times as if to speak, but then closed it without producing a sound. In the face of my passive defiance, he was powerless. If I'd raised my voice or cursed him out or elaborated on my reasons, he would've snapped into drill sergeant mode and berated me into compliance. But this was something altogether puzzling. We locked eyes for half a minute before Chuck turned away, muttering his way back to the office.

I was sure Chuck was writing up my pink slip in the back, but after lunch he left for the week, stomping out without so much as a good-bye or even a glance in my direction. Lester came in later that afternoon to spend his night off playing his favorite game, a sniper simulation that involved shouldering a realistic rifle and taking out bad guys by looking at a little video screen mounted inside the scope. I told him what had happened with Chuck and he explained: it was impossible to find anyone willing to work days (or any other time, really) for the federal minimum wage. They'd been trying for months before I walked through the door. If they fired me, Lester would have to go back to working doubles, and that meant paying him a significant amount of overtime. Overtime came out of the managerial budget, and they'd do almost anything to avoid paying it.

I'd inadvertently called their bluff. Until they found some other poor bastard to man the counter for four dollars an hour (net), I was untouchable. They had no power over me; on the contrary, I had all the power.

As I was punching out that night, I noticed two handwritten

signs on the wall. They hadn't been there that morning. One read *NO READING AT FRONT COUNTER!* and the other read *ATTENDANTS MUST VACUUM UNDER MACHINES EVERY MORNING!* I took them down, tore them into pieces, and left the pieces on the counter.

One evening I was walking to the bus stop when I saw an ex-girlfriend sitting on a bench up ahead. It was dusky and the dead-end street was deserted. I waved, but when I quickened my pace in her direction, she jumped, squinted, and half-turned as if to run the other way. When I drew closer, she relaxed but looked at me with open disbelief.

Didn't you recognize me? I asked.

I thought you were a fratboy rapist, she said, fingering my Tommy Hilfiger rugby shirt and North Face parka. Why are you dressed like that? And have you gained weight?

I'd recently discovered another perk of the job. The mall was staffed almost exclusively with like-minded, underpaid malcontents, and one by one these disgruntled clerks came through the arcade to offer terms. In exchange for a pre-arranged number of free games, I soon had access to a whole panoply of free goods and services. I could have all the free fast food and ice cream I wanted delivered right to the counter, or I could go into any number of stores and shop "free." The clerks called me when their managers were out or otherwise arranged it so I could freely walk out with armloads of jeans, sneakers, hats, books, et cetera. Before long I had put on a spare tire and was dressing like a total fucking asshole. *(Fluorescent green terrycloth cargo pants? Why not? They're free! Orange and purple patent leather Nikes? Welcome to Funkytown!)*

One of the most devoted arcade customers had the bad fortune of working at a kiosk that sold calendars. I thought he was going to cry when I laughingly dismissed his offer of "unlimited free calendars" in exchange for free play. I felt so bad about it that I gave him free games anyway and accepted, at his insistence, an assortment of puppy, hunky fireman, and Corvette calendars. (Which I immediately regifted to my family members for Christmas.)

But despite the increase in money and perks, the job was becoming a real drag. Gone were the days of dozing off in a nest of foam-filled garbage bags in the storeroom, or spending entire shifts on my project of setting record scores on every machine just so I could enter an obscure obscenity when the game prompted me to enter my initials. I now spent my days walking in endless circles around the arcade, soliciting token purchases from anyone with cash in hand. I was essentially an arcade franchisee, at every free moment calculating the daily and weekly revenue projections, and sweating every lull and shortfall. I wasn't opposed on principle to hard work, but if I was going to apply myself, why not in some more worthwhile (and legal) avenue? Endless hustle defeated the whole point of taking a dead end nonjob.

In truth my dissatisfaction went beyond an aversion to the petty hustle, down into the existential realm. In the beginning I'd thought it would be amusingly ironic to work in a mall. It wasn't. Working at the mall was like dating a peroxide blond stripper with breast implants: appealing in theory, an amusing anecdote to tell your friends, but in reality just tacky and annoying. The magical aura I remembered from childhood, the suggestion of endless possibility, had long since dissipated, and what was left was, well, just the mall. The cheap huckster faux-populism and the pathological consumption of the people who shopped there was rotting my soul and sitting in a roomful of trebly speakers turned to maximum volume for forty hours a week had given me a bad case of tinnitus. I slept badly, and thanks to unlimited free food court fare it was more difficult by the week to squeeze through the door to my tiny bedroom.

One night I sat on my sofa to formulate an exit strategy. I figured that if I stepped up my skimming, I could save a few thousand dollars by the end of the summer, quit when the fall slowdown hit, and live on my nest egg while pondering my next move. As I considered the angles, my roommate stood nearby trying to eat a bag of popcorn without using his hands, which were pink and swollen like grapefruit. I asked him what had happened to them and he explained that at his job detailing cars, they were supposed to wear thick plastic gloves to protect their skin from the toxic chemicals, but he had stopped using them.

They say the stuff we use causes cancer, but I can work faster without the gloves, he said. I get paid per car, after all.

Don't ever reproduce, I said.

I'd only saved a couple hundred dollars toward my "retirement" when it all began to fall apart. Upper management found out that Ike was working maybe six hours a week and canned his ass. I suspected that Lester ratted him out, assuming that he'd be promoted to replace Ike. Our embezzling brought our take-home wages up to maybe ten or fifteen dollars an hour, but no real money could be made without access to the safe. We'd both glimpsed the mother lode over Ike's shoulder, huge burlap bags of uncounted and untraceable tokens, literally bursting at the seams. But the one thing Ike had done right was to keep the combination secret. I'd often thought about it myself; the exploitative potential of me or Lester as the manager, with access to safe, time card system, cash, and token machines. It would mean a chance for the guys on the bottom to pillage the company for once, instead of the guys on top.

Unfortunately, Chuck had other ideas. The atmosphere had gone from lax to defiant to openly scornful, and he probably thought that if he handed the keys over to Lester or me, we'd sell the machines for scrap metal, burn the place to the ground, and abscond with the safe to Tijuana. Even Chuck was smart enough to know that you can't promote a guy you used to pay the federal minimum wage and expect him not to turn around and return the fucking.

So they brought in their own man. He was a reformer, a company man. Danny was like Eliot Ness in tie-dye, or Serpico, if Serpico masturbated to tentacle-rape manga. He had a severely articulated bowl cut. He wore combat boots polished to a high shine, into which he tucked his cargo khakis. This was technically a violation of the slacks-and-dress-shoes dress code, but Chuck allowed it, fond, I think, of its undertones of authoritarianism and discipline. He had a calf tattoo of the Incredible Hulk. He reeked of cheap cologne and daddy issues. He was that rarest of creatures—the testosterone nerd. His personality was a toxic cocktail of low self-esteem and megalomania. Given the slightest mandate of authority he immediately began reenacting the same petty melodramas that had soured his own formative years. *Do this! Do that! Faster! It's my way or the highway, pal!*

His first day he called Lester and me into the office and told us that "things were going to be different from now on." We laughed in his face. This was his cue to pull out the new uniforms, paramilitary khaki fatigues to match his own and intentionally ill-fitting company polo shirts with a strangely testicular cartoon Pac-Man sprinting across the chest, a paragon of panting enthusiasm and tireless industry. Clearly, we were supposed to follow Pac-Man's example.

We changed into our new uniforms and then Danny led us through the new opening procedures. As we went around the arcade polishing reflective surfaces and topping off plastic bins of candy and straightening years-old posters, Danny followed us, barking out directions. When one of our shirts became untucked, he called for a complete halt, waited until the offending shirttail had been retucked, and then resumed.

No, no, wipe counterclockwise, he said as I disconsolately

cleaned a game no one had played for at least three years, blowing his sour halitosis in my ear as he grabbed my wrist and showed me just how he wanted it done.

The next order of the day was to clean the filthy carpeting. The floor was caked with a layer of spilled soda, cotton candy, chewing gum, taco meat, mud, and ketchup, months or years old, and ground in every day by the heels of customers. We vacuumed the crumbs up every day but, we told Danny, it would've been impossible to actually clean the carpet. Danny wouldn't hear of it. He brought out a bucket of hot soapy water and a scrub brush and set to work on a particularly large brown stain.

You gotta put some muscle into it, he said, scrubbing away. Lester and I stood over him, arms crossed. After a full minute of sawing away at the stain, he stood up, purple faced and sweating.

See! And you said it was impossible.

I couldn't see that the stain was any less brown than when he'd started. Danny extended the brush to Lester.

Go ahead, give it a try, he said.

I could see that Lester despised Danny's passive-aggressive officiousness as much as I did, but he'd been working at the arcade for years and still hoped to outlast this latest caretaker. I'd had some vague idea that if Lester and I formed a unified front, we could resist the new regime, but I saw now that this was a naïve hope. Lester took the brush, kneeled, and began scrubbing.

Faster! Danny shouted.

Lester scrubbed faster. Danny let him work for a minute and then told him to stand up. Lester stood up, breathing hard, and stood looking at his feet. Danny took the brush out of his hand and extended it to me.

Your turn, he said.

I looked at the brush. I knew that Danny was offering me an opportunity to buy in, a chance to ratify the pecking order without any outright power struggle. I kept my hands in my pockets. Danny gently pulled one of my hands from a pocket and placed the brush in it. Flashing my best shit-eating grin, I relaxed my fingers and let the brush fall to the floor.

Okay, said Danny. That's a write-up.

He went back to the office, leaving Lester and me standing there by the wet spot. Lester looked at me and shrugged and I nodded sympathetically. When Danny came back out he was holding a manila folder full of papers.

It says here you've already got two write-ups, he said. Is that true?

Oh yes, I said. I knew that a third was an automatic firing, which meant I'd most likely get unemployment. I also knew that for that reason management was as averse to firing people as they were to paying overtime or a living wage. I stood there grinning, secure in my endgame.

Danny went back into the office, where we heard him talking on the phone. Lester and I sat down on a broken skee-ball machine and started eating from a box of prize candy under the counter.

He says I'm going to have to wear a turtleneck under my polo, to cover my tattoos, said Lester glumly.

You should sue, I suggested. That violates the First Amendment! And the Second too, now that I think about it.

After a few minutes, Danny emerged from the office and walked over to Lester and me.

I'm sending you home for the day, he said to me. And don't worry about your shifts for the rest of the week. Call in next Monday for the new schedule.

I'd been sure they wouldn't fire me, but this was unexpected. Still, I figured it might be wise to take a short vacation while the new regime blew itself out. I waved to Lester and went to the bus stop.

As I was waiting, the kid who worked at Arby's walked by and said that when his shift was over he was coming in for a couple hours of free play. I explained that we had a new manager and that our deal might have to be suspended for a few weeks. After I delivered the news, I thought he might cry.

No free play, no free roast beefs! he screamed, his voice cracking, as he stomped away.

When I called in the next week, I was only on the schedule for a single shift—Monday evening, the deadest six hours of the week. I knew they hadn't hired any new employees, so who was covering all my shifts? I went to the mall one night at closing time and found Lester working alone. He told me that Danny was covering my shifts himself—off the clock, so as to spare our poor corporate overlords the injustice of having to pay overtime. He was going to keep covering my shifts until I quit, thereby disqualifying myself from receiving unemployment. It was at this point that I realized I would never beat this person. Somehow they'd found the perfect company man to counteract my perpetual slowdown. An employee who will work for free is like a suicide bomber who doesn't care if he lives or dies; there's a level of fanaticism that's the same as invincibility.

I brooded for the next week, calling in sick for my one shift. After all I was only losing twenty dollars, and I was fairly certain Danny would be there to browbeat me all evening. What really stung was that I'd lost a battle of wills with such a craven dolt.

When the next schedule came out, I was again on for only a Monday night shift. When the appointed day arrived, I convinced my sister to drive me to the mall and wait in the parking lot. I went to the food court Taco Bell, exchanged my last roll of tokens for a dozen tacos, and forced myself to eat every single one. Every clot of overstewed mystery meat, every shred of wilted lettuce and surplus cheese food. With my stomach visibly distended, I tottered to the threshold of the arcade and drank a small vial of ipecac I'd gotten from my roommate's anorexic girlfriend. I stood swaying in place, sweating toxins, and within seconds I felt the sickness coming on. I walked as fast as possible to the back of the arcade, where Danny was writing on a clipboard. At my approach he turned and scowled.

You're late, he said. I'm going to have to write you up again.

In reply, I blasted a torrent of steaming, partially masticated taco vomit all over his shoes, his pants, the carpet, and several nearby machines. After all the tacos had been evacuated, I continued to gag up bile. When the spasms had subsided enough for me to straighten up, I blinked away the tears and saw Danny cowering against the wall, his tough-geek façade finally shattered. On his face I saw genuine horror and it was like looking in a mirror. As I hobbled bent over and still heaving out to the car, I took some small satisfaction that I'd finally made one of them feel the way they all made me feel.

I called the arcade the next day and Lester informed me that I was fired. I chalked this up as a win and I'm sure Danny did the same thing. But in fact, we'd both lost. I registered for unemployment, but my benefits, extrapolated from my previous year's (on the book) wages, were less than a hundred dollars a week. Even with my lifestyle, that was unlivable, and I had to hop right back onto the wage-earning treadmill.

Six months later I went by the arcade to see if I could finagle a few free games, and Lester told me that Danny was dead. He'd joined the Army Reserve after 9/11 (his favorite movie was *Rambo 2* and he'd often talked dreamily about "wasting towelheads"), and one weekend while loading a cargo ship, a crane operator under his command had accidentally dropped a one-ton cargo container on him, killing him instantly.

I heard there was just a smear left, Lester said, not unglee-fully.

We used the master key for some free Mortal Kombat.

Whenever one of us pulled off a fatality move, we insisted on calling it a "Danny." This joke did not get old or less delightful, even after several dozen repetitions.

In retrospect, I'm sure Danny's death was no accident. I have no proof of this, but I can all too easily imagine the scenes that preceded the "accident": Danny haranguing the crane operator about his uncreased uniform pants, his microscopically scuffed boots, his posture or diction or insufficient enthusiasm. And then later the crane operator sitting in the cab as Danny obliviously wanders onto the proverbial bull's-eye, the planets aligned for a moment of plausible deniability. Why not? It was the classic crime of passion, unpremeditated and with the most justifiable motive in the world: victim was a douchebag.

Whenever I fear that justice has disappeared from the world, I think of Danny's demise and it gives me hope. You only need to look out your window to see that the universe is inclined toward chaos over order. Though at this point in my life, I hadn't been one to value money very highly, I ascribed my behavior at the arcade to the fact that I was underpaid. The implication being that I possessed buried, unmobilized virtues that would be brought to light by the right financial incentive. That if only I'd been paid more money, I'd have acted properly. Very shortly I was to find that the opposite was true.

CHAPTER 7

Glory(hole) Days

or, The Yellow Pony's Last Ride

In Iowa City there were two porn stores. For some reason they were only a block apart, on facing hills near the railroad yards. Although there was a rivalry implied in their geography, there was a disappointing lack of Jets-and-Sharks-style feuding, no gangs of haggard compulsive masturbators circling each other in the street, brandishing not switchblades but vibrating veined phalluses, swinging not bicycle chains but strings of anal beads glistening with lube. On the east side was the Adult Marketplace, a sad cube-shaped building that sold dusty VHS tapes and was staffed by glowering dead-enders who made a point of never making eye contact with any of the chicken-floggers who came in. The other was the Pleasure Palace, a low-to-the-ground bunker with blacked-out windows that was in no way palatial. It was virtually identical to the Adult Marketplace except in the back there was a huge blacklit chamber of individual coin-operated video booths, the insides of which were glazed with a delicate frosting of dried semen.

With just a few hundred dollars saved from my arcade plundering and my unemployment checks too small for even me to live on, I had to get another job. I knew they were always hiring telemarketers at the MCI call center on the outskirts of town, but I was desperate to avoid this fate. Everyone I knew who'd bottomed out as a meth-fueled jailbird stripper townie had, it seemed, logged a stop at MCI just before the most precipitous segment of their decline, timing that couldn't possibly be coincidental.

I picked up a local paper (remember those?) and was mildly delighted to see that the Pleasure Palace had an opening on the graveyard shift, the midnight to 8 a.m. The position paid only six dollars an hour, but I figured it would be nice and slow, with the fringe benefit of meeting the occasional undersexed bachelorette. The moment I walked in to fill out an application, I knew I'd get the job. I just *fit in* there. I had long greasy hair, a bad mustache, I was sallow and stick-thin, wore faded polyester button-ups and bell-bottomed corduroy Levi's and cordovan ankle boots. The manager must have agreed, because he took one look at me and told me to come back in two hours for my first shift, and by the end of that day I was officially a smut peddler, sitting on a stool behind the counter half-lidded and unperturbable as a buddha, reading Baudrillard as gay scat porn played on a wall-mounted television over my shoulder.

The next night, Chip, the manager, gave me a tour of the facilities. As we sauntered among the video booths, he pointed out that the wall of each booth had a round aperture at about waist height.

These are the ventilation holes, said Chip, giving me a significant look. You get what I'm saying?

I had no earthly idea what he was saying, but I was too embarrassed to admit my naïveté. Oh yes, I said in a winking tone of voice. Strictly for ventilation! Ha ha!

The way these booths work, people buy tokens from you up front and get three minutes for a dollar, Chip said. He squatted down to rattle the steel lockbar that secured the coin box. It was a lot like the arcade games I'd worked with. These things jam up from time to time and you'll have to open it up and refund them. Just use common sense; sometimes guys will say they put in like twenty dollars of tokens and you know they're lying; just give them a couple bucks of time and if they complain, give them my number. Lemme show you how to give credits...

Chip undid the lockbar and opened the front of the cabinet. As he fumbled with the innards, I saw a movement out of the corner of my eye. A fully erect veined penis had emerged, turtle-like, from the ventilation hole, and remained there quivering.

I cleared my throat until Chip looked up and saw our guest.

Yeah, that happens from time to time when you're working back here, he said. Then he went back to work. After a moment, the penis began thrusting itself upward insistently, trying to call attention to its tragic plight, the plight of the unstimulated erection, gouging the air fast and then faster. I realized that the friction generated by open air might, in conjunction with the frotteur's thrill, be enough to induce ejaculation. I took a long step backward and two to the side, out of the splash zone.

Chip looked up from his work and assessed the situation. THIS IS THE MANAGER, he bellowed. IF YOU EJACULATE ON ME YOU WILL BE BARRED FROM THE STORE FOREVER.

The cock froze in midthrust and then meekly withdrew through the gloryhole. I could just barely make out a muffled voice from the other side of the wall. *Sorry, Chip!*

The first thing most people ask when I mention I used to work at a porn store is, Did you have to clean up the booths?

Uh, no. For six dollars an hour? For six dollars an hour, I wouldn't even clean the sleep crust from my eyes. The booths were cleaned by a fellow named Daniel, who came by every morning during the 6 a.m. lull, always clad in the same allover print Darth Maul T-shirt. I wasn't sure if this was his semen cleaning shirt or if he just wore it every day, and in the end I

was afraid to ask. Chip said Daniel cleaned all the porn booths
in a fifty-mile radius, and made a good living doing it. I didn't
begrudge him this one bit; whatever he was making, it wasn't
enough. Daniel was a cheerful fellow, which I thought was
strange considering he had maybe the most undesirable job
on earth.

What's it like? I asked him one morning.

Not bad at all, he said. Once you get used to it. You got to be
careful though.

Careful? Of what?

Just stuff. Sometimes I'll be back there cleaning the floor
and someone'll push their peter through one of them holes,
damn near take my eye out.

That happened to me once.

We stood nodding as we savored this small moment of
brotherhood.

Or sometimes, I'll reach under the seat to wipe it down and
when I pull my hand back there's a syringe sticking out of it.

What?!

Oh yeah, he said. Degenerates.

Jesus. This happens often?

Naw. Not more than once a month usually.

Don't you get worried?

Naw, naw. He leaned against the counter and lowered his
voice to a conspiratorial register. What should I be afeared
of? Germs? You ever seen a germ, brother? Me neither. And
there you have it. It's all a conspiracy by the soap corporations. Shee-it—little tiny invisible animals wanna get into my
body and eat my blood? What do they think I am, a got-damn
idjit?

So you never get sick?

Brother, he said. I feel fucking horrible pretty much all the
time.

*   *   *

One of the more popular items was a tiny flask of some quasi-legal chemical solution that a lot of men liked to snort before engaging in vigorous self-abuse. Chip said it was a VCR cleaning fluid that happened to also be a potent inhalant—basically a poor man's amyl nitrate that Congress hadn't yet gotten around to banning. Unfortunately it sometimes induced the unforeseen side effect of abrupt unconsciousness. Paranoid about liability, the store sold the product but forbade its use on the premises. The men had to come in, buy the little bottles, go out to the back alley, huff the contents, and quickly stagger back inside, lurching stiff-legged and glassy eyed through the place like cripples staggering down the aisle of a faith healer's tent revival. If they made it to the back of the store (it wasn't unusual for them to collapse in the middle of the store), they immediately fell into the first unoccupied booth and went into a masturbatory frenzy, often forgetting to even close the door first. These chemically enhanced episodes of onanism never took very long to complete and often concluded with a long atavistic scream—on one occasion sustained for what seemed like a full minute, everyone in the place rooted wide eyed where they stood, before finally trailing off in a hoarse series of whimpers. It was so intense that at the first opportunity I took one of the tiny bottles down and slipped it into my pocket, determined to try it later in the privacy of my own home. (I passed out cold before I could even unbutton my pants.)

About 3 a.m. on my fourth or fifth night, the moment I'd been waiting for finally came to pass. The door chimed and in walked a trio of twenty-something waitresses from the steakhouse down the street, all of them—why else would they be here in the middle of the night?—grievously undersexed. They were plain and squat, and smelled of fried food, but, well, you've got to play the hand you're dealt. I straightened up in my chair and tried to look "hunky." I briefly considered skipping back to the stockroom to do a quick set of push-ups, just to fill out my shirt a little more, but decided against it. I was already on the raised platform of the checkout counter, literally on a pedestal, and I was confident in the presentation. I had it all planned out to the last word, a foolproof routine that just had to end up in a back-room orgy right out of *Penthouse Letters* (which I'd taken to reading during lulls). In fact, as soon as they left, I'd write my own *Penthouse Letter!* As they browsed the racks of vibrating eggs and jelly penii, I rubbed my hands together with lecherous glee. I'd almost certainly be ravaging all three of them within the hour, though I was willing to settle for just two if need be.

All this confidence melted away the moment two of the women placed their purchases on the counter. They'd picked out the Black Stallion, a shiny obsidian-like twelve-incher rippling with veins, rock hard—no jelly models for these ladies!— and with the same girth as my upper forearm. My own semifirm six-incher (the Yellow Pony?) had nothing on that monster. Flushed with a sudden attack of inadequacy, I discreetly took a half-step to the right, where the cash register would spare my relatively puny package from scrutiny. As I rang up their purchases, the third girl ran up with her own selection, an undulating electronic tongue that promised *lightning-fast flicking action that never got tired!* I got a jaw cramp just looking at it.

To add insult to injury, the return policy dictated that I had to demonstrate all sex toys at the time of purchase (after all, they couldn't return them), so as they stood there I had to open both Black Stallions and the Tornado Tongue, pop in some double-As, and show that they did indeed fulfill their advertised purposes. I stood there for thirty seconds, a large black vibrating plastic cock in each hand, as the waitresses licked their lips and stared vacant eyed at the dildos. Satisfied that they would shortly be satisfied, they took up their purchases and left. Before the door chime had even faded, I'd picked up my notepad.

Dear Penthouse Letters: You won't believe what happened tonight! It was just past 3am when three blondes came into the porn store I manage. They were tens. They looked at the toys but I could tell what they really wanted was, shall we say, a man's touch? Can I help you, I asked them. No English, the tallest one said—I'd traveled extensively overseas in my days as a Green Beret, and I recognized her accent as Swedish—before putting one red-painted fingertip to her glossy lips and, yes, briefly putting just the tip in her mouth before winking as all three of them broke into throaty laughter. Allow me to give you the deluxe tour, I said, putting one hand on the small of her back as I flipped the sign on the front door to Closed with the other, and steered her and her friends toward the palatial velvet-cushioned video booths at the rear of the store ...

This was before everyone had high-speed Internet at home, in the end days of the adult bookstores' smut monopoly; if you wanted porn, you had to come and rent it. From me. I took a particular pride in making all transactions as comfortable and unjudgmental as possible, even when the customers themselves didn't. The cast of characters was almost a cliché; the distinguished professorial old man wearing a wedding ring and guiltily renting gay porn; the kindly old chap in a straw boater and navy blazer with gold buttons, seersucker pants, renting German scat tapes; the morbidly obese fellow with severe Asperger's who'd clearly given up on ever having sex with a real woman and resigned himself to a lifetime of vicarious sex. There was a five-movie-at-a-time limit, and there were dozens of regulars who came in every single day and rented five movies. The movies were three, four hours long, and yet every twenty-four hours they'd be back for five more fresh tapes. Even running every movie consecutively at double speed, they'd barely have time to sleep a couple hours before going to work and then coming back for more tapes. But then, looking at these sunken-eyed onanists shuffling each day up to the counter, that was probably exactly what they were doing.

Many people who work in close proximity to pornography become desensitized to flesh, and their sex drive withers away. An acquaintance of mine worked in the porn industry for a year and said he didn't even look at a woman for months afterward. I didn't have this particular problem, though perhaps I would have eventually had I not been fired so quickly. I was cohabitating at this time with a haughty torpedo-breasted corn-fed blonde, and in the hour or two before my shift ended I'd saunter through the aisles, leafing through uncellophaned magazines and studying the photos on the back of movie boxes, mentally compiling a list of perversions for us to reproduce when I got home. Most nights, I had to sit in the back of the bus with the schizophrenics and Down syndrome people going to the university hospital for clinical studies, so the enormous erection nearly tearing out the front of my pants wouldn't look out of place. She'd be waiting for me in bed or sometimes in a hot bath, though that ended after one particularly strenuous session during which most of the bathwater splashed over the side and in the morning the lawyer who kept an office downstairs arrived to find his desk completely sodden with rose-tinged water.

As I became inured to brazen sexual displays, uptight customers began to annoy me more and more. I tried to ignore them, but their discomfort was contagious. Just as when you see a comedian bombing onstage and you slowly start to squirm and flop-sweat as if it were you up there, so was it with these twitchy repressed nocturnal porn fiends. The worst of them all was a man who came in every night at 4 a.m. It was always the same—the door would chime to signal an entrance, and just as I turned my head I'd see this balding trench-coated guy, head down and face flushed a deep scarlet, arms hanging at his sides as if nerve damaged, scoot in the door and quickly turn, almost at a run, down the first aisle to evade my gaze. As if I gave a fuck! As if we weren't in a business establishment whose openly stated purpose was the dissemination of pornography! I tried to concentrate on my magazine, but his labored simulacra of casualness as he crisscrossed the store was irresistible; his eyes cutting sideways like a skittish dog, actually whistling—whistling!—as in a cartoon, as sweat beaded on his forehead. I'd try to laugh him off, but he was so fucking awkward that I never failed to get nervous, too. Repressed by osmosis! Each night he threw his five rentals on the counter, gave me a ten without making eye contact, snatched his tapes up, and trotted out of the store without his change. It was hard to say who was more relieved at these moments, me or him.

One night I was feeling particularly jaunty when in walked this goddamn Nervous Nelly, skulking in the usual manner and generally making everyone in the store uncomfortable. I glared at him for several minutes, without apparent effect, until he passed in front of the counter on the way to the video booths in the back.

JUST RELAX, MAN, I shouted. YOU'RE MAKING EVERYONE NERVOUS!

In the quiet store my raised voice was very loud, and at this he leaped involuntarily backward into the far wall, bringing several racks of pastel-colored phalli and latex vaginas crashing to the floor.

W-what?

IT'S JUST PORN, MAN! THERE'S NOTHING TO BE ASHAMED OF, SEX IS PERFECTLY NATURAL! JUST FUCKING RELAX!

Cringing as if from a physical blow, Nervous Nelly scrabbled to his feet and made for the exit at a near sprint. A few seconds later I heard gravel flung against the wall of the store as he peeled out of the parking lot.

What was that all about? asked the next customer as he laid his night's rentals on the counter. He was a regular, an obese fellow with a snow-white bowlcut who imported a new Asian mail-order bride every other year.

I dunno, I said, shrugging. I was just trying to help.

The next evening I was restocking returned videos when Chip stomped in.

I just had a very disturbing conversation with one of our regulars, he said. This guy tells me that you yelled at him last night for no reason. That true?

I didn't yell *at* him, I said. I raised my voice, yes, but it was really a very civilized conversation.

What's this shit about "sex is natural" and "there's nothing to be ashamed of?" Chip asked. Tell me you didn't say all that.

But it's true, I protested. You know it's true!

It doesn't matter what's true! Chip shook his head slowly, his lip curled. If this guy thought sex was natural and healthy and nothing to be ashamed of, he'd be out there having it instead of at home with the curtains drawn watching other people do it on film. And then we'd be out of business. You know how much money that guy spends in here? A hundred a week, at least.

It doesn't have to be so lurid, I said. That was my only point...

That's the allure of all this, that it's dirty and shameful and unhealthy and naughty, Chip said. I thought you of all people would understand that. Wholesomeness, no guilt, no shame, nothing forbidden...what is that? What kind of world is that? I mean, come on! Don't you ever look in the mirror? You think I hired you for your cash register experience? You think that buxom blonde I see you downtown with all the time is dating you because you're husband material?

I shrugged. Sorry, I said. I was just trying to help the guy.

Just get out, said Chip. He swung back the counter partition and stood aside for me to pass. I'll mail your check. He shook his head. You let me down, kid. You could've been one of the great ones.

Of all my firings this was the one time I didn't see it coming, and the one that hurt the most. I never dreamed I'd ever be fired for being insufficiently sleazy, and out of all my firings ever, I think this was the most mortifying.

I trudged out the door onto the walk, and at that moment a car slowed right in front of me as it crossed the railroad tracks. An elderly white-haired woman, tiny behind the wheel of her Oldsmobile, looked over, saw me emerging from the Pleasure Palace and sneered, actually recoiled in disgust, from the sight of this obviously godless drug-addled longhair in his natural habitat of orgiastic perversion, before accelerating off into the night. Too upstanding for the Pleasure Palace but still Public Enemy #1 in Grandma Mabel's eyes. I walked home feeling placeless and disconsolate, and by the time I arrived at my girlfriend's apartment I'd resigned myself to a stint as a tele-marketer. My girlfriend said she'd drive me out there the next day to fill out an application, and then spent the rest of the night comforting me with wine and by various other means...

CHAPTER 8

Bullet Dodging Interlude

or, I Was Barely There

All the jobs where I only lasted a month or a week or a day or a half day or an hour or even less. The places where I could see the approaching car wreck with clairvoyant certainty, the bosses who so clearly had been dumped on their entire lives, veritably quivering with unrelieved frustration, and now here I was wandering into the proverbial crosshairs, the desks by the restroom, the cubicle neighbors who talked at double the necessary volume at all times, the break rooms where you had to buy coffee from a vending machine, the eager beaver co-worker who perched on the edge of my desk that first morning, his ass in actuality touching my keyboard, asking me what kind of music I liked and didn't I just espy his iPod peeking out of his far hand, and no matter what I said I'd have to put in his wax-encrusted earbuds to hear this incredible new band he'd discovered, and if I told him that I hated it or that I liked them three years ago but were over them now, I'd have an enemy for life. And if I nodded politely and lied, yeah, this is pretty good, I'd even worse have a friend for life, I'd never even be able to go to Starbucks without him tagging along and badgering me to try the white mocha extra whip, *it sounds faggy but dude it's fucking DELISH, dude,* an overloyal wingman who'd laugh well before the punchline when I was trying to hit on the girl from Marketing at the Christmas party.

The first days or weeks when the taste of recent freedom was just too strong and the boss could see something in me bridle and recoil, all the false enthusiasm I'd mustered for the interview now gone and in its place the unmistakable sneer of a bad apple. And then came the line I know so well, *Franklin, I just don't think it's working out.*

No, no it's not. And thank God.

A nonprofit that sold tacky sweatshop-made T-shirts and tin-cheap pins out of a basement mailroom. During my tour on the first day the head man introduced me to the mailroom clerk. When the clerk went upstairs to sign for a package, the manager took me aside and whispered, Just between you and me, he's not very bright. He held my eyes for just a moment to impress an understanding upon me, and then we moved on.

My job required me to work side by side with the mail clerk, so I got to know him quite well. He was an efficient worker, precise without being overbearing, pleasant but restrained in his banter, and always checked if I needed help with anything before he went on break. And yet all the other employees consistently treated him like an untouchable. Every time he left the room, they'd elbow me and roll their eyes or shake their heads in disappointment, as if to say, the poor bastard just doesn't get it. He was far less oblivious than they thought him, but he bore it all with dignity and resignation.

I was puzzled until one day I spied a group of women in the office huddled around a desk throwing contemptuous glances in the direction of the mail clerk, and something in their postures made me think back to the playground. Like the boy who's shunned by his schoolmates for wearing the wrong brand of shoes, the clerk had been ostracized for no good reason. Completely arbitrarily. A hierarchy demands a whipping boy, and his number had come up.

After I realized this, I stopped trying. The place disgusted me. There but for the grace of God, go I. One day the head man came in to scold me about a transposed figure on a report, and without looking from my computer screen I said, if you don't like it why don't you just fire me? And that's exactly what he did.

The offices of a government program that provided senior citizens free transportation to doctors' visits. Days spent reclined in an office chair, head lolling backward as we waited for the next call. Almost drowsing off and then pulled abruptly back to full consciousness by the squawk of an old lady who didn't even wait for a hello, just went straight into her demands. *I need to be picked up at two thirty to go to my doctor's at 123030 Juniper Boulevard Northwest, across from that shopping center there with the Olive Garden and don't be late and don't send nobody from Red Top, their cabs smell like hot garbage!* And if you asked her to repeat something, a protracted sigh of telegraphed annoyance and then the requested information repeated back at a snail's pace as if to an imbecile, sometimes with such dripping condescension that I couldn't help but accidentally mistype the pickup time for her ride to a cardiologist's appointment. *Hope your heart doesn't explode, you evil bitch!* It was like telemarketing, but worse, as there were no commissions as incentive, just a middling hourly wage.

What added insult to injury was that the job had been sold to me, by a shady employment agency rep, as a *great opportunity!* Okay, I'd said when she'd called to tell me she'd found me a job, but what will I be doing there?

It's a great opportunity!

Okay, that's . . . great. But what will I actually be doing?

It's office work. You'll be in an office. A government office.

Doing what?

Work.

But—

It's a great opportunity! Do you want it or not?

I was broke so I'd said yes. An hour into my first day I realized I'd made a dismal mistake. During a smoke break that midmorning, one of my coworkers had asked me as we huddled under an awning if I thought I'd last there. A dozen faces turned toward me.

I'll be honest, I said. I don't think so.

Not a lot of people do.

What about you?

He scoffed. I'm not going to last much longer.

The really annoying thing, I said, is that this job was sold to me as a great opportunity.

A ripple of laughter went through the smokers. Who told you that, someone asked.

The woman at the employment agency.

This ain't no kind of opportunity, someone said.

But someone must've been a little secretly fond of the job, because two days later I was called into the boss's office first thing in the morning. Miss Johnson was a corpulent middle-aged woman who never ever emerged from behind her desk. When she had something to say she just yelled it out at the top of her lungs, and out in the calling area we had to answer back like little kids.

Someone tells me that you said this job isn't a great opportunity, she said to me after I'd taken a seat.

What?

I hear you don't think this job is a great opportunity.

I stared at her incredulously and found that she was serious. But it's not!

Yes it is, she said.

No, it's not.

Yes it is. If you don't realize that, maybe you don't need to be here.

I couldn't believe my ears. What, liking the job is a condition of employment? Everyone out there hates this fucking job!

Oh really? She spoke toward the open door in a resonant baritone. How you all doing out there?

Doing good, Miss Johnson, came a chorus of replies, doing real good. A wake of titters.

Miss Johnson looked at me triumphantly, the irony in their voices clearly lost on her. See? Great job. Great opportunity.

I had the distinct sense that if I were to recant and agree that yes, this job was indeed a great opportunity, no, a golden opportunity, solid 24-karat gold, and that from here on out I'd seize the day with both hands, that she'd relent and I'd be allowed to go back to my desk and continue doing the semiconscious minimum. After all, she was the boss, but it was still her world, and this was all clearly just a matter of wounded pride. But I had my own pride and I'd rather starve in the street than tell Miss Johnson what she wanted to hear. I rose and made for the door.

Bad job, I said as I exited. Bad opportunity.

It was a little before nine in the morning and as I descended the escalator down into the subway, heading back home to bed, I saw my girlfriend coming bright eyed and hypercaffeinated up the opposite side, pastel sweatered and hair shining and exuding an almost visible degree of enthusiasm, heading to her own job nearby. When we made eye contact I gave her what I thought was a rakishly reassuring smile, but she knew instantly and without words what had happened, and in retrospect that was the first moment she realized I wasn't the man she wanted me to be, and that I never would be…

*   *   *

A library where my job was to type dewey decimals onto those labels you see on the spines of library books. One day my second week my boss came in with a book on the history of wrestling that I'd processed the previous week.

You need to redo this one, she said. You put it in Sports, It should be in History.

It's about wrestling, I said. It belongs in Sports.

It's about the history of wrestling, she said. Therefore, it belongs in History.

All due respect, I said. You're wrong.

I'm right, she said. Redo it.

She placed the book in my TO DO crate. I reached over, picked it up, and tossed it into my DONE crate.

All done, I said.

She looked at me and then walked out. When I left that evening she stopped me in the foyer and told me that I needn't bother coming in again, ever.

A bookstore, for reading on the job.

A five-star restaurant, for not smiling with sincerity.

A record store, for sitting down.

An office so wrong that even the tableau of individual desks seemed to bristle with pure malignant wrongness, the Post-it notes and desk lamps and ergo stools on fire like a Dilbert cartoon rendered by late-period Van Gogh. Less than an hour into my employment I raised one finger during the office tour, freezing my guide in midsentence, and said, Wait one second, I'll be right back. I walked calmly around the corner and then ducked into the stairwell, instantly sprinting mindlessly down the stairs, taking them four and five at a time, careening off walls and fire extinguishers and other stair walkers who shrank against the wall hugging papers to their chests and cursed me as I passed, so frantic that I missed the ground floor entirely and somehow became shunted into the bowels of the building, left to whimper down winding gray subterranean corridors lit by enmeshed bulbs (did this really happen or was it a dream I had?) until I found myself rushing headlong toward a red door marked EMERGENCY ONLY—ALARM WILL SOUND and I don't even hesitate, fuck it, I bang right through at full speed to emerge into a massive loading bay where the sudden commencement of various klaxons and alarm bells have frozen the workmen where they stand in a school child's diorama of blue-collar industry, one man motionless with a cigarette raised halfway to his mouth, and I zigzag through them and out the freight entrance onto a street still congested with commuters going where I've just fled and I can't decide if I should kiss the ground or dance a little jig or whoop in celebration so I try to do all three at once and the crowd shrinks back as a crowd does only in the presence of insanity.

Back to my shitty unheated apartment to starve! And there have never been any doubts, then or now, that I made the right choice, because like the original rebel said, it's better to rule in hell than serve in heaven.

CHAPTER 9

All Sales Is Lies!

or, That Red Bull Is for Closers!

The first thing that struck you when you entered the MCI tele-marketing center was the armed guards. These weren't the usual drowsy gym teachers just looking to pull in a paycheck over the summer as a rent-a-cop, these were serious paramili-tary pig fuckers who looked like they spent spare afternoons in their backyards bayoneting mannequins. Even the female guards had thirty-inch necks. They manned a veritable port-cullis of double Plexiglas doors, and if you didn't have a pass, you were out of luck. Didn't matter if you'd said hello to them five days a week for the past year and were on a first-name basis, no pass no entry, and if you didn't like it they'd be happy to call the cops and you could discuss it with them. And you better believe that if you put them to the trouble of all that paperwork, they were going to press charges for trespass-ing. (Later, when I'd gotten nice and salty, and I was hungover or burned out but had used up all my sick days, I would delib-erately show up with no pass and feign outrage when I was sent home.)

What was their purpose? I often wondered if the guards were perhaps there to keep us in, and not to keep intruders out. (For who'd want to break into a call center?) When we didn't meet our sales quotas, we were technically supposed to stay late until we did. What usually happened was that we stayed five minutes longer than the supervisors and then left. On these occasions I was always fearful that just as I crossed the threshold of the front door I'd be tased, tenderized with steel batons, dragged back inside and handcuffed to my monitor until I hit that last international sales kicker. Somehow we always made it out just fine though.

If we were prisoners, it was only of our own low aptitudes and expectations. MCI was the paycheck of last resort for every burn-out, fuck-up, and dead-ender in town, who settled there after they'd been evicted or fired or burned their last bridge or OD'd, a sorry pilgrimage of real losers really losing. Having arrived there fresh from being fired from a twenty-four-hour porn store, I certainly fit the bill. I was now three years out of college, and while most of my peers were just getting their first promotions, their first raises, their first spouses, I was still floundering, though willingly, sure I wasn't interested in that life, but not yet having discovered any viable alternative.

Telemarketing was so demoralizing that turnover was astronomical, so they were always, always hiring. Even if you had no intention of actually working on the phones, you could always go through the two-week orientation in a pinch and then quit, which many people did multiple times, using borrowed or stolen IDs. The check you got was enough to live on for a few weeks, which for most of the people there (myself included) was substantially further ahead than we were accustomed to thinking. That in fact was my own plan when I first arrived at MCI, fresh from my Pleasure Palace firing—sleepwalk through orientation and walk with a few hundred dollars, which in a town where on any given night a local bar was offering twenty-five-cent beers, was enough to sustain my hazy, meaningless existence for at least another month or two. I was sure I'd be horrible at sales anyway, dependent as it was on the common touch and a kind of dumb relentless persistence, qualities I conspicuously lacked. Common people hated me instinctively on sight (even more so when I tried to affect an aw-shucks "reg'lar guy" persona, so halfhearted were my efforts and so thinly disguised my contempt) and for six dollars an hour, the only motivation I could muster was for napping and embezzling.

Training encompassed six hours a day in a windowless conference room, enduring slideshows and monotone recitations of various nonsensical figures out of three-ring binders. The test at the end was open-book (open-binder?), so there was no need to pay attention. Many of my fellow trainees openly slept, only rousing themselves for the hourly smoke breaks, during which we stood in the parking lot not making eye contact with each other, pretending we weren't about to become telemarketers. On the last day our trainer had us watch the shitty Ben Affleck movie *Boiler Room,* about a group of hard-driving young salesmen who bend every rule and exploit every loophole on their way to massive commissions. Message received.

After training we were assigned to sales teams. There were about a dozen sales teams of fifteen people, each led by an elite salesperson who'd made such exorbitant commissions working on the phones that the head man was forced to promote them to management. They now made a flat salary, with commissions if their units exceeded their sales quota. Because of the constant turnover and the quality of most new employees, meeting these quotas, much less exceeding them, was rare. Most of the teams didn't even try really, the salespeople muttering their sales scripts into their headsets while eating chips as their manager sat playing computer solitaire.

One team, however, was different. Their leader, Jordy, was a lantern-jawed martinet who screamed at underperformers like a drill sergeant. During the trainees' tour on the first day of training, my group came upon Jordy just beginning one of this signature rants and our guide motioned for us to stop and watch.

Jordy stood perfectly still for ten seconds, glaring into the averted faces of his charges, and then struck out with one leg and sent a chair tumbling across the bay. If you want to waste your time, that's fine, he said in a tone of barely controlled rage. It can't even really be called time wasting, as that implies that your time has value, and it isn't, you are worthless lazy failures, your time is worthless, your lives are worthless, YOU are worthless. You should be fired. You should be fired and sterilized so you can't reproduce your worthlessness. Nevertheless I don't care what you do with your worthless lives because fuck you all. HOWEVER! When you waste my time, I care. I care deeply. Because my time, unlike your time, is valuable. My time is more valuable than silver, more valuable than gold, more valuable than true love or newborn babies or a pill that cures cancer and baldness and makes you lose weight without exercise or dieting and makes your dick rock hard and nine inches long. My time is valuable and I will not allow you to waste it. That will not stand. It will not. May God strike you down where you sit wallowing in your stupid lazy worthlessness, and Matt you better put those fucking chips down right now or I will fire your worthless ass I swear on my mother's grave.

At this, a bug-eyed fellow in the back row of Jordy's assembled team meekly withdrew his hand from a bag of Doritos and hung his head.

Look, I'm sorry, continued Jordy. I shouldn't have said those things. I didn't mean any of it, you guys know that. It's just that I care about you guys. I care so fucking much that it hurts, and I know this will sound crazy but when I read the Good Book and it says that Jesus died on the cross to save us, I'm like, Dude, I get it. I totally fucking get it. Because I come here every day and give my all for you guys, all for you and none for me, because I want you to be the best. And you can be the best. Each and every one of you has the seeds of greatness in you and believe me when I say that if we do what we're capable of, they'll be talking about us hundreds, thousands of years from now, in flying saucers and underwater cities and shit. *Team Jordy, they really brung the pain back in the day, didn't they? Oh shit yes they did.* Look, let's not have another week like last week, let's do this thing right. It's time to shit or get off the pot. Let's sell some long-distance. *Let's make history!*

His salespeople dispersed, scooting along to their respective computers in their rolling chairs and donning their headsets.

First person to hit their quota this week gets the executive parking space right out front, said Jordy, in an instant totally relaxed. Park with the big shots, you know you want to. Last person to hit their quota gets fired, and if you don't like that, tell it to someone who cares because by God I don't.

After we filed, startled, back to the training room, someone asked what the team had done to deserve such a dressing-down.

They finished second in the nation last week, said the guide. At our horrified expressions, he went on to explain that while Jordy's rant may have seemed over the top, his management style had made his team the top one for several months running. If we were lucky, our trainer told us with a smirk, we'd be assigned to Jordy's team.

I prayed mightily that I'd be assigned to one of the other teams, any other team, to molder unmolested in slack obscurity before my inevitable end. I remember wondering if any employee had ever not made a single sale for the duration of their employment, and if not I would be the first. I wasn't surprised at all when, on the last day of training, I was assigned to Jordy's team.

Jordy's team consisted of a cross-section of Midwestern archetypes. Ben and Chad were Chicago preppies from good families (one was dating a Miss Illinois runner-up), Earvin was a sloe-eyed east St. Louis ex-con with knife scars, Rainy was an orange-skinned gum-popping ex-stripper, a cowtown refugee who'd do a double penetration with you and a friend just to prove she didn't give a fuck. Aaron and Scott and Matt were awkward doughboys who were terrified of females but came to hypnotic quicksilver life on the phones. They were all happy to have me on their team as my immediate and continuing failure drew Jordy's entire attention and allowed them to slack off a little. I wasn't hopeless so much as I simply didn't care. I was going to quit any day now, so why sweat it? I sat at my desk doing the minimum, reading the company-penned script in a monotone and getting no sales while Jordy spit on the back of my neck screaming or listened in on my calls from his desk, reproducing my timid rebuttals in a mincing lisp for the amusement of my peers.

But Mith Johnthon, he'd sneer, writhing with the contempt shooting through his body like electricity, you never know, if you try it maybe you'll like it, have an open mind! Are you trying to sell her long distance or fuck her in the ass, Schneider? Okay, I underthtand, have a nithe day, thorry to bother. If your daddy had taken no for an answer, you would've ended up in the bottom of a wastebasket in a crumpled Kleenex! And it's too fucking bad that he didn't, isn't it you stupid little sack of recessive junk DNA. How about this, if you don't get a sale in the next ten minutes I'm going to choke you to death with your own headset and in court when the jury sees your sales figures they won't just acquit me, they'll throw me a parade. And if you've got a problem with anything I just said, you can make a formal complaint to the center manager. Here, I'll even dial his number for you; here, I'll even hold the phone up to your ear; here, go ahead and tell him...

And at this he jabs a phone into the side of my head, the faint bewildered voice of the center manager actually audible from the earpiece saying yes, yes, hello, who is this? and I have to cover the mouthpiece of my headset with my hand and whisper to Jordy, stop it man, I've got a live one here, I think she's going to buy.

Oh sorry, Jordy says, hanging up the phone and patting me on the back. Good work, Schneider, great work.

Even with my dead weight, the team continued to make more sales than the rest of the call center combined, and at least once a week our superiors bankrolled some kind of free open bar group outing for us. On these occasions I was always surprised to see that the diverse group got along winningly, though it didn't take long to realize that it wasn't their common humanity that transcended race and class barriers but rather their shared amorality, the willingness and even glee with which each of them overstepped boundaries of decency and fairness in pursuit of meager commissions. Because it was clear from very early on that there was nothing aboveboard about any of this, and that any successful sales technique had to incorporate a healthy degree of outright deception. In fact, the money was beside the point—several of the frat types received a huge monthly allowance from their parents and lived in the poshest building in town—it was the air of transgression itself that drew them. There was a meanness there, a vague undirected predatory instinct coupled with a frank indifference to their fellow men. That they could exercise this instinct while also engaged in a very American sort of commerce was icing on the cake. They were all killers of a sort, and it wasn't long before I realized I was just like them.

Why not give it a try then? After all, it was a shame to sit there day after day and not sell, to let all these good folks go unexploited. And at this point, months into my tenure there, thousands of calls had imprinted my spiel into my brain and given me an almost unconscious sense of how to sell our shitty product.

First, tone was everything. One must strike just the right

tone—assertive but empathetic, a kind of deferential superiority. Nothing is so flattering, so seductive, as a superior who treats you as an equal. (A corollary: never trust a boss who comes bearing smiles.) You got to the point where your spiel, once so stilted, was now almost musical; every intonation and inflection had a purpose, a series of psychological and emotional misdirections, feints, and end-arounds. As much as what you said, it was equally important how you said it. For an advanced salesperson it was really only a contest with oneself; if you executed your spiel to perfection, a sale almost inevitably followed. Conversely, the smallest slip, the most fleeting off-note or false tone, broke the spell and the customer, for reasons unknown even to them, would decline. It got to the point where the second I misspoke, I abruptly terminated the call, not even bothering to wait for the no I knew with certainty was coming...

There were many routines, everyone's was different—the Absolutely Free $50 Calling Card! The Risk-Free Trial Period! The Check We Are Going to Send You!—but they all relied on misdirection, false impressions—let's face it, lies. I called mine the Permanent Record.

The key to it was to imply that you knew more than you actually did and, more important, than the customer did. This wasn't difficult, as most of them knew nothing. All we knew of most of the leads was their name, address, and phone company. As soon as they picked up the phone, I asked them their name.

Is this John McRube?

Yes, he'd say.

Are you still at 1234 Gullible Street, I'd ask, reading off my computer screen.

Yes, he'd say.

And you still have phone service through Western Bell?

Yes.

It's easy to string them along to this point, because they're not sure if you're calling from the phone company or if you're selling something or what, only that you seem to know a lot about them. At this point I would type a few ostentatious keystrokes, loud enough to be audible over the phone, to imply that I was calling up their file, their Permanent Record, tapping into the massive global database (jointly maintained by the U.S. government, the military-industrial complex, and the Freemasons) that contains comprehensive information on everyone. Everyone suspects something like this exists, and with the proper vocal inflection, it's quite easy to imply that with a few keystrokes you've just called up everything from their kindergarten report cards to an FBI surveillance report on their nocturnal masturbatory habits.

Hmmm, I would say, in a tone that was troubled and weary, but hopeful. I'd seen it all before, but I was here to help, and not a moment too soon... A pregnant pause as I tap the return key as if scrolling through page after page of data. Sometimes I tapped for a full minute or more, letting them sweat. Mm-hmm... mm-hmm. Oh gosh. It never took them long to break.

What, what is it? Who is this?

At this point I inhaled abruptly, as if I'd been totally absorbed in my work. Oh! John, can I call you John? This is Franklin from MCI, and believe me when I say I have something that will interest you. It looks like you're still paying (exorbitantly high made-up number—say, a dollar a minute) for long distance, yeah?

This had to be uttered in the interrogative, with a rising emphasis at the end of the line. The law stated explicitly that we couldn't lie to the customer, but if we asked them a question, and they said yes, then that was a perfectly legitimate foundation for the ensuing exchange, even if I knew it wasn't true. Now, I had no idea what they were paying for long distance, but most likely neither did they, and if I'd delivered my spiel correctly, conveyed just the right degree of casual authority, they'd take my question as rhetorical, on the assumption that I already knew everything about them. Once I'd established my credibility, I could put in place any number of false statements (*You're also paying a forty-five-dollar monthly fee??!!*) and go from there. Even an incompetent could close these setups. Compared to their fictitious, dollar-a-minute, 45-dollar-a-month monthly fee plan, our five-cents-a-minute, six-dollars-a-month plan was clearly superior. *Numbers don't lie, Mr. McRube.* And technically, neither did I.

This then was the motif of telemarketing, a kind of passive-aggressive conmanship that obeyed the letter of the law while gleefully pissing all over its spirit. And in truth, isn't this the spirit of all American commerce? Was telemarketing any worse than a car commercial selling you "freedom" or a beer commercial depicting a Budweiser-swilling galoot surrounded by models, or the mythopastoral Vaseline-lensed Marlboro Man ads? The designer jean ads that baited my thirteen-year-old self with sex appeal and coolness and gave me, instead, shoddily constructed denim pants made in Malaysian sweatshops?

And if I was troubled by this reversal, this journey through the looking-glass to become one of the liars who'd once made a fool of me, any guilt I felt was thoroughly papered over by the suddenly quite large, sometimes four-figure checks I received.

The persuasiveness necessary to sell, the amorality, the ability to modulate the impression you made and to anticipate and counter the resistance of the other person, the unassailable confidence, the aggression, the obsession with numbers and rankings and competition—the attributes that made a successful salesperson were the same that made a successful seducer. The salesperson lives in a world of quotas, hourly, daily, weekly, and to survive must have a very short memory.

The problem was that lessons were elided along with rejection, and you lived a kind of animal existence, head down, thoroughly tethered to the moment, never reflecting on the past or anticipating the future. (Probably no coincidence that half the people in the place had unwanted, minimally parented offspring.) No surprise then that MCI was like Caligula with headsets...

You don't find the cream of the intellectual crop in Iowa City telemarketing. Big meat-head horse-cocked farmboys in shapeless clothes, white Eminem-types with perpetually bloodshot eyes who moved their lips when they read, girls with pancake makeup and peroxided hair and drawn-on eyebrows who spent their paychecks on breast implants, one of whom after a hot streak actually bought her own tanning bed. It was going to save her money in the long run, she insisted, since she tanned several times a week. She kept it in her shitty apartment, where it took up most of the living room.

There was Briana, a wide-shouldered wide-hipped small-town girl who'd escaped to the sophisticated metropolis of Iowa City, Iowa. She sat next to me her first day, and as she kneeled on the floor to plug her headset in, caught me ogling her from behind. Her only reaction was to gaze suggestively at me back over her shoulder while remaining on all fours, slowly arching her back to accentuate the curve of her ass. The moment was so absurdly charged that we both broke into laughter. A few days later, two guys on my team who lived together showed me a videotape they'd made one night after bar close. It began in a shower, with two men who as the tape came into focus I realized were my teammates. One was wearing sunglasses, the other a cowboy hat, and neither wore anything else. Kneeling between them was Briana, working vigorously. A hand came from off-camera and slapped her in the face, and she paused in her labors to giggle. The video continued for several more minutes...

Another girl, a potent combination of innocence and pure

voluptuousness, blond hair, rosy cheeks lightly dusted with freckles, with the body of a young Sophia Loren, absurdly well-endowed, perhaps over-endowed (if such a thing is possible), a cartoonish hourglass. The men literally lined up at her desk, but she always very nicely put them off. She sat across from me, separated by a low cubicle divider, and whenever either of us stood up, we always exchanged a smile. After a few months of this, the smiles had begun to take on an implicative aspect. One afternoon I worked myself up and waltzed over to her desk. As I drew near I saw that she had her head bowed in concentration, and upon closer inspection, I saw that she was working on a meticulously detailed and expertly shaded Bruegel-style pencil drawing of a large, veined penis, complete (even now it haunts me) with spurting ejaculate. At this moment she sensed my presence and turned, giving me a completely guileless and unembarrassed smile. I was prepared for anything, literally anything, but this, and all I could do was turn on my heel and slink back to my desk, defeated.

Theodore, a short ogrish fellow who quite simply had the gift. He could talk his way in or out of anything and it barely took him a week to ascend to the call center rankings. He was so persuasive that he regularly convinced women to have sex with him right there in the bar. I can still see him now, dancing that night's girl around the dance floor in concentric circles of increasing size, his spiel timed, just as on the phone, to perfection, so that by the time they reached the threshold of the men's room all questions had been settled, all inhibitions put to the side, and she entered the stall almost gratefully. We all begged him for the secret words, but he assured us we'd never be able to pull it off, and he was probably right.

An eighteen-year-old sales queen, and to this day I'm not sure who seduced who, not that either of us needed all that much convincing. We ran into each other one night in a bar and went simultaneously into modified sales routines.

Lonely tonight, right? Now tell me how this strikes you, Franklin...

You've noticed me, we both know it. You've thought about me. But what really matters is what you do about it, and the time to do something is now, wouldn't you agree?

No risk, no obligation...

It's a win-win.

We left together and on the sidewalk in front of my building she paused and said she had to make a phone call.

Hi, honey, she said into her phone, did I wake you? One of my friends drank too much and I have to walk her home and put her to bed, I'll be home in an hour or two. Love you. It wasn't the lie that struck me so much as those two words, completely unnecessary given the circumstances, and utterly sociopathic; *love you*. Love you?! That one utterance taught me more about human nature than entire decades of my life. As soon as the door closed behind us she coolly stripped down naked, as if she was at a doctor's appointment.

People hated us. They really, really hated us. The telephone had previously been a largely private means of communication; a ringing phone meant Grandma or an invitation to a party or an old friend you hadn't heard from in years. Now suddenly these petty conmen were intruding right into your home, calling up at all hours, sometimes every day, and they wouldn't take no for an answer! Telemarketing as an industry really only flourished for a decade or so before the inevitable backlash, and my entry into the world of petty telephone crime coincided roughly with the beginning of the end. It seems slightly unreal when I think back to those days, when telemarketers were a public menace! Late-night talk shows milked us for jokes and Congress held hearings condemning this latest encroachment on the sacred right of every American for peace, quiet, and privacy (unless of course, that privacy was used to smoke pot or have un-Christian sex). Congress itself, the highest legislative authority in the most powerful country in world history, denouncing us as a bona fide menace to Western civilization. If only they'd known how lurid, how cheap the reality of it actually was. Second-world low-tech sweatshopping, slouching in remaindered office chairs, wearing elastic-waisted pants, our mouths dusted with fluorescent Cheeto particulate, reeking of last night's vomited cocktails, idly picking at our diseased crotches or flipping through a greasy shoplifted magazine while from our mouths issued the very voice of God, sure, deep, and reverberating with an irresistible authority.

I assure you that however much you hated us, we hated you more. We hated you because you were gullible enough to buy what we were selling, or because you were smart enough not to, or because you were just the babysitter and weren't authorized to make any decisions about the phone service, or because we hadn't had a sale in three days and would have to work the weekend to meet our quota, or because our boss was a tremendous asshole and we were just passin' it on, or because it was your world, Mr. and Mrs. Joe Public, of respectable employment and holy matrimony and manicured lawns in the suburbs and all the attendant virtues exalted, and I was just a guest in it, and an unwelcome one at that, left to skulk at the margins scrambling for scraps.

Basically we hated you because we worked in a converted tractor warehouse surrounded by community college dropouts, Asian wankstas, obese Trekkies, and the recently paroled, cheating subnormals and old people out of pennies. When you think about it, you can't really blame us. I have a feeling that American Taliban guy came from similar beginnings.

If a contact screamed and cursed, I apologized for wasting his time, promised to take him off our call list, and then scheduled him for a callback in thirty minutes. The way the routing system was set up, the computer routed the callback to a phone in my group. Many times I convulsed with soundless glee as my cubicle neighbor, Aaron, was blindsided by a certain apoplectic hilljack who, upon hearing the beginning of the now-familiar spiel, immediately began threatening all manner of homicide. ("YOU JUST CALLED HERE HALF A FUCKING HOUR AGO!!") Having caught onto the gag, Aaron would apply all his powers of persuasion to mollifying the furious victim, apologizing profusely for the "computer error" and promising that this time—this time!—he'd make sure the number was taken off the calling list. After several minutes of this, the contact would calm down and sometimes even apologize for losing his head. It's just so irritating, he'd say, I was right in the middle of dinner.

It's all right, sir, Aaron is saying. I'll make sure it doesn't happen again. I can see him now, his voice cartoonishly sincere, but he's grinning as he types in the order for another thirty-minute callback.

We passed many shifts playing this game of hot potato. Once in a while, the thirty-minute callback got routed right back to you, and you could just pick up right where you left off. I remember once a number popped back up on my screen which I recognized as that night's victim. All I had time to say was, "Hey, Doug, me again!" before I was cut off by an agonized ear-splitting howl of impotent rage, like Job screaming into the whirlwind. *In God's name, why me?* I felt a little bad for him so I put in the order for a sixty-minute callback instead of thirty. He sounded like he could use a breather.

We were all salty phone terrorists, and could laugh off just about anything, but sometimes a new guy caught a hot potato. Once, having tormented one particularly vicious mark all evening, we all clock-watched for thirty, thirty-one, thirty-two minutes, puzzled at this uncharacteristic imprecision, until one of us noticed the new girl sitting at her monitor, jaw agape, face slowly flushing at the torrent of bile we could just barely make out seeping thin and trebly from her headphones. She was from small-town Iowa, and from the way she'd tacked up calling region maps and international rate sheets in her cube, we could tell that she thought she was engaged in a legitimate enterprise, if not outright altruism— "saving good people's money." She never saw it coming.

She stuttered her way through an apology as she put him on the Do Not Call list and then retired to the ladies' room for a good cry. A week later she was using every ripoff trick in the book as well as a few of her own, and a week after that a coworker whispered for me to come over to his computer to see a picture he'd taken the night before. It was the new girl, staring directly into the camera with a dazzling smile on her face, her legs behind her head, naked from the waist down.

Another night, I caught the hot potato, but when the mark picked up the phone he was strangely calm. He listened to my spiel and then asked me where I was.

What do you mean?

Are you at the Denver call center? I saw on my screen that he lived in Greeley, a suburb of Denver. Your name is Franklin, right?

Sure, I said. I'm in Denver. Why do you ask?

You get off around ten, right, Franklin?

That's right.

I'll be waiting for you in the parking lot, Franklin, the man said in a matter-of-fact tone. I'm going to have my shotgun with me. And when you walk out those doors at ten o'clock, I'm going to blow your fucking head off.

He hung up. Ah, I thought as I scheduled Mr. Shotgun for a seven-thirty *A.M.* Saturday callback, so that's what all the security guards out front are for.

*   *   *

We read the occasional anti-telemarketing newspaper articles with amusement, rolling our eyes at the inception of a national Do Not Call list and the promises of tighter regulation. If it had any effect at all, it made things worse. If the party was about to end, why exercise any restraint at all? Why not rob everyone blind, sell to seniles and nine-year-olds and house sitters? After all, a hundred dollars may not be much when you're flush, but if this place got shut down in six months, it might be the eventual difference between working at McDonald's and another month of daytime television. Jordy wouldn't say it outright, but he hinted that things were going to change soon. Don't leave any money on the table, he told us, we may not be here next week you worthless used condoms full of gonorrheal semen, I'm sorry guys, you know I love you all. (Breaks down crying.)

Many regional phone companies, to discourage the kind of capricious serial company-switching that the telemarketing industry thrived on (there was a sizable body of people who switched companies every few months, lured by the latest incentive dangled before their noses—tote bags, T-shirts, refrigerator magnets), wrote a mandatory switching fee into their contracts. Usually this was a small token fee, but in rural areas, where the company had to dispatch a lineman out to the Appalachian hinterlands to manually switch the cables every time some penny-pinching senior citizen switched from MCI to Sprint and back to MCI again, they set the fee forbiddingly high. In these cases, this information was included on the contact's info screen, often in oversize, blinking font. At this time MCI sent checks to new customers for one dollar and fifty cents, a token effort to "offset" (the company-mandated euphemism) the switching fee.

One day a lead popped up on my screen from small-town Tennessee. The switching fee was an enormous prohibitive sum, several hundred dollars. The old man had been looking to switch long distance companies for a while but, he said, he knew that his company would charge him a huge switching fee.

Yes, I said in a somber tone, it's five hundred dollars. A moment of silence on the line. But it's your lucky day, I went on, because we are going to send you a check for the switching fee.

Really?! He was shocked. You'd do that for me?

We are sending you a check, I repeated in an almost parodic tone of reassurance. You will receive a check in the mail. From our hearts to your wallet, that's our motto.

The law, after all, only stated that we could tell no lies, and technically I was telling the truth.

He was genuinely grateful as I closed the sale. He couldn't believe we'd do that. That's the free market for you, I told him unironically as I entered in his information. Capitalism in action! God bless America!

Did I ever feel guilty about any of this? Oh no. No, no, no, no, no. The salesman's rationalization is that if people are so foolish and gullible to allow themselves to be convinced by a stranger on the phone, they deserve to be taken advantage of. And why not? After all, is there any cure for naïveté other than bitter experience? In a way I saw myself as performing a valuable public service. For years, I'd considered the aftermath of my post-detasseling shopping spree as the end of something, but as I got older I realized it was actually the beginning. A cynical people are a strong people, a people ready finally to do what needs to be done. But first the gauntlet! Every single person who bought phone service from me, I'm certain, was one less person who'd believe later that rust-proofing the undercarriage was worth the extra grand, that the politician on television really did care about them, that all it took was a few hundred dollars and a trip to the mall to acquire "cool," that the person they'd met at the bar that night had just been tested, so don't worry about a condom. That's right, I saved lives. Lifesaver!

If anything, I wanted to do more. Opening a phone bill to find half a dozen unforeseen charges is annoying, but not quite transformative. There was bigger game out there, larger delusions to puncture. Wasn't there some way to send an electric shock through the phone lines, jolt them out of their stupors? What was the keyboard shortcut to remotely burn their houses down, incinerate their cars and coffee table books and closets full of artificially weathered clothing, relieve them of their misbegotten signifiers of taste and substance and importance? Your new long distance service will start in four to six weeks, you should be getting the informational packet and free $50 calling card by Friday, and by the way, your values are misconceived, your beliefs are nothing but lead weights, your miseries are self-created, you cling to them like an addict to his pipe, the tomorrow you spend all your time preparing for will never come, the institutions you support will grind you to dust, and does your thrift not just mask a profounder sort of poverty? Thank you, have a nice day.

While the qualities of the ideal salesperson that I've described—the amorality, the confidence—were a prerequisite for success, they were far from a guarantee. It was impossible to predict who'd excel and who'd fail. The most aggressive, honey-throated smooth talkers often produced zeroes across the board, and there were more than a few nasal pushovers who seemed to consistently stumble upon easy sales, rich old ladies who said they'd been wanting to switch over for months and took the highest-priced plans with all the options. Effort was no guarantee, either. It was known around town that if you were successful, telemarketing could be incredibly lucrative, and every week there was another crop of eager beavers just panting to get in on the action. They sat at their desks

well aftcr their shifts were over, memorizing scripts and resistance busters and rebuttal trees while silently moving their
lips, sure they were about to crack the code. Almost none of
them ever did, and after a few weeks their seat would be empty
and we'd all move in to cannibalize their inkpens and foam
headphone covers.

One of the most elite salesmen was a near-mythical figure
in the world of telemarketing, who traveled around the country full-time to different call centers demonstrating his technique. The higher-ups had been dangling plum management
positions in front of him for years, but he refused them all. He
was consistently making high four figures, sometimes five,
working twenty hours a week and besides, he liked the challenge of working the phones. What was management supposed to do, fire their best salesman? At a loss, they shuffled
him around the country, to drain the local commission's
budget before being "transferred" to another city, a kind of
white elephant, an employee so successful that he threatened
to bankrupt the company itself.

His name was Steve, and in person he was of almost con-
frontational plainness, a bespectacled slump-shouldered white
guy who perpetually wore an ensemble of T-shirt, baggy denim
shorts, and tube socks. He never made eye contact with anyone and smelled like onions. On the phones, he spoke in a
braying lisp, plodding through the company script at ear-
shattering volume and systematically going down the list of
company-penned rebuttals.

I HEAR WHAT YOU'RE SAYING, MRS. JOHNSON, BUT CON-
SIDER THIS, THAT WE CAN SAVE YOU MONEY, YEAH?!

Within a week he'd broken every local record. We all lived
in mortal terror that he'd sit in an adjacent cubicle, from
which his grating high-volume spiel completely overpowered
and unsettled everyone within earshot. We studied him
closely, but could detect nothing innovative or unique about

his manner, and yet week in week out he put up impossible figures.

Of course he does, said Rainy one day during a smoke break. When she'd started at MCI, she'd been a fair-skinned brunette, but now her skin was tanned several shades darker than her peroxided hair, which seemed to sear my retinas in the dreary afternoon. That's what the masses want, she said, that bland watered-down corporate focus-grouped generic script.

That's true, said Aaron, sucking on a menthol as he huddled in his filthy hockey jersey streaked with snack dust. The guy may make a lot of money, but he's a hack.

Exactly! Me, I'm an artist, said Rainy. Word had leaked out that I had ambitions to be a writer, and Rainy looked at me for confirmation.

That's right, I said.

Me, I'm like John Coltrane on the phones, said Rainy. The mark thinks I'm going to take him here, but no, I take him there. He wants reassurances, promises? I give him more questions. Shit, if he wants ass kissing and a mushy feeling inside, he can go to a car dealership. Talk about hack work. They're still recycling closers from the fifties at the car lots. As soon as one of those guys opens his mouth, you know exactly where it's going to end. I'm in the moment, man, riding the wave, I'm just a medium, it comes from some other place, a higher place.

You're definitely breaking new ground, said Aaron. But you don't make a lot of commissions, do you?

Of course not, dear, said Rainy, flinging away her magenta lipstick-stained butt. I'm ahead of my time. The masses never appreciate a true artist until he's gone.

In the end, what mattered most—and this is probably true in all things—was luck. The final lesson of sales is submission,

submission to the random. You have to weather the droughts, to believe that things will turn around even as the guy sitting next to you is making sale after sale using a spiel he stole from you, right down to the last syllable, the last accent; he even talks like you off the phone; he's even started dressing like you. It's easy to do this when you're just coming off a hot streak, but as the days and weeks stretch on, when you're basically working for six dollars an hour, a completely insufficient wage for absorbing rejection from cretins with *Wheel of Fortune* blaring in the background, your patience wears thin and you realize even that there is no guarantee at all that things will turn around. Odds are in favor of it of course, but then you've already beaten long odds in making it this long without a sale, and theoretically the drought could go on forever. There have been people who've won the lottery two days in a row, and there are people who've been struck by lightning on consecutive days. Comparatively it doesn't seem all that implausible for the universe to decide that you're not getting any more sales, ever.

This line of thinking led only to dark places—crying jags, tantrums, and abrupt, shouted resignations. As soon as someone became mired in a slump, we'd begin speculating on how long it would be before they quit. It was almost always sooner than we thought. Quiet and then a sudden exclamation of *Fuck this place!!* followed by the sound of a headset being flung against a computer monitor and then, long after the footsteps had receded, the last door slammed, the car peeled out of the parking lot, a ripple of evil little schadenfreudian titters across the sales floor. More leads for us!

One of the all-time salesmen was a towering black man in his fifties named Billy, a former football player with a rich baritone. He wore snakeskin loafers and Cosby sweaters and used to do a little jig at his desk when he was closing a sale. Sometimes he danced all day. He had a wife and two kids and often worked through breaks reeling in a prospect; girls would bring him cups of iced sodas, which he would acknowledge with a wink. He was always among the top finishers every week, until he wasn't. At first he continued on as always, dutifully reciting his pitch, but then he got sad, and then angry, and then started asking us in a conspiratorial whisper if it was possible for the supervisors to control who got what leads, because he thinks he may have pissed off the wrong hombre, a fucking hypnotist couldn't sell the deadbeats he was getting.

Billy's end came when a prospect backed out of the sale at the last minute. One part of industry regulation was a system of third-party operators who'd come on the line after you'd closed a sale and make sure you'd disclosed all the fine print. It was really just a formality, but this woman, the first sale Billy'd had in weeks, reconsidered at the last minute and told the third-party operator to forget the whole thing. Billy called her back a few minutes later, pitched her all over again and, after extracting repeated assurances from her that she really wanted to go through with it, sent her back to third-party. Of course, she changed her mind a second time. Billy called her back, cajoled, begged, and finally started screaming at her. And then, *Fuck this place!!*, headset flung against computer monitor, footsteps receding, doors slamming, car peeling out, and so on. He was well liked and we watched him storm out ruefully but also with some excitement, for the center as a group always made about the same number of sales week to week, it was only the individual names and figures that fluctuated, and we knew instinctively that a leader faltering was opportunity for the rest of us.

As it happens, one of the main beneficiaries of Billy's fall was myself. Nothing changed except that one day they all started saying yes. As I said, luck. My spiel was just the same—I couldn't have changed it at that point even if I wanted to, so deeply was it etched onto my synapses. The streak doubled then quadrupled my paychecks and then doubled them again. I was hitting my weekly quotas before lunch on Monday.

Underperforming colleagues were yanked off the phones and forced to sit in on my calls, to "learn." There was nothing to learn, as they soon found out. I was using the same general blueprint they were, telling the same lies. Bullshit, they muttered as they sat there, hopelessly behind on their quotas as I was making sale after sale after sale. Yes, bullshit, I agreed, but wasn't it all bullshit anyway? Now that it favored me I could be a little more philosophical about it. When we went out, drinks were on me, the bosses took to announcing my figures on the PA system. One week I actually sold more than any other telemarketer in the country. I got a paper certificate and for that week the use of the executive parking space in the very front of the parking lot. When word got out that I took the bus to work, people lined up at my desk petitioning to be my chauffeur.

Looking back, I'm not sure why I stayed so long. Clearly, the work catered to my sadistic side, and it provided a convenient and lucrative outlet for my free-floating resentment. If I had to work, my thinking went, why not at a job where I could exact revenge, one call at a time, on my unwitting jailers, that great mass of consumers that underwrote the system that so chafed me? And in the beginning, it was exciting, pulling the wool over their eyes, reveling in the feeling of superiority, of getting away with murder. But like all jobs, it eventually grew tedious. The best salespeople, the absolute elite of the elite, sold maybe 4 percent of the people they talked to in a given day. The flipside of that is that 96 percent of the people they talked to slammed the phone down in their ear after informing them they were a motherless piece of dog shit. Every day people went to lunch and never came back. Most who stayed were just too depressed to find another job, too downtrodden and raw from the up-close blast furnace of dealing with the "public," of squeezing blood from stones.

People dealt with it in various ways. At least once a week we'd all be called into the break room where the shift supervisor would brandish an empty liquor bottle in her latex-gloved hand.

We know someone is drinking in the men's room on shift, she said. If we catch you, you'll be fired on the spot! This has to stop!

It never did. Whoever it was, they favored Black Velvet.

Others spent the breaks driving around the block in shitty hatchbacks with mismatched quarterpanels or dangling fenders, smoking enormous twists of paranoia-inducing ditchweed, chewing jimson seeds or mushrooms of questionable provenance, anything to dull the mind, to transport us however temporarily or halfassedly from our dismal reality. Once someone was passing around a bottle of prescription pills, everyone downing a few, but when the bottle got to me I read the label and announced that we were taking antibiotics. They just shrugged, they weren't discouraged in the least.

And of course there is the romance of rock bottom. There are worse situations to be in, but still telemarketing was a kind of endpoint, the last rung of token normalcy before the indisputable failure of sleeping in your car or moving back in with your parents. Here now was life stripped of all illusion and pretension, down to just a bare scaffolding of desperation and imperative. No glad-handing or networking or angling for that promotion, because nobody cared what school you went to and there were no promotions to be had, just a quasi-legal minute-to-minute, hour-to-hour grind, here in the ghetto of the free market. The minivans in the parking lot with trash bags duct-taped over the shattered window, shards of windowglass still glittering from the baby's car seat, the skittish parolees standing with their backs to the wall in the break room, the junkies fresh from rehab clutching their menthols with hands out of a Bruegel, just biding their time until the next relapse. Here now is a girl fight in the parking lot, two fat girls in a frenzy gone far beyond hair pulling and well into manual scalping, they don't even really want to fight anymore, but the crowd wants blood! Here now is the coworker who invites you to come see his band perform; when you ask what instrument he plays he says he goes onstage at the midpoint of each set and drinks from a gallon jug of milk until he vomits. Here now the beautiful alcoholic who couldn't hold her liquor, she's stumbly by noon, she has a bad habit of going home with men and shitting in their beds. Here now is a fellow in the break room, down on his luck, surreptitiously scanning the floor around the vending area for dropped change because he's broke that day and hungry, drinking glass after glass of water to make his stomach feel full and pocketing napkins to use as toilet paper at home. (Wait, that fellow is me!)

I didn't love these small-town desperadoes, but I admired them for their indifference. People always say that it takes courage to care, but I've found that it take far more to not care, to say *fuck it* and mean it and live it. Though I had little in common with them, I felt at times that I was among my people, people who had no great love for life, who felt as I did that it was something to be endured, and even that only because what else is there?

I was in a dive one night, a bar of bare concrete floors and three-legged lawn chairs and greasy fingerprinted pint glasses, a drunk passed out on the toilet and other patrons pissing into his lap, screw him, where just that week I'd seen a grizzled construction worker choke almost to death a college student who'd wandered in looking just a bit too well scrubbed, a bit too assured of a brighter future than the rest of us there. (After he'd been dragged off the kid by a half-dozen other patrons, the guy bellied up to the bar next to me for a post-assault drink, looked over, and asked, "What do you think of that?"

After a moment's hesitation I said, "I think you're a tough motherfucker." He laughed, threw his arm around my shoulders, and bought me a beer.)

Someone sat next to me and when I looked over it was Billy. He smiled at me and he looked unwell. He took out a cigarette and held it filter up to the light.

Do you know why a Parliament has a recessed filter?

I sure don't, I said.

He held the cigarette under his nose, snorted sharply, and broke out into tremendously unjoyous laughter. I nodded.

So can you hook me up?

I wasn't into coke but in my circles I knew it could be had. I had a feeling that I'd regret being drawn into Billy's nocturnal machinations—if he'd come here, to me, it was safe to say that desperation was running high—but I felt a touch of survivor's guilt about how he'd bombed out of MCI, the sole bread-winner for a wife and kids, done in by a streak of bad luck that could have claimed any one of us. I made a few calls and arranged a delivery to a nearby parking garage. Since Billy was a stranger I had to be at the meet.

Billy had some friends with him, but they ignored me. We sat in the car listening to the radio while we waited for the man. When we finally got the coke it was horrible shit, like cold medicine chopped up and cut with talcum powder. I felt slightly embarrassed to be associated with product of such quality, but no one said anything. I took one line to be polite and sat back.

I heard you're the new top dog now, Billy said after a while, wiping his nose.

I said I guess I was.

How much did you pull in last week?

I told him. He let out a low whistle. Not bad, he said. I bet you got that parking spot now. That used to be my parking spot. Last summer, all last summer, every week.

He did a bump out of the filter end of his cigarette and then lit it.

Top of the world, he said, cashing the big checks, getting that good pussy, I bet. I was there, too. Just remember—it don't last. It don't last.

His eyes were watery, though probably only from the lines. Now get the fuck out of my car, white boy, he said.

How long could it last? Not much longer, as it happened. The entire production was built on sand from the very beginning. Yes, we were making massive commissions on our sales, but they were taxed to death by the 50 percent incentive tax. Even the prizes we won in the weekly sales contests, gift cards and cheap electronics, were taxed out of our paychecks, even if we didn't want them, even if we pitched them directly into the garbage upon receipt. And of course there were the customers, opening bills every day somewhere across the country, the blood draining out of their face as they read the fine print, tallied up surcharge after surcharge, and then sat right down to write an angry letter to their congressperson. The managers were making more off our sales than we were, but then we were so shady that we were killing their golden goose with each sale. *You don't sell a guy one car, you sell a guy ten cars over fifty years,* as the line goes. Well, not only were we selling the customers just one car, as soon as they drove around the corner their proverbial lemon burst into flames and all four wheels shot off their axles simultaneously. It's possible, thinking back, that I never made a single completely legitimate, fine-print fully disclosed sale.

It was rotten to the core, and yet we really had no idea. Stories began appearing in the newspaper about WorldCom, MCI's parent company, and its founder Bernie Ebbers. Authorities said he'd cooked the books to inflate earnings and minimize expenses, overstating company profit by billions of dollars. The stock collapsed and the company went into bankruptcy. The nation at large expressed shock and Ebbers was demonized, but we were only amused. We engaged in the same kind of petty, sloppy fraud every day. Our lies were simply on a smaller scale. When it became obvious that the company was going under, the prevailing sentiment in the cubicles was outrage. To lie, cheat, obfuscate, exaggerate, steal—was this not the essence of business? What could be more American? To game the system couldn't be a crime, for wasn't it rigged already?

As bankruptcy proceeded we geared up for one last pass, one last ruthless fork-tongued pillaging of all the military wives and old ladies on fixed incomes, before the entire company was shuttered. It never even got started. Suddenly broke, the company stopped buying sales leads and instead recycled the dregs of past years. In sales, complaints about the quality of the leads is a constant refrain (shades of *Glengarry Glen Ross*), but this one time it was actually true. This was garbage, worse than garbage—deaf people and pay phones and wrong numbers and receptionists at office towers, and once in a while, just a stone-cold refusenik, someone who wouldn't entertain your lies even for a one second before slamming the phone down. (They were probably ex-telemarketers.) Every day now there were several instances of *Fuck this place!!,* headset flung against a computer monitor, footsteps receding, door slamming, car peeling out of the parking lot. Only this time there was no subsequent ripple of smug titters across the sales floor—we weren't survivors, we'd been left behind.

To make matters worse, now that the feds had the company over a barrel, the top men got paranoid about their dirty little cash cow. In the past they'd turned a blind eye to our methods, but now everyone was in full-on "cover your ass" mode, and they decided that if MCI were to emerge as a viable company, it had to clean up its act. Outside regulators began monitoring our calls; you could tell they'd tapped in when the line took on a hollow, echoey quality. We received new scripts, new binders full of required disclosures and approved openers and legal jargon in all capitals detailing what would happen if we deviated from these new rules. We threw them in the garbage unread.

People started quitting, taking flat-wage jobs at malls or drive-through windows. It was clear to us that this new regime had no future, with its recycled leads, its stultifying rules, its contemptible naïve insistence on full disclosure and honesty. The product was shit! This is what the higher-ups didn't understand. The product was shit and as such it couldn't be sold even to an idiot except by deception. And this is exactly what I told the center manager when I was called into his office for repeated recorded instances of "unapproved sales methods."

Where do you think I learned these unapproved sales methods, Doug, I asked when I was called into the center manager's office. I learned them here, Doug. From Day One. You can't just one day tell us that everything you've taught us is no longer allowed, and good luck.

That's exactly what we're telling you. A real salesperson adapts to whatever situation—

Salesperson? There are no salespeople out there, Doug. We're just liars and conmen. Go ahead, say it. Liars and conmen. Say it for me.

He shrugged and sat back in his chair. He'd worked on the phones himself, years ago, and he knew what we were, but he also had a family and his cushy salaried job was suddenly in very real peril. I was not going to be a monkey wrench in the new machine he was building.

Within eighteen months the place would be completely emptied, the motivational banners in the landfill, the furniture remaindered for pennies on the dollar, the building itself used for bulldozer storage, and a few years after that the tele-marketing industry itself would be dead, killed by cell phones and Do Not Call lists, discarded on the trash heap of industrial history along with coal scuttlers and milkmen. But of course we didn't know that then. He called security to escort me from the building.

Oh, so *that's* what those security guards are for, I thought. The two now-familiar guards meekly stood at each side of my chair and asked me to stand up.

Many people, when they were fired, took the opportunity to settle old scores, to vent months or years of pent-up complaints. This was their chance to tell everyone what they really thought. I only felt relief. When I passed Jordy's section on the way out, flanked by security guards, I stopped and on an impulse, bowed. Everyone smiled and waved and gave me unironic thumbs-ups, their eyes at least sincere as their lips kept moving, dispensing lies to strangers...

CHAPTER 10

Aftermath Interlude

or, The Other Thing

I once spent the Fourth (and Fifth) of July in an overcrowded small-town jail after an argument with several police officers in which I thought being right would somehow protect me from arrest. They packed thirty or forty people into a space meant for maybe a dozen, students and dead-enders and big bull-necked farmboys with singed palms from holding fire-crackers just a split second too long, red faced and blind drunk and fucking pissed because it was Independence Day in the greatest democracy in the history of mankind and still somehow their lives fucking sucked. We were each given a thin five-foot-long sleeping pad and herded into a small con-crete room with small windows ten feet up the walls. We had to lie head-to-feet in close-set rows, and all night I laid there slowly sobering up, parch-mouthed, as they tossed and writhed all around me in their sleep, kicking me in the head, bellowing about various unresolved grievances in their dreams, pissing themselves. When I sat up to catch a breath of fresh air above the rank fetid heat of all those men, a speaker crackled to life and ordered me to lie back down. When 8 a.m.

finally came they herded us all into the common area. We
were to be out-processed in alphabetical order, but because of
the crowd, it would take all day. Most of us were still drunk or
just hitting the worst of hangovers and tempers were short.
One guy vomited and then scuffled with a guard, both of them
slipping and sliding and finally pratfalling together into the
warm throw-up. The vomiter was promptly strapped into a
restraint chair and a hood of fine mesh was put over his head.
He proceeded to scream and struggle against his restraints all
morning, pausing occasionally to regurgitate a mouthful of
bile, which congealed in the inside front of the mesh hood
until his face was completely obscured. The other prisoners
exchanged meth recipes and counseled each other on the
finer points of home invasion (did you know most burglar
alarms can be disabled with nothing more than aluminum
foil?) as I sat around trying to look tough. My posing was
undercut by the fact that they'd confiscated my glasses, so I
was left to shuffle around squinting like Mr. Magoo. Late in
the afternoon I was almost shanked when I mistook a fat man
for a chair and tried to sit in his lap...

When I finally got out that evening, hungover, starving,
filthy, and blessedly unsodomized, I felt a relief that bordered
on euphoria. But—and here's my point—it was nothing, nothing at all, compared to how I felt being fired from each and
every one of those shitty jobs...

Hoo-ee!! Because a jail is just a building, but when you've
got to work, the jail is your life. The Man might let you wear
jeans on Fridays, but your ass is still company property. To be
fired is to receive the gift of everything; of freedom, of time, of
life. Even as I laid in bed for hours after my arcade ipecac incident, heaving yesterday's lunch and then just bile and then
actual blood into a wastebasket, I couldn't stop smiling,
because I was free again, and that scene has repeated itself
every time I've been fired.

But like any abrupt transition, it can come as a shock. It's like getting dumped by a girlfriend who you're sick to death of anyway—underneath the thrill of liberation, there's still that twinge of *YOU'RE dumping ME? I should be dumping YOU!* The key in these situations (both a firing and a dumping) is to draw a line between your new life and your old one; I always went on a monthlong drunk, just to get recalibrated and clean house.

One recent firing took place first thing in the morning and I was home by noon, ready to get down to some serious drinking. I'd long since discovered that you could drink much faster if you just poured the forty into a punch bowl—with luck I could get the whole two and a half beers down in less than a minute. I hadn't eaten breakfast that morning and the first sweet wave of drunkenness hit within minutes, a buzz of poisoned neurons withering and dying as months of unnecessary nonsense got sloughed off into oblivion; how to do a mail merge, MLA style, Excel keyboard shortcuts, the name of my ex-boss's little microcephalic pants-shitters. Good-bye and good riddance!

In my enthusiasm, I'd spilled down the front of my powder-blue button-up, my red silk tie, my flat-front khakis. I started to pat them down but then remembered that no, I wouldn't be needing these clothes again anytime soon, so who gives a shit about staining? This thought so delighted me that I allowed my jaw to slacken and I dribbled another half-mouthful of beer down the front of my outfit. Why, I might never have to wear this hateful goon suit again, ever! I could burn it, for all that it mattered. And as soon as this thought entered my mind I knew I had to do it. A little symbolism never hurt anyone, did it?

I stripped down and donned my red velour anchors-and-sailboats bathrobe and took the clothes out into the backyard. Under a tarp I found the vestiges of a grilling phase my ex-girlfriend Sadie and I had briefly entertained: tongs, charcoal, lighter fluid. I threw the clothes in the grass, soaked them down with lighter fluid, and threw on a match. They went up with a whoosh and I stood there savoring the smell of poly-cotton blend and starch and antiperspirant-caked pit stains and asexual mediocrity going up in flames, my upward mobility incinerated in a second.

I heard a door open and turned and saw my neighbor emerge out onto his deck. He was a smiley garrulous blond fellow who owned a boat and was perpetually remodeling his house.

Hey neighbor! What are you up to?

Burning some clothes, I said, staring into the fire.

Oh. Seconds passed as he waited for me to elaborate. Why are you doing that?

They're dirty.

Oh. He emitted a forced chuckle. Okay. By the way, I haven't seen that girlfriend of yours around for a while. She used to keep the front yard so pretty, now it's all grown out. Is everything all right?

Sadie and I broke up, Mitch, I said. She left town. She won't be back, ever, I said. I spit a mouthful of beer onto the burning clothes. When that didn't have the desired inflammatory effect, I squirted on a long stream of lighter fluid, and the flames flared upward. She's gone, Mitch, I said. And good riddance.

Mitch looked wide eyed from the burning clothes to me, back to the burning clothes, and then retreated back into his apartment.

I stood there sipping from my second forty, my head swimming, watching the clothes curl and blacken and disintegrate. When they were all but gone I toed the pile of ashes with one foot and grunted. Well, *that* wasn't me anymore, not that it ever really had been. But then what was left? The answer seemed obvious but on the other hand I could feel through the fog of intoxication a distinct urge for a four-dollar cup of burnt Starbucks, followed by ninety minutes of eBay auction monitoring and then a 1500-calorie lunch of Asian-fusion strip mall fare. Who exactly had I become? I thought this over as I stood in the yard scattering the ashes of my former uniform. There was a chunk of something in the middle that just wouldn't break up, and when I finally troubled it apart I found that it was my wallet, melted into a solid clot of plastic and faux leather and scorched small bills, the contents beyond rescue, all the metro cards with fifteen cents on them and business cards of "contacts" I'd "networked" (OH NOES) and coffee punch cards. I bent and plucked out the melted remains of my driver's license and left the rest of it for the birds, or identity thieves, or crackheads, or whoever...

For the next week I was delirious with liberation, out on the town every night, but then something else set in. Not necessarily a depression or a sadness, but more like an uncomfortable ambiguity. One of the most unfortunate aspects of human nature is that you never feel more yourself than when you're surrounded by that which you despise. Freud felt the personality was a hostile, reactionary impulse, and the aftermaths of my firings seemed to confirm that. After all, it's easy to feel good about yourself when you're surrounded by loud-talking salesmen with "These Colors Don't Run!" bumper stickers, orange-skinned girls from Marketing who never stop smiling, even under anesthesia, venal yes-men middle managers with bad pants and worse haircuts so steeped in corporatespeak that no one has understood a single fucking thing that's come out of their mouths for years, literally years. The typical office is like a living breathing answer to the oldest of philosophical inquiries. *What should one do?* Anything but this! Clarity like that is hard to come by. But suddenly without all these people around demonstrating for me exactly what not to do, I backslid into fuzzy self-doubt and a kind of general malaise. Many a late post-firing afternoon found me trotting up and down my hallway in my bathrobe, doing a little shadow-boxing and saying to myself, shrug it off, Franklin, turn back the clock, back to better times, better Franklin, the front of my robe sodden with beer overspill.

What to do with myself? This was the question that tormented me as I spent entire days and then weeks on the sofa or in bed, vowing to get up in ten minutes and do something, and live, but the next thing I knew it was dark and then it was time to go back to bed. I wasn't depressed, but I was paralyzed by something.

I remembered the first time I worked up the guts to cut school, back in the fourth grade. We'd been reading about explorers; De Leon, who died searching for the Fountain of Youth, Magellan, the legendary circumnavigator! I felt that I was capable of similar things, great things, if only I could shake off the limits put on me by well-meaning adults. One morning during recess I slipped around the corner of the building and sprinted to the alley, crouching behind a parked car until I heard the rest of the students file back inside to resume their schoolday. As I walked the deserted Iowa mid-morning streets, I was filled with euphoria. Finally, the world was mine to experience, with no parents or teachers or minders filtering and mediating my every perception, oppressing me with their palpable worry-vibes. Should I go to the arcade? The candy store? Down to the river? An undeveloped ravine lay on the edge of town where, according to rumor, there was a Model T half-sunk in a swamp. If I found it and returned to school with an ancient hood ornament, my playground standing would be secured.

All of these options had their own appeal, but for some reason I couldn't decide on just one. It wasn't that I couldn't decide between my options, it was that I didn't know how to make a decision. I'd spent my childhood in school, trudging in single-file lines down interminable hallways, moving from room to room at the prompting of a bell or klaxon, coloring inside the lines and asking permission to use the restroom. I chafed at these constant restraints, but once I was free of them I found that I was unequipped to deal with freedom. After standing paralyzed in the beautiful spring morning for perhaps thirty minutes, I shuffled back to school and turned myself in at the office, where they at that moment were making panicked phone calls to the local police, who were preparing to pull over every unmarked van in a fifty-mile radius. When they asked why I'd gone, I just shrugged. No one ever thought to ask why I'd come back, which I found disturbing even then.

And now I had the same problem. It was freedom that oppressed me! Thinking back on my previous year of clock-punching, it all seemed like just a blur of commuting and meetings and and overpriced lunches with people I didn't like but didn't quite hate either. And I guess I could see now why some people loved to work, had to work. Working was the ultimate winnowing-down of choices—once you settled in somewhere, almost every hour of your day was now designated for sleeping or working or getting to and from work or gymgoing or blowing off steam through harmless little pre-approved outlet activities. Once you plugged in, you could go for the rest of your life without ever having to make a choice more substantial than soup or salad, brown shoes or black. Get a raise? Buy property. Get a promotion? Start golfing. Hit thirty? Get married. Hate your marriage? Have some kids. Two wrongs make a right, three wrongs make two rights, four make three, ad infinitum.

The ugly truth is that despite our politicians' ritual incantations about "freedom" and officially licensed "Home of the Free" bumper stickers, ten-gallon hats, and fanny-packs available in red, white or blue and available on every streetcorner, we are not a people who love freedom. We love the idea of freedom, we love it in the abstract, but when it comes to the messy reality of freedom, we recoil in horror. Is this our fault? Maybe, maybe not. After all, from day one we're conditioned to do as we're told. By the time the average American has graduated college, he's spent seventeen years sweating deadlines, clockwatching, currying favor from authority figures, following instructions, paying attention to detail, coloring inside the lines. He's utterly unprepared to do anything but take orders. Growing up, one generally realizes after it's already too late, is the abdication of freedom, done in increments so small that we hardly notice its loss. It's marvelous training to be a bean-counter, but generally quite poor preparation for life.

Weaning myself off of that dependence was by far the hardest thing I've ever done. And I guess this is the part when I'm expected to offer you the reader some valuable advice or a secret formula or an itemized lists of strategies to follow in my footsteps, what color is whoever moved your cheese, the lost insights of Jesus or Mohammed or Xenu. Unfortunately, this isn't that sort of book.

What do you want to know? How to live? I can't help you there. I can show you how *not* to live. (Just look out your window.) There's no easy solution to this problem, you just have to puzzle it out. What should one do and how should one do it? You've just got to puzzle it out, and that takes thought, which takes time, which means you can't be spending your days making the rich richer by rubberstamping invoices or writing ad copy to sell pet rocks or constructing dynamic online portals or et cetera et cetera ad infinitum. In a very real sense, you have to decide if you're going to have a job or a life, if you're going to be a worker or a human being.

And don't tell anyone I said this, but I'm glad that I'm incapable of holding down a job, because if I could, I probably would. Because there are no guarantees in life, and you could spend decades trying to puzzle it out and still end up dying miserable and alone under a bridge where little kids will find you and poke your corpse with sticks before it's cremated by the city and the ashes disposed of in a mass anonymous grave for unclaimed decedents. Because choosing to live, to live for oneself, means you take on a tremendous burden of responsibility. No one else can be held accountable for your happiness, your freedom, your anything, and that's not a burden many people are willing to shoulder. It's much easier to go sit in a cubicle for eight, nine hours a day, receive a little disposable income to buy yourself clothes at the mall and a new car on the installment plan and pay-per-view wrestling matches on Saturday nights to make you feel like you're DOIN' THE DARN THANG, and just kind of comfortably putter along for the rest of your days. And then die. Which is what most people do.

Or, you could do the other thing.

But before you hit that painful transitional phase, nothing can touch those first white hot hours after a firing, when you're giddy from sudden liberation and everything seems possible. After my impromptu biz-cazsh cookout I sat on my fire escape in the shattering midday sun, and had another celebratory round, savoring the first happiness I'd felt in months. I knew I had the whole summer and fall off, financed by unemployment checks. Just like when I was a kid, only better. My fire escape overlooks a blind alley, and as I sat there with a tallboy of malt liquor in each hand, a homeless fellow came around the corner. My stretch of alley can't be seen from either street, and people often gravitated there to pass the pipe or settle a dispute with fists or box cutters or pinch a furtive loaf or for a quick transactional fuck. As I sat watching from above, the man took two tallboys out of his garbage bag, cracked them open, and stood there taking nips from one and then the other, the relief on his face visible even at a distance. After a moment he looked around and spied me in my perch. Seeing the same distinctive silver cans of Steel Reserve in my hands, he raised his tallboys in a salute and then took a long draught from each one. I did the same and we both laughed, a moment of genuine affinity that trumped any break-room or desk-side chat I ever had. As he tottered into one of the abandoned houses, dragging behind his garbage bag of possessions, I realized I'd truly crossed over...

CHAPTER 11

The Metamorphosis

or, It's Never Too Early, but It's Almost Always Too Late

My firing from MCI had been a textbook example of how not to get unemployment—they'd chronicled all of my transgressions and I'd clearly broken every rule on the (cooked) books. I was resigned to getting another shitty job but thought there might be a small chance I could use my newfound persuasive powers to fast-talk my way through an arbitration hearing. I was of course delighted when MCI, already under fire from all sides for their own transgressions, deemed my unemployment hearing to be an inadvisable use of their limited time and resources, and failed to show up. I won by default and incredibly, I found myself fully funded for the next year or so.

Given this rare opportunity for self-improvement and life enrichment, I proceeded to spend it on aimless debauchery.

I have only hazy impressions from this period, as I was truly drifting and on top of that fucked up pretty much all the time. There was a shower orgy in which one of the female participants slipped on the wet porcelain and cracked her head on the floor hard enough to lose consciousness. The other participants only paused long enough to drag her onto the bathroom floor, where she lay face down next to the toilet as they recommenced their sodomies. Sprawled on a sofa in some party house at some undetermined hour of night with some temporary companion, moved almost to tears when we discover a stash of drugs inside a hollowed-out wooden figurine. Later that night as we're lying semi-catatonic in an unfurnished room somewhere, we seem to have a shared hallucination that the door is being kicked down, but our delirious laughter turns to horror when we realize, no, the owner of the pilfered goods has somehow tracked us down and is in fact kicking the door in, and he is not at all happy. A party where a skinhead is escorted from the premises (thrown off the porch, actually) for getting unruly, and he returns shortly with half a dozen friends who proceed to beat everyone in the house, even the harmless bespectacled fellow who hadn't even been there at the time of the ejection, who clung to their lower legs and wept as they bludgeoned him, even the girl who stood in the center of the carnage and screamed, over and over, *please, no violence!* until she was abruptly cut off by a ham-sized fist that knocked her out cold. Only I escaped unscathed; I was childhood friends with the head skinhead's girlfriend, and at the outset of the carnage he'd pointed at me and turned to his cronies and said I was to be left unharmed. It saved me a bloody nose, but my reputation around town was shot from that point on, as I was thereafter suspected of secret fascist leanings.

Throughout this period, I was living a sort of double life. I was seeing a girl who lived in Washington, D.C., and we were in love. She had a white-collar job in a downtown office and an apartment in her own name and good credit and health insurance and an IRA, and though she swore otherwise, as time passed it became apparent that if I didn't join her in adulthood I would lose her. I'd never considered this before, but Iowa City was a very small town and now that I'd been fired from MCI, there literally wasn't anywhere else to work. The steady stream of unemployment checks was the perfect cushion for a move, and I was sick of my life anyway. When I brought it up to Sadie, she agreed immediately, and in short order I'd given away everything I owned except for a suitcase of books and clothes, and moved to D.C.

I cut my hair, shaved, donned my most shapeless khakis and pastel button-up, and struck out on the job interview circuit. It was a rude introduction to the workaday world; swaying on the train at rush hour, ass to crotch with the other zombies reeking of aftershave, always late, sucking down burnt Starbucks (why is it always burnt?) just to stay awake, walking through cubicle farms and being eyed up and down by sour-faced fat women eating Cups-a-Soup. My recently acquired sales skills came in handy and by the end of each interview I was chortling and shaking hands with my prospective bosses, with whom I was already on a first-name basis. *Tell me about it, Bill, a good worker is hard to find.* It was obvious they didn't know anything, and like all know-nothings, were eager to believe anything they were told.

One place, some trade association in the Virginia suburbs, where I was such a hit they had me take their aptitude test on the spot.

Ace this and the job is yours, my interviewer told me, and to this day I swear he liked me so much because we wore the same color shirt.

I sat down at the computer and clicked "begin." Word association; questions about surreal, dreamlike hypothetical situations; Rorschach blots. After rolling my eyes at the prefatory admonition to "be honest in your answers," I of course proceeded to choose the answers that would get me the job. ("Night" is to "dark" as "You" are to: (a) "honest"; (b) "dishonest.") But later, as I thought more and more about what taking that job would mean—the long commute, the annoying boss—I began to regret my decision. And so when they called and said that my test results had been lost and would I mind taking it again, I did so with relish. I still had unemployment coming in, so what did I care? This time, I picked all the wrong answers. My girlfriend sat with me at my computer, and we laughed as I deliberately spiked the test. If I were angry at a coworker, would I rationally and calmly discuss my grievance, or would I bottle it up and brood? If I pass someone in a hallway, do I make eye contact and greet him or ignore him? Anything that might paint me as antisocial, lazy, unstable, indifferent, or rebellious, I picked.

A woman called the next day. Could I start Monday? I was flabbergasted.

I don't think I want the job, I said.

What? Then why did you take the test?

A good question, I thought. I stood thinking for a moment, but couldn't come up with anything, so I gently, gently replaced the phone in its cradle and turned the ringer off.

Back to the job search. My plan was to hold out for something ideal, but as the weeks wore on, Sadie became impatient for me to follow her into legitimacy. I didn't want to disappoint her so, though I had misgivings, I accepted the next job I was offered.

INCOMP had been contracted by the federal government to oversee the renovations on a massive and iconic federal arts center, the government itself being too beholden to its own redundant bureaucracy and dedicated inefficiencies to properly administer such a project. The private sector, the free market, clearly, was the only way to go. INCOMP in turn subcontracted the project out piecemeal to various other private sector vendors and companies, in each case the lowest bidder taking the pot, each tier of market-driven competence further winnowing away inefficiency and waste until, in theory at least, the renovation would pretty much build itself, the cranes and jackhammers and cement trucks propelling themselves across the landscape with a jaunty diligence, like the platoon of brooms in that *Sorcerer's Apprentice* cartoon, except the animating force in this case was not sorcery but the free market, a motive no less magical and, as it turned out, no less imaginary.

Hee hee! Even now I can't think back on the long list of grievances and bunglings without a titter. The project managers would never tell you straight out what had gone wrong—after all, it was their fault—but as in any office, the help liked to gossip. The rumors I heard were truly mind boggling, but were supported by paperwork that passed my desk or overheard snatches of conversation or furious screaming exchanges in the office next door. A mistyped proposal would be sent out and a year later a massive concrete plaza, tons of material and thousands of man-hours, would have to be demolished and redone—the numbers for length and width had been transposed when the plans had been transmitted. Another ill-conceived plaza was slated to be built on an adjacent plot of land but the newly acquired property had been the site of a large shittily maintained gas station for decades and the soil itself was incandescently toxic from years of fuel leaks. Before anything could be built, INCOMP was legally obligated to remove the toxic soil. When the specialized waste handlers arrived, festooned in biohazard suits and piloting special triple-layered hermetically sealed tankers, they found that oops, someone had mixed up the scheduling and the plaza had already been built and could they perhaps carefully dig the poisonous soil out from under the gleaming new multi-million-dollar plaza?

A new addition either incorrectly blueprinted or the plans incorrectly executed—the new and old simply didn't fit together, entire buildings one or six or eighteen inches off-kilter. Rebuild or repair? And whose fault was it? Who was to foot the bill for the extra work? This problem—and every problem—would be settled in court, after months or years of suits and countersuits. Nothing, absolutely nothing, worked out properly, and no one would admit fault even when it was obvious whose fault it was. That, of course, being what court was for, because who knows, with a slick enough lawyer you might be able to weasel out of something and hey, saving or not saving the company five million dollars was the difference between a promotion and a pink slip. Because it didn't matter what you knew, it mattered what you could prove, and the gap between the two was often quite sizable.

My job, other than the occasional writing or editing, was to archive the documents that passed between INCOMP and various subcontractors. (That they trusted a nobody like me to fill out these million-dollar work orders should give you a sense of why they were always fucking up.) When a new document came into the office—and dozens of them crossed my desk every single day—another guy in the office scanned it onto the server and then it was my job to file the hard copy in one of perhaps a hundred binders placed in, on, and in a heap at the foot of, a massive sagging complex of bookshelves. Which binder was the proper one was determined by consulting a long prioritized list of various topics, projects, subcontractors, and job sites, and even then half the time it came down to a judgment call. Then you had to locate the proper binder in which to file the document, which itself could take hours.

To say this job was dull would be an understatement. Most days I felt like Bartleby the Scrivener. But if I had any second thoughts, they were quickly erased by Sadie's evident pride in my recent ascension from layabout to salaryman, and if things got bad and I found myself yearning for my days of unemployment, reading in bed until late afternoon and staying out all night, enough paper moved across my desk each day that I could easily immerse myself in work to the point where I simply had no time to think.

The bulk of the project was divided between three project managers—Tom, Larry, and Bill. Or was it Tim, Gary, and Will? Or Ted, Jerry, and Phil? I was never able to remember their right names or really even tell them apart. They were the men in charge, not only in the office but in a larger sense, though usually they tried not to gloat too obviously. They were men's men, ex-military, ex-athletes, they had white-collar jobs in a blue-collar field, monstrous cars, cavernous houses in the exurbs, wives who (they said) gave masterful blowjobs, virile mustaches, high and tight haircuts, a wardrobe of earth tones that was bought new every year but was in a style that was neither in nor out of fashion. Most of them white but a few of them black, which gave all parties a warm feeling of diverse affirmation, never mind that it was the falsest most superficial kind of diversity—you could've switched out their brains and I don't think anyone would have noticed, not least the men themselves, who all dressed and talked and thought exactly alike.

The lone woman who worked in the office was an amazonian forty-something engineer named Lurleen. She'd once been attractive, but now she dressed like a twelve-year-old at a ballerina-themed slumber party and talked mainly of her "boyfriend," the actor Kiefer Sutherland, whom she'd never met. At least once a day she'd launch into a breathless, weirdly angry monologue about what she'd do to Kiefer, given the chance. Her fantasies always started with a description of what he'd be wearing (khakis, leather bomber jacket) and proceeded to encompass a nighttime motorcycle ride, candlelight dinner, and a hotel room. But just when things were on the brink of getting explicit, she'd break off with a guttural menopausal whinny and fall morbidly silent, leaving everyone in earshot to turn back to their computers and shudder, as we involuntarily extrapolated all the carnal acts she was at that moment imagining just a few feet away. At these moments I always breathed through my mouth, just in case she experienced an attack of explosive lust-induced incontinence.

The only other person in the office was Abraham, an unremarkable bespectacled white guy. Technically he had the same job as I did, but had fashioned a patchwork set of duties for himself, typing up memos for Gary, who was impatient and could only hunt and peck, fetching coffee for Edwin, the head man, screening phone calls for Lurleen. He'd achieved total job security, at the mere cost of his dignity. Under his façade of aggressive normalcy bubbled, predictably, some rather deviant urges. He spent hours a day at his desk surfing the nether regions of the Internet, watching grainy surveillance videos of people being run down in the street by garbage trucks, homeless people set afire by teens, Islamists cutting off the hands of shoplifters. He seemed to glean real enjoyment from these videos, wiggling in his chair and exclaiming *awesome!* when the blood and guts erupted.

Also, he talked incessantly of fucking. Fucking fucking fucking, men and women of all ages and sizes in every imaginable orifice and setting; a standing 69 in a janitor's closet, a rusty trombone in a Red Lobster bathroom, a golden shower under the bleachers at a monster truck rally. If he was walking down the street and saw a rotten cantaloupe in the garbage, I have no doubt that he'd stop, cut a hole in one end, drop his pants, and fuck it into pulp right there on the sidewalk. My second Monday on the job I was at my desk furtively eating a breakfast sandwich from a nearby deli when he walked up with a stack of papers.

These are the papers for the south addition, he said. Edwin wants you to look over the cover letter and then file it with the rest of the south addition stuff. Oh, also—I fucked the cable guy last weekend.

I stopped midbite. What?

Yeah, said Abraham. He came by on Saturday morning to hook up my cable and I asked him if he was freaky and the next thing I knew, he was all over my dick like it was a lollipop. Then he came back the next day with his wife and we played all day. We even did a DP. Do you know what that is?

What am I, a Mennonite? Of course I know what that is.

Ugh. I looked down at my breakfast sandwich, frozen halfway to my mouth. The pink folded pastrami and viscous melted cheese had begun to take on a rather unsavory aspect. I turned the sandwich sideways to spare myself the sight, and was confronted with the vaguely puckered orifice in the middle of the bagel. I set it down on the edge of my desk and tried to clear my head.

You have a girlfriend, don't you? Abraham asked slyly. What are you guys doing this weekend?

No, my girlfriend's dead, I said. She died of bowel cancer. And I have AIDS.

Abraham heaved a sigh. Has anyone ever told you that you have nice lips, he asked.

While this undiscriminating lust could be irritating, by far his worst characteristic was his singing. Every office has one person who sings as they go about making copies or coffee, and in this one it was Abraham. Encouraged by Lurleen, whose failing self-esteem he propped up with the occasional sexual proposition, he sometimes spent half the day belting out Top 40 hits and gospel songs with a lack of self-consciousness usually only seen in people with organic brain injuries. Of course he had no idea that he sounded fucking horrible. His vibrato-soaked alto might have gotten him to the second round of *American Idol* but to a discerning listener it was rather like having a racehorse urinate in your ear.

The most infuriating aspect of this habit was when he'd show up at my desk and give an unsolicited recital. How to react? At first I tried to ignore him but this only egged him on, as he sang louder and vampier, embellishing each line with a flourish of jazz hands and a soft-shoe. Finally, when ignoring him proved futile, I turned in my chair and watched, which was somehow even worse. What to do for those interminable minutes as he drew out each soaring note, staring off into the middle distance? As I sat with my face arranged in an expression of polite acknowledgment, I began to hate him and then hate myself for not quite having the guts to haul off and punch him in mid-crescendo.

After a few weeks of this, I finally interrupted one day and told him that I had work to do, and could he save it, and on second thought, could he just never ever sing at my desk again and ideally never in the office again, and thank you very much now fuck off you passive-aggressive little shitmidget.

He just gaped at me—not even hurt, but incredulous. In his mind it was as if I'd pissed up onto the Sistine Chapel...after a moment he turned on his heel and stomped back to his desk, where he sat arms crossed, softly singing the chorus of a song popular at that time, *I am beautiful, no matter what they say...*

The project managers' jobs were to oversee the work that was being done, which meant that they themselves never did any actual work. Instead, they spent a lot of time on the phone cajoling various foremen and site managers in the voice of the Father in a black-and-white sitcom: *Can you do this for me? I'm counting on you—don't let me down.* When they weren't in meetings, they'd gather to shoot the shit in the conference room mere inches from my desk. These episodes of office camaraderie began with the token chitchat—how's the wife, the kids, and so on—but quickly and invariably moved to talk of their latest toys. One of them would whip out his new cell phone and enumerate all the fantastic unnecessary features as the rest of them pretended to be interested, all the while mentally rehearsing their own exhibitions. This would continue until each of them had shown off their new laptop, phone, wristwatch, PDA, camera, car, truck, et cetera. This was all done in the tone of a father showing off pictures of a new baby, and after a particularly triumphant debut—Tim's underwater camcorder very nearly induced aneurysms of jealousy in the others—I sincerely expected him to offer around a post-congratulatory box of cigars.

One afternoon while Tim was at a meeting, Abraham crept into his office and brought out his latest purchases, which he'd been parading around the office that morning, a professional-quality digital camera and the latest iPod.

How do you look at the photos he's taken? Abraham asked. I bet he's got nude pictures of his wife on there!

Back up, man, I said. He was already massaging the front of his jeans. Sadie had a similar camera, and I was able to bring up the Pictures folder. The only picture was a grainy shot he'd taken of his computer monitor, from the vantage point of his chair. We put the camera down and turned to the iPod. The only thing on it was an audiobook of *7 Habits of Highly Effective People*. Almost a thousand dollars' worth of hardware, and they may as well have been paperweights.

Oh man, I said to Abraham as we sauntered back to our desks. This guy is barely even human. He's like a meat robot from the planet Square!

Ooh, meat, said Abraham, rubbing his crotch with renewed fervor.

The head of this circus was an executive named Edwin, a snappish, rosacea-faced penguin who split his time between D.C. and Florida, blowing into town every other week or so to conduct damage control and gauge the project's plummeting fortunes. As soon he walked in the door he began shouting at the top of his lungs about this or that fuck-up, demanding to see a blueprint or a proposal, and hurry up you incompetents, and everyone in the office save myself would sit bolt upright and begin running in frantic little circles in front of their desks, like malfunctioned floor buffers. In a way, I guess he couldn't be blamed for being in such a foul mood all the time; he was in charge of a multi-million-dollar project that was being thoroughly and astonishingly bungled. I might even have sympathized with him had he not taken a particular interest in me and my minute-to-minute activities. It was an eerie flashback to my arcade days, but even more galling. Chuck, my arcade manager, had in his defense that he at least had nothing better to do than torture me, whereas Edwin actually had vast sums of money and a literal army of highly compensated tradesmen riding on his performance.

One day my phone rang, which was somewhat unusual in itself. The only people who ever called me were my girlfriend or Abraham, to tell me how he'd sodomized his grandmother's bridge partner in a Dumpster behind a pawn shop or something.

This is Frank, I said.

No, said a nasal voice I immediately recognized as Edwin's. It's "Good morning, this is Frank. How may I help you?" And you say it like you mean it. Got it?

Yeah, I got it, I said, and hung up. A second later, the phone rang again.

This is Frank, I said.

There was silence on the line. Then, someone clearing his throat. *Ahem, ahem.*

"Good morning, this is Frank. How may I help you?" Edwin said, his voice rising an octave and a half with false perkiness. This is your last warning. Got it? That's how you answer the phone from now on.

Okay, boss, I said. He hung up. A second later, the phone rang.

This is Frank, I said.

"Good morning! This is Frank! How may I help you?!" He was nearly screaming now. Say it! Right now, repeat after me! "Good morning!"

Good morning, I said in a slurring monotone, trying to keep the glee out of my voice.

Say it like you mean it! His voice rose again into shrillness. "Good morning!" Say it now, and you better mean it!

Have I ever not done my job satisfactorily, Edwin? I asked.

There was a moment of silence on the line, and then he

hung up. When it rang again a second later, I let it ring. If the project was losing, at a conservative estimate, a half million dollars a month, then the thirty minutes he spent haranguing me cost the company ten grand. I thought about writing a cost analysis and forwarding it to his office in Florida, but thought better of it.

Home life was no less nonsensical. Every day brought a new absurdity and I could almost see our domesticity curdling as I bridled at this new life. Separate the trash, cans and bottles here and paper there, never mind that you've seen them throw it all into the same truck, this bin goes out on the third Monday, the others on the second and fourth Thursday, this bill needs to be paid by the ninth, and this one by the tenth which means it has to be mailed on the sixth at the latest, it's Tuesday so we have to clean the kitchen tonight, never mind that it's not dirty, Tuesday night is kitchen cleaning night and its Tuesday night, also we should trim the backyard, its getting a little long, never mind that its fenced in and no one can even see it, we can see it, and that's all that matters, it's a matter of self-respect, don't leave your dishes in the sink, Jesus will know, a place for everything and everything in its place, shower every day even though you never break a sweat, and I hope you don't have any plans tomorrow, I wanted to go over our retirement accounts, we have to start making contributions now, you know, it's never too early but it's always almost too late.

This was life lived for the future, never the present, and for other people, never yourself. A life turned outward, with nothing at the center but a void. It was a cowardly lifestyle, as it was motivated entirely by fear—fear of disapproval, fear of discomfort, fear of standing out, fear of failure. But I'd been flat broke and down and out, and I feared none of this. In fact it struck me all as the concerns of a child, the definition of an adult being, I thought, someone who accepts the risk inherent in life and soldiers on anyway. But no, I found now that my lifelong effort to shed my irrational childlike fear had somehow disqualified me for adult life.

Worse yet, sitting at a computer eight hours a day under flickering fluorescent lighting had completely burned out my capacity for any kind of subtle pleasure. My weekdays spent in deprivation left me with an irrepressible hunger for the coarse. Now I understood Abraham's fascination with the grotesque, his thirst for sensation, any kind of sensation. Suddenly everything had to be turned up to 11, soaked in butter, in HD, and with giant undulating double-E implants. After work my girlfriend and I moved with our peers to food courts and chain restaurants to consume food laced with corn syrup and MSG, and then retired to watch television or better yet, to the multiplex! (Fuck *books*!) More explosions, more rotating camerawork, Dutch angles, epilepsy-inducing ratatat cuts, more robots, more skin, more tits, more mushroom clouds, more everything! Oh, a sequel? Even better, we won't be bothered with exposition or characters, no thinking needed, we know from the first scene exactly how everything is going to play out, and not only does this plodding populist determinism not detract from the experience, it intensifies it. Because far more important than the interesting is the familiar—security, at all costs! And we sat there in the dark surrounded by our fellow Americans clutching the armrests as our entire bodies reverberated with THX surround-sound, 8,000 volts of speakers and a bass cannon the size of a harpoon launcher all to give you, the paying customer, the sensation of *being there*. Being where? Why in the moment of course, the one truly forbidden no-man's-land in this era of illusory freedom. The present, the one mode of consciousness that must be avoided at all costs, for that's where the dirty business of living is actually carried out. Because really, who could look into that void? Who could take the truth of their own life, the vacuity of those endless commutes, the fluorescent-lit days? The only time you get to live in your skin is vicariously, through the exploits of others, large or small screen, the preciously petty contestants of reality TV or the bland archetypes of the silver screen, an hour or two of vicarious swashbuckling, vied over by multiple desirable suitors, fighting for the cause of righteousness, smiting your enemies in orgies of casual mayhem, risking it all and coming through (though just barely) in the end. An hour or two of a simulacra of life and then back to your hidey-hole to lay your clothes out for the next day and to fall into a restless sleep, tortured by the almost unbearable vividness of your dreams...

Adult life was not agreeing with me. I was too smart for it, or too dumb, or too strong, or too weak, one or the other.

The first thing I did when I arrived each morning around 8:30 was to brew a pot of double-strength Folgers, and by ten minutes until nine, having ingested two cups of bitter, syrup-thick coffee, I was teetering on the brink of explosive incontinence. At this point I would rise from my desk and stride purposefully out of the office, often leaving Abraham or Lurleen standing next to my chair frozen in midblather. (And I often mused on my walks to the bathroom that it was quite possible that they continued their monologue uninterrupted, so fundamentally irrelevant was an audience to their chatter.) Deep in the bowels (heh) of the building was a massive bathroom, on the same scale as the facilities found in stadiums or prisons. With unadorned stone walls, yellowed ancient lighting, and a seemingly endless row of stalls, it had the ambiance of a Soviet army barracks, and was the perfect setting in which to engage in serious voiding. The toilets were wonderfully overpowered to the point that with each flush I had to absent myself upward, for fear of my intestines being sucked out of my body by the turbinelike suction.

I often spent thirty minutes in this dungeon, reading a magazine or pleasantly staring off into space or constructing tiny origami animals out of the coarse, low-grade toilet paper. On this fateful day I'd just finished my second tiny crane of the morning (pull the tailfeathers and the wings flap!) when the outer door banged open and a raucous crowd entered. From the variety of accents and finely maintained footwear I glimpsed under the door, I deduced that it was the house orchestra, apparently on break. I often heard them practicing as I wound my way through the labyrinthine corridors, some-times noodling away or occasionally rising in synchrony to blast out some menacing Wagnerian riff. Now it sounded like every male in the orchestra was banging into the stalls on every side. After a mass clinking of belt buckles and an omi-nous moment of rustling as a score of pants were dropped in unison, the bathroom was all at once filled with an unholy cacophony of intestinal explosions, a spectrum of noise rang-ing from piercing, almost ultrasonic dolphinlike squeakings to whimsical calliope-esque tooting to midrange staccato trumpeting to long sustained bleatings in basso profundo, all of it counterpointed by the jaunty ploppings of deposits of various size and integrity being dropped into water-filled porcelain bowls.

I sat slack jawed and frozen in my stall, looking very much like the subject of Munch's famous painting, except naked from the waist down. And then the smell hit me. A pot-pourri—a poo-purri—of the vilest order, of fermented organic matter, fresh from a four-day alchemic sojourn through the humid ninety-eight-degree superhighway of digestion, now bursting dark and steaming back into terrestrial light. The waste products of two, three dozen people all at once, min-gling in malicious olfactory synergy. Almost before the odor registered consciously, I was bent over and dry-heaving between my legs. And through it all not a single flush! I pounded each wall of my stall with my fists, bellowing, *courtesy flush! courtesy flush!* only to be answered largely by silence, a few puzzled snatches of some Slavic language, an angry exclamation in Russian, but no flushes, no flushes at all! I flushed my own toilet several times to illustrate my request, but only succeeded in thoroughly misting my own ass with blue-tinged water...

Pulling up my pants (no wipe, no time for that!), I careened out of my stall, past several turtle-necked fellows blithely reading orange-tinted foreign-language newspapers while waiting for a toilet to open up, and out into the hall. I stood there fastening my pants for a moment and then headed up the stairs back to the office. The next day I brought in a two-liter of Mountain Dew—no more coffee, not at work! From then on I sipped caffeinated soda all day, and ate light lunches, and still by five o'clock I'd be breaking out in a cold sweat, clenching my teeth along with my sphincter on the train home, taking the last stretch of sidewalk up to my house at a full sprint, up the stairs two and three at a time, my pants already down around my knees by the time I hit the bathroom.

Would the indignities ever end?

My friends and I, in the time-honored tradition, often convened at a local dive after work for happy hour. While "happy hour" may not technically be a misnomer, it certainly requires some qualification. The happiness found at happy hour is of the sick, unwholesome sort of the sailor on shore leave, or the prisoner on a day pass, a desperate headlong rush to unconsciousness and the kind of intoxication that erased all the day's memories.

At these gatherings, I often bitched about my coworkers to Sadie, who laughed but always insisted that I wasn't, I couldn't be, depicting my coworkers fairly.

As you describe them, she would say, with a dimpled look of adoring patronization, they're basically one-dimensional cartoons. The way you describe them, they're not even human.

But this was exactly my point! It wasn't my telling that reduced them to inhumanity, but their own... well, inhumanity. They'd reduced themselves, I ranted, by their obsessive toeing of various lines, by investing themselves wholeheartedly in the workings of a soulless bureaucracy, by the passive acceptance of bankrupt establishment petit-bourgeois culture, mindless consumerism to compensate for their insecurities and inadequacies, comfort at the expense of freedom, security at the expense of thought, et cetera.

One night as I was treading over this familiar ground, Sadie rose from the table and went to stand at the bar alone. After a few minutes I joined her and asked what was wrong.

Don't you realize, she said, that I'm one of those people you're always deriding?

That's not true, I said, rubbing her back with one hand. That's not true at all.

But it seemed that with each (let's be honest) disingenuous caress I saw with a little more clarity that she was right. How had this fact escaped me for so long and, more importantly, what was I to do about it?

Name one thing, other than my body, Sadie said, that you like about me. Just one thing.

That's easy, I said. I thought about it and thought about it and after a minute or two I sat down on a stool at the bar and thought about it some more and after a while I'd finished my beer, so I ordered another one and thought about it some more while drinking this fresh beer, and about halfway through that pint, while I was still racking my brain and honestly felt like something was right on the tip of my tongue, just give me a few more minutes, Sadie stood up and walked out.

The next morning I was at my desk when Lurleen sidled over to me and said, psst. I glanced up and she was biting her lower lip. From her office suddenly came an explosion of giggling, which she immediately silenced with a sidelong glance of warning.

Ask Edwin to load the copy machine, she whispered. Tell him you just can't figure it out and that he's the expert. When he bends down, look at his behind.

She turned on her heel and returned to her office, where much whispering and muffled laughter commenced. I turned back to my game of Solitaire. What did I want to see Edwin's sweaty plumber's crack for? Thirty minutes later Abraham came down the hall and paused next to my desk to tie his shoe.

Do it, he whispered urgently. He squeezed my arm to impart the seriousness of the situation. Trust me. Do it!

Then he was gone.

I sauntered over to the copy machine and conspicuously rattled the paper tray for a few seconds. Then I stepped over to Edwin's office and knocked on the door frame.

Can you load this copier? Lurleen said you were the expert.

He snuffled irritably and stood, hauling up his sweaty khakis. This is the third time today, he said. What the hell is everyone copying? This isn't personal use is it?

Oh no, I said. Company business.

Muttering under his breath, he grabbed a ream of $8^{1}/_{2}$ x 11 and went to one knee. As he pulled out the tray and slid in the stack of paper, I surreptitiously glanced down and saw, arcing out of the top of his pants, the unmistakable y-shape of a fluorescent pink G-string, of the sort favored by female strippers and porn actresses. My eyebrows crawled up my forehead in astonishment, and it was all I could do to keep myself from exclaiming out loud.

The problem is, said Edwin as he stood up. Is that all you people ask me how to do it and then you don't watch and learn for yourself. You're like children, you just want to be taken care of.

I nodded happily in agreement as he stomped back to his office. For the rest of the day everyone exchanged knowing winks and half-smiles, and for that afternoon it was almost like we didn't hate each other.

This freaky semi-insight into Edwin's deep dark psyche did lend him a somewhat human aspect, and the next few times he harangued me I took it with a touch more equanimity. This quickly wore off though—he was an annoying little son of a bitch—and before long, my empathy gave way to fantasies of blackmail. I even broached the subject to Abraham a few weeks later.

Blackmail him for what? Abraham asked, eyebrow raised.

Money, what else?

Abraham scoffed. He doesn't have any money. You couldn't even get a hundred dollars out of him.

That can't be true, I said. He must make mid- to high six figures.

He does. But he's got two mortgages, a fleet of cars that he barely ever drives because he's on the road all the time; he eats out at expensive restaurants for every meal, stays only in five-star hotels, and has a trophy wife in Orlando who spends whatever's left over. Trust me, I open his mail—the guy's barely breaking even. Why do you think he's so fucking pissed all the time?

I thought he just had chronic panty rash, I said.

Mmm, panties, murmured Abraham. His eyes drifted off to the middle distance and his hand brushed across the front of his jeans. Give me thirty minutes in a windowless room with Edwin and his pink G-string, and I'll show you panty rash.

What does that even mean, I asked.

A few days later I was coming back from lunch with Abraham and Tim. We were taking a shortcut through the back corridors of the center when a set of double doors up ahead burst open and a dozen or so female dancers emerged, flushed from rehearsal and glistening with sweat, jostling each other in delicate camaraderie. My God, what creatures!

At their approach, my middle-aged companions immediately sucked in their guts and stuck out their chests, but the girls didn't so much as glance over as they passed. It wasn't that they didn't admire us (that would've been understandable)—they looked right through and past us as if we were nonentities. It couldn't have been a matter of looks—Tim at least had been an athlete and still looked it, tall and lantern jawed and wide shouldered. I cut a glance sideways to try to see what they'd seen and it hit me—us striding along in our slacks, daintily pinching our plastic bindles of leftovers, pressed shirts and fresh haircuts and clean shaven, a degree and sort of grooming that cried out for, demanded, approval. We were just dickless office drones in their eyes, not even worthy of contempt. It would've been far better at that moment to have been anything else, anything at all. Even a homeless man—at least he'd have a bank of anecdotes, *I didn't like the way he was eyeing my trash bag poncho, so I shivved him and jumped a train south,* and what woman isn't intrigued by danger? And that's the thing, we were the opposite of danger, we were the embodiment of security at all costs, at the cost of everything else, at the cost of life itself, and these women, devoted as they were to the pursuit of art, saw that immediately.

This was more disheartening than any busywork, any screamed rebuke, any empty wasted day. I was so crestfallen that I felt like curling up in the stairwell for a good cry, but even as the dancers' chimelike laughter echoed back through the corridor, my comrades were unrattled.

Probably lesbians, said Tim, his voice dripping with contempt as we turned the corner.

Rooting through my desk looking for a pen one afternoon, I opened a large bottom drawer and found a foot-thick stack of documents I thought I'd filed months ago. Vaguely I remembered a frenzied morning we'd spent preparing for a visit from upper management, straightening pictures and buttoning our top buttons and cleaning our desks. The top of my desk had been buried under garbage and stacks of papers and I'd shoved everything into the drawers just minutes before the walk-through. I'd forgotten about the papers until now.

I leafed through the pile and saw that they were in fact important proposals, most of them pertaining to hotly contested fuck-ups and various high-urgency projects that were now in the terminal phases of completion. In fact, I remembered Edwin demanding just days before one of the documents I now held; he'd cursorily rummaged through a few binders and then gone on the server to look at the scanned copy. (The complexity of the filing system was such that people almost always just looked at the scanned documents; finding the hard copy of anything required the guidance of the archivist (myself) and I was always busy filing the daily flood of documents.)

I called up Abraham to conduct a little experiment.

Edwin wants to see the Compco proposal for the fountain, I said. In fact, I held that proposal in my hand.

Tell him to look at the pdf, he said. It's in the Compco folder online.

He wants the hard copy, I insisted.

The what? The pdf is the hard copy. It's the same thing. Tell him we lost the hard copy or whatever and to just look at the pdf. Unless you want to root through the piles and find him the hard copy. If he insists, just call Compco and have them fax over a copy. They're on top of all that shit.

They keep archives, too?

Oh man, they're all professional and shit, said Abraham. That's what I do when one of these guys asks for hard copy, I just call the vendor and have them fax it over. I can't find shit in those binders.

Gotcha, I said.

I looked through the rest of the pile. In total, I had the work orders for five million dollars of work in my hands. I looked left and right; Edwin was out of town, and the others were at a meeting. The only other person in the office was Abraham, and he was completely oblivious. Whistling, I sauntered over to the garbage can, tore the proposals into tiny pieces, and let them flutter down. Five million dollars' worth of contracts, a week's worth of filing, gone. I went back to my desk and put my feet up; as far as I could detect, nothing had changed in the universe, no balance had been tipped, no virtue stained. God really *was* dead!

Clearly, there were no consequences if I stopped doing the work, so I stopped doing it. How could I continue going through the motions, knowing that no one would suffer if I didn't, no process disrupted, no revenue stream stanched, and maintain even a shred of self-respect? From that day on, each hour of each workday I'd secret away a small stack of that day's documents into my desk. By the end of each day the inbox would be completely empty, completing the illusion of my diligence. I passed several weeks in this manner, reading e-books at my desk and taking long, frequent breaks, until one day I went to stash another stack and found that my desk was filled to capacity. I stood up and tried to jostle it, but the desk was completely immobile. It was essentially a huge dense stack of paper with a thin skin of tin around it. This presented a new more difficult challenge: how to dispose of the steady influx of documents?

I was blearily drinking my fifth or sixth Mountain Dew that afternoon, racking my brain for a solution, when my eye alighted on something crammed behind the coffee machine. A document shredder! The others were at a meeting, so I gleefully carried it back to my desk and set it up. I experimentally fed a single sheet into the teeth of the machine, and after an ear-splitting buzz, it emerged from the other end as confetti. Seldom has technology delivered a more tailor-made solution to my fingertips. I spent the next two weeks waiting until everyone was out and then shredding through the backlogged proposals. On non-meeting days the only time I was alone in the office was over lunch, so I had to spend many midday hours with hastily assembled, condimentless baloney sandwiches in one hand while using the other to feed million-dollar proposals stamped URGENT! into the shredder.

This worked wonderfully until after two weeks or so the overworked shredder died an abrupt, smoking death.

Tuesday was Lurleen's birthday so on Monday Abraham brought us together while she was at a meeting to organize a surprise party.

Tim, he said, I need you to bring some cookies or something. Can you do that?

Sure, said Tim. He took out his beloved smart phone and keyed something into his address book.

Just don't forget, Lurleen is allergic to peanuts. So nothing with peanuts. Got it?

Got it.

Jerry, he said, shouting over to where Jerry sat at his desk, transfixed by his blank screen. Can you bring flowers?

Sure, said Jerry. Got it.

Bill, can you bring a couple two liters of soda? Maybe some sparkling grape juice?

I can do that, said Bill.

Next Abraham turned to me. One of us should bring a small cake, he said, and one of us should bring plates and forks and napkins and cups. What would you prefer?

I take the subway here, so it'd be easier if I brought plates and stuff.

Okay, said Abraham, making a notation on his action plan. I'll put you down for plates and myself for cake.

The next day we acted diffident all morning, and when Lurleen went grumbling and disappointed to lunch, Abraham brought us all together in the conference room.

So let's see it guys, he said.

Shit, said Bill, I thought you said next Tuesday. It's today?

Yes, Bill, it's today.

Bill shrugged. You should've communicated that to me more effectively, he said.

Tim scoffed derisively and, elbowing Bill aside, placed a tray of cookies on the table.

Here you are, he said.

Abraham leaned forward and scrutinized the label. These are peanut butter cookies, he said. I told you, she's allergic to peanuts.

I thought you said she liked peanuts, Tim said. Bill snorted contemptuously.

No, said Abraham. These cookies would kill her.

Tim picked up a cookie, sniffed it, and took a tentative bite. Tastes fine to me, he said.

How about you, Jerry, said Abraham.

Jerry slammed a heavy shopping bag down on the conference table. Abraham opened it to reveal a ten-pound bag of flour.

Flowers, said Abraham. You were supposed to bring flowers, not flour.

Oh, said Jerry. I thought we were going to bake her a cake or something.

Where would we bake a cake, asked Abraham, indicating the office with a sweep of his arm. Do you see an oven in here?

Jerry just shrugged as if to say, ain't my fault.

What an idiot, said Tim.

Fuck you, snapped Jerry.

Abraham heaved a sigh and turned to me. Tell me you didn't let me down, he said.

I rolled my eyes and put the plates and forks and cups and napkins on the table. Abraham blanched and slowly placed the contents of his own bag on the table—more plates and forks and cups and napkins.

I thought you were bringing cake, he said.

No, I was supposed to bring this stuff. I take the subway, so it'd be inconvenient for me to carry a cake to work, remember that conversation?

Abraham just stared at the assortment of ill-conceived party favors on the table, the sack of flour, the deadly cookies, the hundreds of plates and forks for an office of just five, without anything edible to even place on them. These fucking people really couldn't get anything right, I thought.

One of us has to run to the store and get stuff, said Abraham. Who's it going to be? I have to wait here for a call from Edwin.

We all stared at our feet and cleared our throats and waited for someone, anyone else to volunteer or be designated, and just at that moment the door opened and in walked Lurleen with a Styrofoam takeout container.

What's going on, she asked, eyeing the table.

Surprise! Abraham shouted. He threw his arms around her in a pelvis-grinding bearhug as the rest of us tried to look passably festive. Over Abraham's shoulder, Lurleen looked from the table to each of us, unconvinced.

The situation was about to slip from farce to tragedy if something wasn't done. The garbage can next to my desk hadn't been emptied for days and it was filled to the brim with shredded proposals. I pivoted, grabbed the can, and upended thirty gallons of makeshift confetti over the six of us.

Happy Birthday! I shouted at the top of my lungs.

This had the desired effect and everyone roared with laughter and when the blizzard subsided we all sat around the table eating peanut butter cookies and drinking paper cups of tap water while Lurleen picked at her lunch and told us Kiefer Sutherland trivia (Did you know he's an accomplished rodeo rider?) and for the rest of the day, unbeknownst to them, my coworkers were picking out of their hair and from their shoulders and the folds of their pants tiny bits of their life's work.

* * *

Now what? I could refill my desk, but that was just delaying the inevitable. I couldn't throw the proposals in the garbage—someone would be sure to find them. The same went for walking out of the office bearing armloads or trashbags full of papers; sooner or later someone was sure to ask what I was doing, and that would be it. In desperation I even began filing some of them, but my conscience wouldn't let me engage in such futility. In the meantime, the inflow never stopped, dozens or hundreds of pages a day, now piling conspicuously up on top of my desk.

I brought in Sadie's massive alpine backpack the next week; when my coworkers asked about it, I told them I was joining a gym. I waited until everyone left for the day, stuffed all the reaccumulated papers in the backpack, hoisted it onto my back, and then walked to the subway, bent nearly double under almost a hundred pounds of papers. On the train I sat next to a wingtipped lawyer poring over a brief, his briefcase full to bursting, and it occurred to me that we were both taking our work home, but for opposite reasons.

It was well after sundown when I reached the abandoned house next to mine, and I tottered uncertainly under my load through the brick-strewn backyard and down into the shell of the house. We'd heard squatters there several nights in a row. Their fire pit was in the churned dirt floor of the basement, a blackened crater surrounded by overturned milk crates and concrete blocks, configured around the fire in a nearly identical fashion as Sadie's and my furniture was arrayed in front of the television.

I emptied the proposals into the fire pit and hurried home before Sadie got suspicious. That night as we sat on our loveseat watching a crime drama, I went to the kitchen to get us drinks and heard through the window the homeless people next door, whooping around a roaring fire. They sounded like they were having much more fun than we were.

*   *   *

At about this time, I grew tired of everything; the job, playing house, everything. I especially resented Abraham's continuing musical antics. It was bad enough I had a starring role in a bad satire of domesticity, that I had to work this fucking dismal job with all these dismal people, that I'd moved to a new (boring) city to find that my girlfriend was in fact one of *them*—on top of all that, why should I also have to tolerate this tin-eared Philistine crooning in my fucking ear every day?

Inspired by an upsurge of venom, I'd come up with a plan to deal with Abraham. The project managers often had to tour a jobsite, and in the corner of the office nestled a crate filled with reflective vests, hardhats, tape measures, and other trades-man's accessories. I retrieved from the bottom of this crate something wonderful, which I secreted away in my desk until just the right opportunity presented itself.

All day I sat as patient as a toad as my tormentor shuffled from copier to supply closet, crooning his usual midmorning ballad. I was determined to wait for just the right moment. It didn't take long. He'd just set up beside my desk, leaning back with eyes closed and breaking into the majestic chorus of a Celine Dion song when I withdrew a hundred decibel air horn from my desk and blew a tremendous blast inches from his face.

In the immediate aftermath my ears were ringing violently, and in retrospect I was lucky I hadn't deafened him. I tried to maintain an expression of righteous satisfaction, but when I saw Abraham's shocked face, his hair riffled back from his forehead by the force of the air horn, I couldn't help but break into a gale of laughter. This, of course, was my mistake. Ridiculous people can never tolerate being ridiculed.

You'll pay for this, he said softly, and went back to his desk. I could tell he meant it, and that I'd made an enemy for life, but on the other hand, I noticed with not a little satisfaction that he wasn't singing anymore.

*   *   *

Each Wednesday Edwin and the project managers were summoned to a weekly meeting with the building administrators. Ostensibly the purpose of these meetings was to update all parties on the latest developments, but in reality they were just a symbolic exercise in sadism. Abraham went along each week to take notes and told me about how the government people berated Edwin and Tom and Gary and Lurleen, asking the same questions over and over ("How could this have happened?"), and only quitting just before the unlucky victim broke into tears. They'd been chewed out by their own superiors over the faltering renovations, presumably taking it all with a smile and a "Please, sir, I want some more." and Wednesdays were their one opportunity to vent all that pent-up anger.

This was just the type of pointless officiousness that I hated, and Abraham knew it. The next Wednesday afternoon, an hour or so before the big meeting, Abraham announced that he was "too busy" to attend that day.

But Franklin can go along, he said to Edwin, speaking just loud enough that I could hear him from my desk. This was his payback for my punitive air horning and he wanted me to know it.

Edwin acknowledged him with a grunt; I don't think anyone ever even glanced at Abraham's weekly packet of notes, and I had the distinct feeling they only took the fifth man along to equal the other side's contingent of people, a kind of tribal calculus of bodies in the room. In the event that pandemonium broke out, I guess Abraham or I was supposed to break off a chair leg and bludgeon his counterpart on the other side of the table, who as I recall was a diminutive brunette with a faint mustache who studied art history at Middlebury.

Edwin and Lurleen and the managers and I caravanned up to the conference room, with me lagging sulkily behind. In the elevator Lurleen reenacted the previous night's episode of *24* in real time, shaking her head in mock disbelief at Kiefer's lethal efficiency. ("I just don't know how he managed to get out of that one!") She seemed to be under the impression that the show was a documentary, and I couldn't bring myself to disappoint her...

We filed into the conference room, where our betters awaited us. I was amused to note that they were essentially Edwin and company, plus ten years and slightly better clothes, a dash of salt and pepper and Banana Republic instead of Dockers. As my coworkers sat down, I made for the refreshments table and assembled a peanut butter and jelly everything bagel. When I got back to the table, my counterpart, the aforementioned mustached brunette, handed me a meeting minutes printout, which I thanked her for and then used to wipe my mouth. She rolled her eyes and turned pointedly away.

The head of the other team was a silver-haired architect with gold-rimmed glasses. He had the upper hand and this gave him a bottomless sort of patriarchal solicitude as he looked smilingly upon his selection of victims. Finally he settled on Tim.

So Tim, said Silver Fox, what's causing the holdup at the south fountain?

As the attention of the table turned to Tim, I actually saw his pores constrict as he began to glisten with panic sweat, like a jostled poison toad releasing venom.

Well, the vendor is having trouble getting the marble cut, Tim said. There aren't a lot of stonecutters in this area, and they're backed up.

I understand that, said Silver Fox, gently, as if talking to a confused child. But you've had the contract for months. It was your responsibility to make sure these things were scheduled.

He had him there. Tim was the putative project manager, and this clearly fell under the aegis of "project management." Tim opened his mouth as if to say something, but no sound emerged. And what was there to say? He'd fucked up; he knew it, Silver Fox knew it, I knew it, everyone knew it. Everyone looked elsewhere as the awkward silence lengthened, but I couldn't take my eyes away. From my seat at the back of the contingent I saw Tim's fingers creep of their own volition down to his belt, where they ran delicately over the keys of his super phone. If only it had a smokescreen function, so he could creep out under cover of obscurity and avoid this whole humiliating scene, to vault through the air ducts like an action hero and emerge on the other side onto a golf course or, better yet, a Best Buy flagship store. Or a key prompt to shoot a tiny needle into the pad of his thumb and administer an injection of competence and snappy comebacks. *Let's see your precious gadgets save you now,* I wanted to cackle, like a Silver Age comic-book villain. I couldn't imagine how he was going to get out of this one, and so I was understandably surprised when he turned to me.

Hand me the south fountain proposal, he said.

What...?

I told you to bring the south fountain proposal. Don't tell me you forgot.

He'd of course done no such thing. What a fucker!

Ah. I, uh...don't have it, I said.

Tim made an irritated noise and turned shrugging back to Silver Fox. I'd show you in the contract where it says we're not liable for vendor availability, he said, but Franklin forgot to bring the proposal.

I could see that Silver Fox didn't believe him, but he wasn't willing to pursue the matter any further. He turned next to Edwin.

And *what* is going on at the southeast annex? Do you even know?

What came next was an exhibition of the highest order. When Silver Fox accused him of negligence, Edwin pleaded incompetence. When Silver Fox accused him of incompetence, Edwin pleaded ignorance. When Silver Fox accused him of ignorance, Edwin deftly changed the subject. This rhetorical game of cat-and-mouse continued on for nearly half an hour, and by the end, Edwin had somehow given an account of himself as consistently better than his accusers made him out to be—aggrieved, a bit persecuted, and even innocent. Even I was won over, and I hated the fucker! As we filed out of the meeting room even Silver Fox seemed a bit in awe, his closing handshake softened by a note of apologetic sympathy.

No one talked on the way back to the office. We knew that we'd only staved off the inevitable. Even Edwin's preternatural composure had drained away, and he stood in the corner of the elevator muttering. What had his performance actually accomplished, after all? Edwin's job was to manage, and having failed at that, he'd turned out to be brilliant at obfuscating his grievous mismanagement. The renovation was an unsalvageable disaster, so from Edwin's own perspective, his job was now to not get caught not doing his job, and at that I had to admit he was masterful. But it was all just a shell game now, and we all knew that things would get very ugly when it all caught up to him.

The parallels to my own situation were not lost on me. My own furtive paperwork disposal wasn't so very different from Edwin's mobius strip-like monologues, and I realized then that in time I too would be caught. In my own mind I'd been clinging to a vision of myself that was in fundamental opposition to the Kafkaesque bureaucrats and straw men of the office, but in reality I was no different. I'd "joined the team" in the only way that mattered. I had a bright future in middle management if I was interested. To any observer I appeared to be industrious, efficient, and busy, my inbox empty at the end of each day. And did it really even matter that my actual duties were going undone, that it was all a sham? Did it? I'd learned before now that appearance is more important than performance in the office, and had I been filing away diligently the past months but coming in untucked and bedraggled, I'd no doubt have been fired months ago. But now it dawned on me that perhaps appearance was not just the most important thing, but the only thing, and that much like the rest of these people, my life had become nothing more than an avoidance strategy, a lot of sound and fury and paper shuffling, signifying nothing.

The mood was dour when we arrived back at the office and we each shuffled demoralized back to our desks. I was reading yet another email from my girlfriend detailing my responsibilities in her new yard work action plan ("Acquire list of invasive plants from local botanical society. Arrange tree trimming. Weed brick sidewalk by hand every Sunday.") when my phone rang.

This is Franklin, I said.

I heard Edwin sigh angrily. I'm going to need the notes from the meeting typed up by the end of the day, he said.

Oh. I looked at the blank legal pad I'd taken to the meeting. I forgot to take any, I said.

The next day I strode in at my usual time of ten after eight. As soon as I sat down, I heard Edwin calling from his office.

What time is it, Franklin?

It's eight, I said, rolling my eyes.

No, it's not, he said. What time is it?

Oh look, it's seven forty-five, I said. Let me slide under my desk real quick for a fifteen-minute nap.

It is eight eleven, said Edwin, unperturbed. You're supposed to be here at eight o'clock, are you not?

I'll stay until five-eleven, I said. How's that?

I don't want you here until five-eleven, Edwin said. I want you here at eight o'clock, like you're supposed to be.

I'm sorry, I said. Just tell me what happened in the last eleven minutes that required my urgent attention, I'll get on it double-time.

That's not the point, Edwin snapped.

Then what is the point?

And here, finally, was the crux of the conversation. My question hung in the air like a stench, I could almost see Edwin recoiling with a grimace from its implications. I found that my practiced veneer of office blankness had been cracked by a surge of real anger, because this was the question that hung over the entire world I'd entered into—*what was the point?* When half a minute had passed with no answer, I got up and went over to stand in Edwin's doorway.

Well? I said. I think I deserve an answer to that question.

Edwin had half-turned and now sat frozen in his chair, one pudgy finger raised daintily to click his mouse, taken aback at my confrontation.

What?

What's the point of getting here at eight o'clock sharp? The work I do isn't time sensitive, and truth be told there isn't much work to be done at all. I mean, let's be honest, no one in this office really does anything of importance. If this office was smote with a meteor from outer space, not only would our replacement be unnecessary, the entire project would probably move forward at double speed and with half the problems. Shit, the only person in this office who does anything at all is Abraham, and that's just picking up your dry-cleaning and Starbucks runs.

Edwin opened his mouth to speak, but closed it and cradled his chin in his hand. I suppose his first impulse was to issue the standard denials—Maybe you don't do any work around here, but the rest of us have put our heart and soul into this blah blah blah etc.!—but to his credit he was smart enough to realize this conversation had moved beyond that point. As the seconds mounted, I was genuinely curious to hear his answer.

The point is, he said. There was just the barest moment of hesitation. The point is, I said so!

Even Edwin knew how ridiculous it sounded, as soon as it came out of his mouth. But what else would he have said? As far as I was concerned, I'd won. I went back to my desk, put my feet up, and waited.

It didn't take long. The next morning I was getting a cup of coffee when I noticed something strange. As I walked back to my desk, I perked my ears and noticed that as I got farther from the coffee machine, which was outside Edwin's office, he seemed to resume a conversation. I turned on my heel and went back to the coffee machine, where I topped off my mug. As soon as I entered Edwin's sightline, he stopped talking. I went back to my desk, and just to fuck with him, went back for creamer. This time he slammed his office door closed. Definitely something going on, and I had a good idea what it was.

When he went to lunch, I crept into his office and found a business card on his desk from a staffing agency. I dialed the number on the card. A woman picked up.

Yes?

Hi, I'm calling from INCOMP on behalf of Edwin James. He lost the notes he took from your call and wanted me to confirm the dates again.

That's no problem, said the woman. Your new editor will be there on Monday at eight.

Thanks, I said. I'll pass it on.

I couldn't say I was really surprised. I spent the rest of the day waiting to be called into Edwin's office, but it never happened. If anything, the two-faced bastard was chattier than usual, making small talk at the copier and asking if I wanted anything when Abraham went on his Starbucks run. So that's how he was going to play it.

That night at home I stood in our spare bedroom, which had become a repository for our unwanted clothes and books and broken vaccuum cleaners and back-mangling futons and cracked wall mirrors and shitty Guatemalan hammocks and filterless humidifiers and old film projectors and several bicycles that had had a wheel stolen when left out locked up

overnight. I was rooting through the drifts of this miscellaneous junk when Sadie poked her head in.

Dinner's ready, she said.

What? I can't right now, I'm looking for something important.

What are you looking for?

The VHS tape eraser. Do you know where it is?

No, she said. Is this going to take long?

Why?

Ann and her boyfriend are coming over at eight. Can you be
ready for company by then?

What? Why are they coming over here?

To visit, she said, and rolled her eyes. That's what adults do,
you know. They socialize.

Oh, Jesus, I said. I'm really not in the mood to discuss their
latest promotions and exchange appropriate cultural signifiers and listen to them regurgitate opinions they read online.

You've got problems, Sadie said, turning off the light and
closing the door behind her, leaving me in darkness and
waist-deep in garbage.

Do I, though, I yelled. Is it me with the problems, or is it
everyone else?

She didn't answer.

I arrived at the office early the next morning, just after seven.
(What an industrious fellow I was, with the proper motivation!) The place was deserted as I stood running the electro-
magnetic VHS tape eraser in slow circles over the metal skin
of the computer tower that housed all the electronic documents, with a delicacy that was almost loving. They probably
had off-site backups, and at worst they could just request
copies from the vendors, but my little prank would be good for
at least a momentary panic, a little adrenaline to clear the
blood.

When Edwin walked in a half-hour later and saw me at my

desk already typing away, he nodded and looked upon me
with benevolence.

Good to see you here so early, he said. *But it's not going to
save you,* I could see him thinking.

Good to be here, I answered. *If you think you're smarter than
me, you're even stupider than you look,* I thought.

He paused, perhaps detecting a bit of contrary oversincerity
in my voice, but shrugged it off and continued into his office. I
waited until he called for a proposal, once and then twice and
then he finally said, screw it, I'll just look at the backup online,
and right then I gathered my things and walked out.

I slept for eighteen hours and, by the end of the week, was
back to my relaxed, bright-eyed self. I'd saved up a tidy nest
egg and for the first time in months, I felt good about my
future. As the fog cleared from my brain, I even saw Sadie in a
new more forgiving light, and attributed most of her objec-
tionable qualities to her job. I urged her to quit, and once she
saw the change in my own temperament from irritable and
inert back to warm and alive, she did.

Unfortunately, the damage had already been done. Though
we tried to start fresh, we were each a constant reminder to
the other of our recent failure. Not working and on a shoe-
string budget, cooped up all day and most nights in the house,
it didn't take long for the finger-pointing to start. Whose idea
had it been anyway, this abortive attempt at adulthood?

It was yours, I assured her late one night as we sat in our
apartment. It had fallen into chaos, piles of twisted clothing
and rancid Styrofoam takeout containers and the kitchen sink
clogged for weeks, filled with black chunky water. In the middle of the living room a floor lamp lay sideways on the floor,
where we stepped over it faux-obliviously each day, just to
spite the other. You loved having money to buy stuff, I continued. Anytime you felt bad, you'd just buy a pair of shoes or go

out to dinner or see a movie. You're just like all the other idiots...

She inhaled as if struck physically. You were no better, she hissed. You loved working with all those incompetents, you talked about them all the time, the "meat robots," it made you feel so superior! You were addicted to stupid people!

We sat in silence, nursing our figurative wounds. Nothing hurts more than the truth.

This became a motif of sorts; this smoking ruin of a life had to be someone's fault, and the one thing we both agreed upon was that it wasn't our own. We lived in a long narrow apartment in half a row house and one night we stood at opposite ends of the apartment screaming at each other yet again as the neighbors pounded on the wall.

You ruined my life, Sadie screamed.

She drew back and kicked her pointed wooden clog off her foot, down the long hallway and directly into my crotch. I screamed and folded at the waist, curling myself around my throbbing genitals and whining like a spooked horse. Energized with rage, I managed to straighten up just long enough to kick my own house shoe down the hallway and, guided perhaps by some amused vengeful higher power, it struck her full in the mouth, which immediately began to swell up and ooze blood. We stood at our respective ends of the hallway, clutching our wounded parts and panting, looking at each other now with open contempt and not a little terror, and with the question scrawled across our faces, as it perpetually was at that point, how the fuck had we gotten here?

CHAPTER 12

The Greatest Pleasure in Life Interlude

or, Rock-Throwing and Rocks-Blowing

A gainfully-employed friend had offered to take me out to dinner and afterwards over drinks he took me aside and in a paternal tone told me, *I know it must be hard, you're probably depressed, you don't know what to do with yourself, you probably want to jump back in feet first as soon as possible, right? Why don't we get together to buff up the ol' résumé and I happen to know someone who's looking to hire someone in the new year blah blah blah.* And as the conversation unspooled it became clearer and clearer that it was himself he was consoling, not me, that *he* needed desperately to believe that not working was hard and depressing and that I was chomping at the bit to get back on the proverbial treadmill, because the alternative was too horrible to consider—that not working is easy and I've never felt better and that it's actually his life that's dismal and wrecked. But if I'd told him all that I would've murdered the friendship, so I just nodded and smiled and thanked him for the dinner.

And then after he went home at 10:30 for bed, I sat at the bar and when a boozy blonde asked where my friend had gone, I said he'd gone home because it's a school night, and we both laughed at him and rolled our eyes, and before our laughter has quite petered out I've already slid over onto the stool next to her, and it's true what I always suspected as a child, that everything interesting happens after all the good little boys have gone to bed...

As it happens, she's unemployed, too, and we talk about our old jobs (the conversation proceeding in fits and starts, as it was so long ago that we have trouble dredging up specifics), and at the end of the night we leave together. As we walk up the long hill to her neighborhood, she confesses sheepishly that she lives in an upscale condo tower, a purchase from her heady days of gainful employment, and she hopes that I won't judge her for it. In reply I rest my hand on her ass and that's the end of that. Halfway there we've been pawing at each other like eighth-graders and we're overcome with the need to do it now now now and in the absence of an alley or a recessed doorway, we spot a portapotty at a nearby construction site and make for it.

The last thing I expected when I swung the door open was to find it occupied but in fact it was, by a bearded ponytailed fellow sitting on the toilet. We begin to apologize but then we notice he's asleep or possibly dead, and we quietly close the door and walk away, and if he's dead I'm sure his eternal soul will understand that while it's all over for him, we the living still have things to do (now now now!), urges to satisfy, and the worms can wait a little longer for their food. And as these two adults now scramble up the walk and into the lobby and up the stairs to engage in adult business, let our attentions wander away, dear reader, like the prudish camera in an old black-and-white movie panning over to the moonlit window as the stars embrace...

Sex, the greatest pleasure in life! Numbers two through infinity put together aren't half as good, aren't a hundredth as good, and if you don't agree you're not doing it right. (And in fact most of you aren't doing it right, but that's another book.) The

greatest pleasure in life, and it's free. And if you had to point
to one piece of utterly damning evidence against the idea of
capitalism, there you have it. What, there's more to life than
sex? Like what, funnel cakes? Dune buggies? Scandinavian furniture? How about you take all that shit to an island, and I'll
take all the 25-year-old Brazilian yoga instructors to another
island, and let's see who's trying to emigrate to whose island
after a week.

The best part about not working is how decadence begets
decadence. The austere diet of poverty like a boxer's, to make
the body strong, sleeping late and sitting all afternoon at a
sidewalk cafe, watching women walk by as the imagination
and pulse quicken, retiring to a bar at sundown to drink cheap
beer, just strong enough to maintain a pleasant buzz but not
so strong as to weaken the system. And what's more attractive
than the glow of contentedness? If you're lucky enough to go
home with a fellow unemployed, you can both sleep late and
rouse at noon for an encore performance, and if you're lucky
you can time it so that just as your office rival from your last
job sits down to his ten-dollar salad, perusing the USA Today
pie chart ("What's your favorite season? Eighty-two percent
said 'summer'!") as he grumbles about that morning's meeting, *Why do I always have to operate the projector, I went to Dart-
mouth,* right at that moment you could be PULLING OUT OH
SHIT THAT WAS A CLOSE ONE! And isn't it horrible how one's
pleasure is enhanced by another's suffering?

My God, I can't think of one downside to being unemployed. Of course, there are always women who won't have
anything to do with you because you don't have a job, don't
drive an imported car, don't make money, but these aren't
women exactly, these are prostitutes. I was always puzzled by
my friends who caught women's attentions with their Rolexes
and Corvettes and Italian suits and five hundred dollar bottles
of wine. What exactly are you trying to convey here? And then
fast forward a few years and I'm sitting in a bar with my shell-

shocked pal, the divorce just went through that afternoon, and he's drunk and on the brink of tears. *Where did I go wrong,* he's asking no one in particular, and it's all I can do to not say, *Maybe when you BOUGHT HER.*

Because what makes sex sex is that it's not business, like everything else is on a fundamental level, that it's the free interplay of desires uncorrupted by the calculations and leveraging and obligations of the market mentality that rules so much of the rest of our lives. It's something you do to benefit yourself, right now, as opposed to benefiting someone else, in the future or in perpetuity. When you make it into a transaction, you miss the entire fucking point of fucking, which is that there is no point, you just do it because you want to.

As in so many things, it's the purity of motive that determines the end result. I've fucked in five-star hotel rooms and mountain chalets, but all of my fondest memories have grittier backdrops. Ravishing an immaculately made-up princess on a pile of crumpled laundry in my unheated apartment, our increasingly heated labors accompanied by the metronomic plinking of various roof leaks into half-filled pots and pans throughout the house. Another time, after Sadie had kicked me out of the house and I was temporarily squatting in an unfinished basement with no electricity and five-foot ceilings. I met a beautiful girl in a bar and we retired to my makeshift bed of egg-crate foam on a sheet of plywood, elevated off the dirt floor on concrete blocks. We had to pull the sheet up over our heads to keep the silverfish from swarming us. It was "that time of month," but that didn't stop us either, and afterwards, as we lay there panting on the menses-sodden foam as vermin scurried around us in the dark, I remember thinking that I'd never again feel desire so urgent, so singleminded...

When I was working my libido shriveled up to a tiny guttering flame, I was always tired and overcaffeinated and pissed because profits had dropped 5 percent the previous quarter and Williams had stolen my three-hole punch yet again and I'd forgotten to pick up my dry cleaning. And no matter how determined I was, I could never go out except on the weekends or I'd have to take naps under my desk over my lunch hour and even then I'd be completely useless, and how are you supposed to meet anyone going out one or two nights a week? I remember complaining about this to a colleague once and she suggested I join a church, meet someone there, and I laughed so hard that I scalded the back of my throat and nasal passages with the hot coffee I was tentatively sipping at the moment.

It made sense why all my coworkers, though young, were so eager to pair off with the first adequate person they met. It wasn't so much that working was incompatible with sex, it was that it was the opposite of sex, and when you combined the two, what resulted was a horrible abortive travesty.

At the Internet startup I worked at, deadlines always spelled disaster. When a product launch loomed and we all started working sixty, seventy, eighty hours a week, our social life shrank down to break room chitchat and meaningful looks across conference room tables. The summer the company teetered on bankruptcy, two completely incompatible coworkers started coupling, dashing home after company picnics to have abbreviated missionary intercourse on IKEA futons as CNBC blared in the background. It was the logical desperate endpoint of all the bored cubicle snacking, the compulsive online shopping, a move made from weakness and desperation that was bound for disaster...

Of course, she got pregnant (what is it about incompatibility that makes couples fertile?) and they feuded bitterly over what to do. He wanted to do the honorable, sensible thing and (Schwarzenegger voice) TERMINATE IT, but she insisted on having the baby and giving it up for adoption.

This caused my friend no small amount of angst, and the annual updates he receives about his offspring generally set off a week or two of nonstop drinking. We were sitting in a dive after one of these missives, staring morosely into our beers, and I tried to cheer him.

Well, I said, at least the sex was good...?

It was horrible, he said.

Really?

Everything had to be bargained for—five minutes on top for me, then five minutes for her, unless either party climaxes, at which point right of position selection cedes to the other party. I kept waiting for her to make a spreadsheet for our sexual encounters. That's what you get for sleeping with someone who works in Sales.

Oh.

Sometimes she watched her shows while we did it. She really liked her shows.

At this same job and for roughly the same reasons I took up with a woman in management. She was a responsible upstanding churchgoing girl from a good family and I was, well, me, but we were both miserable in our jobs and misery loves company. Our conversations inevitably degraded into shouting matches, but we were fucking sometimes every hour on the hour. It wasn't sex for enjoyment but only as stimulation, just like the horrible food we gorged ourselves on or the horrible movies we watched saucereyed at the multiplexes— we did it because we were unhappy and were looking for some respite. And even climaxing wasn't so much pleasurable as much as an all-too-temporary distraction from our miseries.

I remember one Friday driving home with her from work, snapping at each other between songs but otherwise riding in silence, going straight to a bar for happy hour to loosen up, but each drink just made us progressively more sullen. We went to her apartment, she entered first and went straight to the kitchen and as I was taking my shoes off she came out with a huge jar of honey which she flung at my head. I dodged and the jar shattered against the wall above the bed, soaking the

pillows with honey, and before I could even say *what the fuck
did you do that for*, she was on me, hitting me with both hands,
not slapping but punching with small hard fists and lean gym-
trained muscles, and even though I could already taste blood,
being a twenty-first-century gentleman I was somewhat reluctant to strike a woman, even if she struck me first, and as I
stood there being admirable and chivalrous and restrained
she continued to beat me about the face and ears and neck,
hissing a high frantic animal whine through clenched teeth
and thrusting wild knees at my groin, and when I finally got
her turned around and pinned her arms to her sides she
reared back and sunk her teeth into my earlobe so hard that I
screamed and threw her across the room and checked my ear
and when I looked at my fingers there was blood on them.
When she charged me again, all my misgivings had been put
aside and when we collided I threw her onto the floor and
bore down on her with my entire weight until she couldn't
move and could barely breathe and forced her to say uncle
and then just laid on top of her as we both panted and recovered our strength. Soon our clothes came off and we continued our combat in a slightly different arena, though with no
less hostility, and afterwards, since it was Friday and we'd
built up a week of sleep debt, we slept all night and late into
Saturday afternoon. When I finally woke up the sun was just
setting and I looked over and she was still out cold, purple
finger-shaped bruises on her arms and neck like a sex-crime
victim, lying slackjawed with her hair in a puddle of honey.
The weekend was already half gone and I knew I had to change
my life.

I reemerge from the building hours later, bleary eyed and
sated and noodle legged into the very end of night, the first
blush of dawn on the horizon like some fetal hope that for
now at least I don't need.

Where am I going again? Where am I? A shitty bombed-out

neighborhood of condo towers surrounded by vacant lots lau-
reled with barbed wire and ammoniacal urine fumes wafting
from every alcove and doorway. But I'm not worried, it's so
late even the muggers are asleep. Everyone's asleep, everyone
except me.

And at moments like this it seems more obvious than ever
that so much of what I've struggled against my whole life
exists almost entirely to preclude this very moment, this very
night; get a job, keep a job, early to bed, early to rise, wait for
the train, wait for five o'clock, wait for a promotion, wait for
your ship to come in, always passive never active, get a wife,
keep a wife, be content with television and porn and surround-
sound and sports in HD, vicarious third-hand defanged plea-
sures, just enough and no more, fill your hours and minutes
with them and just do it, just fucking do it, never think. Get
something and hold onto it with both hands, choke it to fucking death if you have to. Place your trust in tradition and insti-
tutions and authority and shirk your true responsibilities
entirely, other people know what's best for you. And if you
should ever feel any wayward impulses, just think of your
ancestors watching from above, floating ghostly in pristine
robes on clouds, playing harps, and behind them a big old
bearded all-powerful Man who keeps track in a little book, not
just knows but actually *cares*, how many times you jack it in
the shower or covet the female attendant at the gym, or tell
your girlfriend you were at work late when you were really at
happy hour and on and on...

Above all, you must never feel your innate power, the
power of the individual doing what he pleases. Because
despite all the platitudes bandied about regarding freedom
and America and individuals, the last thing they want is for
someone to deviate from the program, because the world
doesn't run on freedom and happiness; it runs on resignation
and obedience and mediocrity and *thou shalt not*. And like all
machines its functioning depends on repetition, on regular

predictable prescribed movement, on the precise motility of individual parts in unison and if just one of those cogs goes off the reservation just once, the thinking goes, and forgets to hunker down and stay scared, and picks up or is picked up by a beautiful girl in a bar without either party extracting or giving any promises, if they enjoy a few hours together with neither worse for it but on the contrary, better for it, that cog might think afterward as he swaggers perhaps down a deserted street in the vestigial dawn, *perhaps life is something to be lived and not just endured! Perhaps the rules are not for my benefit, but theirs!* And if that kind of thinking were to spread there's no telling what would happen; cubicle farms deserted and assembly lines stilled and empty freeways and all manner of yokes shrugged off en masse and people staying on unemployment for years, literally years! People might start doing what they wanted instead of what they were supposed to do, might start fucking instead of making love, cohabitating instead of marrying, pursuing happiness instead of just the absence of unhappiness, not working instead of working, and then what would happen?! For Christ's sake, we've got a GDP to maintain!

Ah yes, Martin Luther to Joan of Arc to Nathan Hale to Che to Martin Luther King Jr. to Mandela, the line goes right through them and down to me. That's right, I'm a goddamn revolutionary! And who would've thought at the outset of the centuries-long struggle against oppression that in the year 2009 the simple act of sexual intercourse could be, in a sociohistorical context, on par with a rock thrown at a tank? It beats getting burned at the stake, that's for sure.

And if I'm perhaps inclined toward overfeverish rhetoric, please excuse me, dear reader, as I'm always surprised to find another unanaesthetized soul in the world, and I'm still a little giddy. I'm walking down the street looking for a cab when I hear my name and I look up and see her high above standing at her sliding door in a robe, looking down at me backlit, and I stop and wave and I wait and wait and just when I think she doesn't see me or doesn't want to see me, she raises her hand and opens her robe and *there it is.* The greatest thing in life, maybe the only good thing. I'm filled with a childish glee and I break into a little appreciative salutatory jig and I don't want to stop and so why should I? I tap away, boots jingling in the stillness on the fractured asphalt, long-forgotten maneuvers from childhood dance classes, the double buffalo, the triple buffalo, the manhattan, counting one-two-three under my breath, one-two-step, one-two-shuffle...

The next time I look up she's gone back inside, but that's fine, because the point isn't the witnessing of the act but the act itself, and to prove the point I start dancing again and then she reemerges onto her balcony. She raises one hand and in it she seems to be holding a tiny mote of light. What is that, a lighter? Is she giving me the rock concert salute? It seems a little corny, but oh well, I can appreciate the gesture. I make a vague confirmatory gesture with my arms, hoping for maybe another glimpse inside the robe, and suddenly the lighter seems to be falling through the air toward my face, tumbling end over end and somehow managing to stay lit and at the last moment I dodge sideways as it shatters on the sidewalk.

What the fuck? I look down at the plastic shards scattered on the pavement and, seeing something familiar, bend closer and oh shit, it was my cell phone. Shit.

Sorry, she says, her voice floating down. I thought you were going to catch it.

It's okay, I shout.

And why should this night be ruined by the destruction, the inadvertent and well-intentioned destruction, of consumer electronics? To prove the point I start to dance again, but the moment has passed and I feel foolish. Just then a police car cruises by and slows down at the sight of this black-clad pencil-mustached watch-capped ectomorph doing a half-hearted jig in the street, who in truth looks like a living cari-cature of a French cat burglar. At which point I stop dancing, throw a cursory wave to my audience above, and stroll genial-ly downhill, away from the police car, because if they asked I'm not sure I'd be able to explain what I was doing and why.

CHAPTER 13

Hindenburg.com

or, Failure Isn't Everything, It's the Only Thing

Twenty million dollars of venture capital had been spent, producing no discernible effect on Commotion's viability. In retrospect the smart thing to do would've been to just auction off the ergonomic kneeling chairs and single-serving coffee machines, but upper management wanted to give it one more try. After all, it's not like they had to pay any of the money back. They brought in BJ, a turnaround guru, for a "relaunch."

It was made known through office back channels that each person in the department was expected, like primates laying meat at the feet of a new alpha male, to visit BJ in his office for an "asset assessment" session. Everyone started polishing up their résumés. When I finally got around to meeting with him, he was sitting at his desk looking at a stack of papers. From his expression, they might have been autopsy photos, but as I drew near I saw they were printouts of some of the articles I'd written for the website.

As I sat down, BJ turned and we locked gazes. This is a standard "new boss" test: if you look away or mumble some insipid ice-breaking small talk, he knows you'll be easily cowed. On the other hand, if you stare back for too long, he'll take it as a challenge and preemptively marginalize you. The only non-confrontational "win" I could ever come up with was to wear sunglasses to the first meeting (which I once did at a previous job, claiming that I'd had my pupils dilated at the doctor's office that morning). Unfortunately, I hadn't had as much foresight today, so I looked away after a few seconds. He didn't strike me as the type to take any perceived challenge sitting down. Like many executives, he was a short, slightly built fellow who made up for it by exuding an intense, palpable ass-holery. He talked too loud, cultivated irritatingly precise "xtreme" facial hair, and wore wide-shouldered sport jackets so aggressively structured that from behind it looked like he'd forgotten to remove the hanger. One of the first things he'd done after he got the job was to decorate his office with all the plaques and trophies he'd won at various martial arts tournaments. Clearly, this was not a man to be trifled with. Hold his gaze too long and you'd get the pink slip, if not a swift blow to the solar plexus followed by a chokehold.

After a few preliminary questions, he said that the first thing he wanted me to do was to draw up a spreadsheet documenting my creative process.

You mean my writing process? Like, introduction, thesis, body, conclusion?

No, no, you're thinking too small, he said. I want you to formalize your actual creative process in a spreadsheet.

I told him I still didn't understand, and he explained. The idea, he said, was to create a step-by-step blueprint that anyone (read: my eventual replacement) could use to produce an idea, any idea.

For example, he said. Let's say that the first step is getting a "notion," probably from some media source. Next, you have to hone that notion into a "concept." Once you have a concept, you have to laterally build it up or something. Get the idea?

I got the idea...*Creativity for Dummies,* in the form of an

Excel spreadsheet. It was the white-collar equivalent of medieval alchemy! I was sure that once I'd made the creativity blueprint, once I'd commodified the one contribution I had to make, I'd be given the boot. Of course, that might be the best possible outcome. If the rumors were true, and BJ was under orders to cut the workforce by half, I might never get a better opportunity for a bloodless firing, complete with severance pay.

All right, I said. Give me a couple of days.

I went back to my desk and made that spreadsheet. I started to dig. I started to dig my own grave.

After my firing from INCOMP, I'd filed for unemployment, but I'd been found ineligible on a technicality. Luckily, I'd squirreled away a moderate amount of money and was able to take the next ten months off. I never missed having a job, but during that year of idleness I began to detect a creeping suspicion that perhaps there was something about my last firing that I wasn't admitting to myself. I'd always reserved a special sort of contempt for people who derided what was unavailable to them—uncharismatic schlubs who hated women, repressed squares who resented bohemians. In high school I'd rolled my eyes at the popular kids with the rest of my friends, but I was never able to wholeheartedly turn my back on them until I'd fought my way up the ladder myself and confirmed that sphere's vapidity firsthand.

And I'd begun to regard office life the same way. Did I hate it because it was empty and demoralizing and arbitrary or because I just couldn't hack it? After all, I had to admit that I'd deserved to get fired from INCOMP, just as much as all the other people there who spent their days hiding the fact that they weren't doing their jobs. As much as I was disgusted by the idea of getting another job, I knew I'd never be completely sure about my motives until I'd legitimately held down a job through my own diligence. In my own mind, I'd already started laying the groundwork to walk away from working forever, but first I knew there were questions I had to answer.

I shot-gunned my highly fluffed résumé all over the Internet, signed up for every online hiring website and even responded to ads in the newspaper. I'd say this had approximately the same degree of effectiveness as going up to random women and asking them if they wanted to fuck. After three months and hundreds of résumés I'd received zero callbacks, so when a "rising Internet start-up" asked me to interview for an opportunity to "get in on the ground floor of the next Google," I didn't even ask what they did.

The interview process was brutal: I had to submit a series of writing samples to clear the first cut and then pass an individual and a group interview to qualify for a conditional one-month trial run, during which I could be let go for any or no reason. While onerous, I figured that any company with such a rigorous hiring process would be staffed with only the best of the best, and considering that my hiring included a chunk of stock options, that could only be a good thing.

The Commotion building was a massive glass ziggurat that squatted way out in the exurbs. Surrounded by an orange gravel moat, its loins were girded with strange lunar office-park shrubbery that required no maintenance or sustenance but were, technically, alive. This office park had been built in a regional spasm of mindless speculative enthusiasm and was, for the most part, vacant. The identical building next to ours was completely unused except for a banner advertising three-cent-a-minute phone cards draped across its highway-facing façade.

Management made out with cheap rent, but the workers, as usual, got screwed. It wasn't unusual to spend two soul-killing hours in transit, each way. I started my trip in the inner city and arrived two hours later way out by the airport (always a red flag), in an area that was frankly rural, where just a few hundred yards from our offices, rusting vans sat on blocks in front yards and people walked beside the highway carrying trash bags. On the way home from my final interview, the bus passed a dead deer on the side of the freeway, half-crushed and with viscera exploding from its mouth. A little farther on we passed the fawn, similarly mangled. A sickened silence descended on the bus. In retrospect I should've heeded this omen.

Commotion's million-dollar idea was to license music and movies, install servers on college campuses, and charge students a fee for high-speed access. It was kind of like iTunes, only shittier. The media portal crashed constantly and media libraries were spotty at best, but the company had an ace in the hole. Horton, the CEO, was said to be lobbying on Capitol Hill to get extremely harsh penalties legislated for online piracy, while also lobbying colleges to ban file-sharing programs. If he succeeded, a captive audience of millions would be clamoring to pay twenty dollars a month for our shitty product, and we'd all retire at thirty. The plan was fundamentally despicable but kind of brilliant from a business standpoint; if they couldn't entice the consumer herd into the pasture, they'd just fence them in and force them to graze at the end of an electric prod.

My role in all this was peripheral at best. Someone had decided that the portal would be storefronted with a kind of online magazine, with articles and essays and whatnot to entice customers. This was my job; I was to produce or supervise the production of all this content. There were plenty of rather obvious flaws in the business plan, but I kept my head down and did the job. Viewed with the right kind of narrow-sightedness, it was a dream job; all I had to do was think up and write articles, with no editorial oversight or censorship. And around the company it was considered not just possible but inevitable that all our stock options would very soon become worth millions of dollars. One day as I rode the train home after another fourteen-hour day, I realized that for once I wasn't just doing the minimum; on the contrary, I was doing the maximum. I strained to detect any warm fuzzy feeling from this application of the good ol' Protestant work ethic, but I felt nothing but a slight nausea from drinking coffee all day.

The ringleader and metaphorical underwriter of Commotion was Horton, the CEO. Horton had made a cool half-billion or so on the first tech wave and since then had worked as an executive-for-hire and top-dollar consultant at various tech companies. His wealth was accepted as de jure evidence of his brilliance; to the poor, money is the greatest and perhaps only virtue. People spoke in awed whispers of his black AmEx card (you have to spend a quarter-mil a year to get one), his palatial estate, how he'd sometimes round up a dozen friends and treat them to a luxury tour of Tokyo or Amsterdam. In person he was a hangdog taciturn fellow, equal parts hubris and Asperger's. Senior management treated him with sickening deference; when he came into meetings, they addressed him as a genius or visionary and then sat grinning open mouthed, panting with sycophantic mania like heat-stricken dogs. On the rare occasions he spoke, it was usually to issue cryptic statements of such staggering obviousness that they took on an almost mystical quality. ("Consumers want products.")

No matter how bad it got, no matter how we teetered on the brink of ruin, Horton's mere presence gave the whole debacle an imprimatur of legitimacy. Which, in retrospect, was all he really contributed. After all, he already had more money than he could ever spend; did he really care if Commotion succeeded? He showed up now and then to drop his tech-savant bon mots, but he was the head of the company in title alone. The real authority passed into the hands of Hilda, the VP of Human Resources and Horton's trusted right-hand woman. Hilda was a kind of corporate remora who'd attached herself to Horton early in his career and accompanied him to every subsequent stop. While Horton flew around the country by private jet, massaging the moneymen, Hilda got her hands bloody running the day-to-day operations. Though technically low on the totem pole, it was understood that she had Horton's backing and ear, so she was grudgingly treated with the same deference he was. In meetings she would often end debate by mentioning, offhandedly, that she and Horton had recently discussed the very same subject and came to "x" conclusion, and what did they all think of that? Of course no one dared confirm any of these discussions with Horton, so the extent of his actual backing in these instances was left to our imaginations. And of course, these manipulations went both ways. As Horton's main source of information about happenings on the ground, she was able to shape his perceptions on everything from hiring and firing to the company logo. Because she had all parties at an equal double-blind disadvantage, she had what amounted to absolute power. A lot of comparisons to Bush/Cheney were made around the office, only half-jokingly.

Given this almost unlimited mandate, Hilda treated the company in the manner of a scolded child given an ant farm and a magnifying glass. Under the aegis of "Human Resources," she subjected us to an endless series of group activities, offsite day camps, and seminars, ostensibly for motivational purposes but more likely out of pure sadism. Since most everyone was already doing the work of two people, the only logical conclusion was that she did it all just because she could. Like many who spend their life in proximity to power, she'd also developed delusions of grandeur. A female coworker who'd gone to her home after happy hour one night reported that the main wall of her condo was festooned with paintings of herself, a grid of multicolored Warhol-style portraits strategically placed to catch the first light of dawn. She was a white-collar Rasputin, though instead of a psychotic monk with red glowing eyes, she was a short, obese woman with a bowl cut, an unfortunate assortment of facial warts, and a wardrobe that tended toward Nehru-collared, pastel-colored body tarps from Ann Taylor Loft.

At the close of my first Wednesday, just as I was about to go home, an e-mail appeared in my inbox announcing that "THE SMACKDOWN WILL COMENCE [sic] IN TEN MINUTES!!!!" I asked a coworker about the e-mail, on the off-chance it wasn't spam. He informed that me that every Wednesday Hilda, the VP of Human Resources, led a company-wide pep rally featuring whimsical PowerPoint presentations, chanting of inspirational slogans, and lots of open-mouthed grinning.

You'll notice that a lot of people schedule dentist's appointments on Wednesday afternoons, he said.

Do we have to go?

Read the e-mail, he said, trying to smile.

I scrolled down past the animated balloons clip art and there at the bottom I saw: "Participation is not mandatory—HOWEVER, ATTENDANCE WILL BE TAKEN!"

My heart sank. You've got to be kidding, I said.

He opened his mouth to reply, but was cut off by the opening riff of "Eye of the Tiger" blasting out of the PA system at ear-shattering volume.

All the employees who hadn't been able to come up with an excuse shuffled into the conference hall, the hyper-aggressive guitar chords an ironic counterpoint to the slumped shoulders and dead eyes. The back rows filled up first.

Plenty of room up front! Hilda chirped.

The lights fell. There was a slideshow featuring a lot of incomprehensible acronyms ("Always PNIP your work!"), clip art, and pie charts. Bored, I eyed my coworkers in the dimmed light. Their faces ranged from dumb animal blankness to a resignation that approached beatitude. I almost envied them;

I myself was new enough to be angry at the wasting of my time.

The slideshow ended with a list of the stock prices of various Internet start-ups made good; Google, Sun, and so on. The market hadn't crashed yet, and these numbers were still impressive. The next slide was a list of the stock-option rates: the average multiplier of an option to the eventual stock price was tens if not hundreds. The implication being that the people in that room were all imminent millionaires, many times over. I could see it in my coworkers' faces, the loose-eyed madness of avarice as they each stared off into space, lips moving mutely as they carried the one and found their prospective net worth to be in the high seven figures. As we scattered back to our desks, energized for four hours of unpaid overtime, I heard snatches of conversations about cars, pools, yachts…

The production schedule required me to write several articles a day as well as edit the output of the other "writers." I use this term sarcastically because the writing staff was a repository for all the lackeys and hangers-on and investors' children who had been taken on as a favor to somebody. Why is it that everyone thinks they can write? *But dude, I've written tons of stuff! For example—grocery lists! Every week for years!* My first day I was charged with cleaning up drafts of "How to Waterproff (sic) Your Shoes" and a laborious thousand-word rendering of the construction and opening of a suspension bridge in rural France. Upon reading them I immediately concluded that I was the victim of a practical joke and began searching for hidden cameras.

Alas, this was not to be. I went to the authors of the articles and told them I needed revisions. I told Jen, the niece of a major investor, that her bridge article needed to be a little more "dynamic" and Chris, the CEO's ex-caddy, that his shoe-waterproofing article needed to be fleshed out. They looked puzzled but set to it. An hour later their second drafts appeared in my inbox. Jen had added five hundred words about the physics of suspension bridges and Chris had converted the text of his article to a larger font. I decided it would be easier to just do the rewrites myself.

When the other writers saw that I was rewriting their articles almost from scratch, their first drafts got sloppier and sloppier until they were just turning in numbered lists, half-pages of cryptic sentence fragments separated by ellipses and, finally, Word documents blank except for a title at the top. I could've complained to the department head, but I would've been just as likely to get fired—they were all connected up and I was just some guy who had the audacity to be qualified for his job. In the end I just did it all myself.

Stumbling in one morning after another public transportation gauntlet, I nearly did a latte spit-take when I found everyone in my department emptying their desks into boxes. Jesus, I knew start-ups were volatile, but I never imagined it would go under overnight.

No, it's nothing like that, explained my cubicle neighbor when I asked him if we'd been axed en masse. He explained that Hilda was spearheading a "creativity" initiative for our department; the cubicles were to be reconfigured into a hexagonal pattern, with massive silk parachutes draped over the entire area. Above the silk parachutes, a battery of multicolored strobe lights mounted on the ceiling would stimulate our synapses with randomly timed flashes, and each writer would have one of those yuppie-zen water-trickling-onto-rocks contraptions on their desk.

That's the stupidest thing I've ever heard, I said.

My coworkers shrugged and kept packing.

I went to my desk; there was a box on my chair for my things. I dumped it onto the floor and sat down. In a company of engineers and bean counters, the creative department was already regarded with a measure of eye-rolling. Now we were going to be an outright laughingstock. It was bad enough I was doing the work of four people—now I had to endure the snickers of ponytailed carabiner-jingling math geeks and rosacea-faced fifty-year-old virgins in sweater vests? And to what end? Last I checked, humiliation wasn't conducive to creativity.

Hilda came by shortly before lunch to check on our progress. Everyone had packed up except for me. She ambled over and asked me why I hadn't packed.

Before I could answer, one of my office rivals chimed in to inform her that it was because I thought her redecoration idea was stupid and demeaning. I made a mental note to key his car at lunch.

Hilda flashed me a humorless smile. Oh really? She asked. And why is that?

This isn't going to make anyone any more creative, I said. It's going to be like working on the set of *Romper Room*. I mean, if you're not happy with the quality of our work, there are other ways to address that.

All the keyboards had stopped tapping as the rest of the department listened in. Well, Hilda said, why don't we just try it for a month and see what happens?

As reasonable as that sounded, I wasn't really willing to compromise. Besides, we both knew that once her plan was put in place, it was going to stay that way.

Why don't we not try it at all? I asked. We're going to look stupid and feel stupid. That's not going to improve our productivity. Quite the opposite. Let's just forget the whole thing and move on.

I'll have you know, Hilda said through gritted teeth, that this idea is based on the theories of Buckminster Fuller.

She stood there with hands on hips, waiting. I realized that this was my cue to withdraw my argument and apologize, thus validating her idea in the eyes of the onlookers. Of course, I couldn't do that. I repeated, in somewhat diplomatic terms, that I didn't think it was a good idea and besides, didn't true creativity come from within?

Wild eyed, Hilda turned on her heel and stomped back to her office. I made a powerful enemy that day, and it would come back to bite me many times in the coming months. On the other hand, the "creativity initiative" was quietly scrapped and I was able to continue to work in an office that was legitimate in appearance if not substance.

The start-up's constant financial instability—we once came within forty-eight hours of shutting down forever—made us regress into a state of adolescent hypersensitivity. We alternated between hours of fevered confessional cubicle huddling and eruptions of undirected resentment. Once, after a contentious meeting, I returned from lunch to find that someone had etched the word "FAG" into my computer monitor. After confirming the identity of the culprit, I waited until he went outside for a smoke, went up to the top floor of the parking garage, and dumped a mugful of urine on him. The IT woman, an Eastern European ex-hacker who wore the same outfit every single day, looked the other way so we could snag the list of office passwords and we spent an afternoon putting up Craigslist personal ads for various senior management figures detailing their fantasy of being urinated on by a filthy obese man. (*I work second shift so make sure you call after midnight! Alternately, just show up at my home address, given below!*)

Shouting matches, often elevating into scuffles, were a weekly if not daily occurrence and when we went out for drinks after work there was always a fistfight (usually followed by tearful reconciliation and man hugs all around). The same absence of management that allowed the chaos to flourish also insulated the higher-ups from any real awareness of how bad it was on the ground, though occasionally they caught a glimpse of the cubicle anarchy. The suits commissioned a promotional film extolling the virtues of the firm, and after weeks of interviews and shooting, the entire company gathered in a conference room to screen the finished product. Everything was fine until about halfway through. Certain details that had gone unnoticed on the videographer's small editing window were rather conspicuous on the big screen, as when during a talking-head interview, two designers could clearly be seen in the background engaged in a furious, teary-eyed slapfight.

Walking back to our section after the screening, I shrugged and told the video editor that it wasn't his fault.

Besides, you can just edit that out, right?

Yeah, he said. But what are we going to do about the fifteen hundred DVDs we've already sent out?

One morning I was frantically hammering out a past-due article when a plastic ball whistled past my ear and shattered my monitor. I whirled around but the thrower had already dropped back down into his cubicle. A wave of tittering fluttered across our section.

Someone had placed several cans of racquetballs in our section—I vaguely remember an accompanying managerial mass e-mail about the stress-relieving benefits of juggling. Before long we'd made a practice of randomly winging the balls as hard as we could at the back of each other's heads as we sat at our computers. Why? Why not? Though everyone agreed that throwing a racquetball at the back of your unwitting coworker's skull was unacceptable, unprofessional, dangerous, and infantile, once you yourself had been hit with the ball, you suddenly felt you had an unalienable right to retribution. *I'm going to throw this ball, but only to set things right, and God willing let this be the last time.* It was kind of like the Israel-Palestine situation, albeit on a slightly smaller scale.

The only person in our section who objected to this game was Jill, the writer of the infamous suspension bridge article, a very prim religious three-hundred-pound Duke grad who kept pictures of Prince William pinned up in her cubicle. After one near miss, she complained to management, and the entire department got chewed out that afternoon.

Jill has a heart condition and she mustn't become excited, the department head said while Jill was at lunch. That's why she's so heavy—she takes steroids to stimulate her weak heart, but she can't exercise, so she just puts on weight. No more ball throwing! Do you have any idea what a clusterfuck the liability issues would be?

We contritely handed over the balls but at lunch some resentful bastard with a welt on his scalp went out and bought another can. By the end of the day we were all huddling in fear again.

Weak heart, a coworker snorted on the train that night. She's just fat.

The next morning, just as Jill was getting up from her desk for another cup of herbal tea, a racquetball ricocheted off my forehead and hit her in the face. Purple faced and in tears, she bawled us out and stomped off to the bathroom. About an hour later she had a seizure at her desk and was carried off on a stretcher.

At lunch that day, some of us debated who was responsible. Half the table thought that if she died, the original thrower of the ball would be charged with murder. The other half was of the opinion that since I was the last one to touch the ball before it hit Jill, I would be the one on the hook, though possibly only for manslaughter since the ball had only bounced off my forehead.

Maybe you can plead temporary insanity due to sleep deprivation, suggested the video editor.

I don't mind the idea of prison, I said. As long as you killed someone in the first week so no one fucked with you, I don't think it would be that bad. I could get a lot of reading done.

She told me she's never been kissed, someone said.

That could mean anything. I've had sex with tons of people I never actually kissed.

If she dies, this next round of funding will never come through.

God, this job is depressing, I said. I gazed out at the parking lot and considered the karmic ramifications of having committed murder-by-shenanigan. A racquetball caromed off the side of my head and overturned a basket of tortilla chips and several glasses of water onto the floor as everyone howled like chimps. When we paid the check, the cashier told us maybe we should find another Mexican restaurant. Luckily there were two more just like it in that strip mall alone.

The next week, word spread that Horton's lobbying had failed—no prison sentences for downloaders. This was a crippling blow, and it came at the worst possible time. The new version of the product had all the appeal of pubic lice and crashed as often as a drunk Asian lady trying to parallel park. Early reports from test groups ranged from indifference to disgust, and people began taking jobs elsewhere. Morale plummeted, so Hilda scheduled more and more motivational jamborees, which of course drove morale even lower.

One day as I was sweating the latest deadline, the entire company was summoned to the middle of the office to find several crates of oranges stacked next to the elevators. Hilda explained to us that the company was failing because we were bad at multitasking and cooperation. She gave us each two oranges, formed us into a series of circles, and had us toss the oranges back and forth to "refine our collaborative skills." This went on for fifteen, thirty, forty-five minutes, with various changes in configuration. The HR VP and her male secretary circulated among the groups with joyless hawkish grins making sure everyone was exhibiting the required degree of enthusiasm. At one point, the guy next to me was purple faced and nearly choking with rage as he frantically caught and threw oranges.

I'm two weeks behind deadline, he said through gritted teeth. Why am I spending my afternoon tossing fruit?

I shared this sentiment. I still had a thousand words to write that day. I spied one of the nonwriter writers in the next circle, leisurely juggling oranges with an open-mouthed grin. Of course he was relaxed; I did all his work. I waited until he looked in the other direction and winged an orange at the side of his head.

The tossing became more competitive, and Hilda began eliminating weaker tossers/catchers. At the end, it came down to the company accountant and the orange-faced woman who answered the phones. As they juggled half a dozen oranges back and forth, Hilda clapped her hands gleefully and everyone else stood around looking at their watches. You could tell neither of the tossers really wanted to continue, but they couldn't just quit with the VP watching so closely. Believe me, you don't know anything about dignity and the human condition until you've seen a frantic, sweat-drenched fifty-five-year-old accountant juggle oranges in front of a hundred fifty peers as "Eye of the Tiger" blasts in the background.

It seemed to go on forever, and I briefly considered the possibility that it would, that we'd all stand there eternally, wasting away from starvation, our pants filling with shit, watching with dimmed eyes as the two of them tossed their desiccated citrus husks back and forth, each of us falling dead in our tracks until only Hilda was left, clapping and marching in interminable figure-eights among the corpses, perhaps even growing younger as the years passed, sustained and vitalized by nothing more than her inexhaustible idiotic positivity. Under the circumstances, it sounded preferable to returning to my desk.

Eventually, though, the accountant had to push his glasses

up, and he missed an orange. After a moment of anticlimactic relieved silence, the secretary was declared the winner. For her efforts she received a generic victory certificate Hilda had created with MS Paint. She hung it in her cubicle, right between the picture of a shirtless Jon Bon Jovi and her son's high school senior portrait in which he posed dead eyed against a red, white, and blue backdrop, casually flashing a gang sign.

When we needed a break from the office, we headed to a circle of picnic tables on the unlandscapable margin of the office park, separated from the freeway by a patchy screen of malnourished trees. You could sit there, engulfed in a thick fog of car exhaust but far from the prying ears of Hilda and her spy network, and pretend momentarily that you weren't at work. Office couples went there to bicker and little gossip groups went there to air a particularly sensitive or spiteful complaint against the company.

One afternoon after another motivational jamboree (Hilda had analyzed everyone in the company according to some pop-psychology pseudomedieval archetypes. She of course had been a "White Wizard," benevolent and all-knowing. I'd been a "Black Knight," the only one in the company—evil, chaotic and destructive! I'd been insulted until one of my coworkers had been dubbed a "Yellow Squire"—ineffectual, submissive, probably syphilitic.) I was sitting on a bench by myself, when a coworker walked up and sat across from me.

Greg was a recent college grad, an earnest worker bee thrilled to be making twenty-four thousand dollars a year doing eighty hours of data entry a week. Of everyone at the company, he'd bought in the most. He came in on the weekends, he fetched bagels, he wore Commotion-branded apparel unironically, he was the first one in and the last one to leave. He was so naïvely eager that I couldn't despise him, even when he made earnest suggestions on how to enhance my performance or wove elaborate rationalizations to explain away the company's latest fuck-ups.

That morning, he looked profoundly shaken, pale, and uncharacteristically sloppy and unshaven, clutching his forehead as if he'd been struck there.

Are you okay, I asked.

He looked up, startled. He looked over each shoulder and leaned closer. I heard something terrible yesterday, he whispered.

After work, a group of people had gone to a nearby restaurant. Most of upper management was there, including the founder. Greg was thrilled when he found himself, hours and dozens of bottles in, seated next to the founder. A dedicated brown-noser, he immediately started in with his spiel about how he was sure Commotion was only experiencing temporary adversity and would certainly emerge a strong, prosperous company. The founder, deep in his cups, fixed him with a bemused eye and said, no, the company was most certainly going to fail. He'd known that from the beginning. Commotion would not be a success, but it was the first company of its kind, and there was tremendous value in that—for him, the founder. It was quite the feather in his cap to have deflowered that particular industry before anyone else. That's how it was in every field; the first always failed, but they were the first.

Greg looked at me, waiting for an explanation. I was mildly appalled to see genuine hurt in his eyes. But what about all that unpaid overtime? What about all the talk, encouraged by our superiors, of stock options, mansions, yachts? Was it possible, he seemed to be asking, that management had been less than forthright and honest? Was it possible that they didn't have the workers' best interests in mind?

We sat at the bench thinking our private thoughts. My God, in that light, all those motivational seminars looked downright sadistic! We were little more than guinea pigs, subjected to all the latest managerial fads just to gather data for Hilda's next consultant gig. And Jesus, I'd been writing two thousand words a day! I'd been taking it day by day out of sheer survival, so it's not as if I'd had the opportunity to build up any grandiose expectations of success, but still. I really was wasting my time, not just metaphorically but literally!

A well-placed colleague assured me later that day that this wasn't unusual in the least. There's a hard-core group of nomadic start-up executives who flit from start-up to start-up, drawing exorbitant salaries for a couple of years before going to the next sinking ship. Since everything is done in the spirit of reinventing the wheel, no one blinks at the hyperinflated salaries or unchecked nepotism, which is rationalized as "incentivizing" or "bringing in assets of trust." Since the vast majority of start-ups fail anyway, no one is surprised when the house burns down in three years and everyone migrates to the next gravy train. The venture capitalists don't care, what's ten million dollars of seed money to them? This made perfect sense; there were executives at Commotion who'd worked at ten, twelve failed companies, and everyone from the security guards to the VPs were someone's frat brother, someone's cousin. In the meantime, why not chase that 1 percent chance at billions by flogging the worker bees into grinding out eighty hour weeks?

As I turned to leave, Greg said he'd promised not to tell anyone, so could I keep it a secret? I promised I would and I did, pretty much. I only told two or three coworkers, who immediately told two or three more coworkers, ad infinitum. By lunchtime, the entire company knew. A lot of people went home early that day.

There was another motivational jamboree the next day (!) and, in light of developments, I didn't think I could stomach it. I called in sick and spent the day on my sofa eating Vicodin left over from a root canal and nodding off into purplish spite-filled reveries.

Jesus! So many hours spent staring off into space in that air-locked building, tossing a Nerf ball against the wall, hundreds and then thousands of times, typing somnambulistically in case a manager happened by while inwardly weaving increasingly baroque sexual fantasies, fashioning banquets from complementary break room snacks, horrible Frankensteinian atrocities: tiramisu made with half-and-half, flattened Twinkies, and week-old coffee reduced down by evaporation, salsa made with black pepper and V8. Furtively looking at little snatches of pornography just to goose the soul into a momentary frisson, restarting a smoking habit just to have an excuse to leave the building every thirty minutes, taking the last train home to sleep and do it all over again the next day. All those months of my life, all spent under false pretenses, and all of them gone!

At some point you have the horrifying epiphany that this is your job, yes, but it's also your life! Tabulating strings of uncontextualized figures, peddling trash to overstimulated grown-up children; it's best to avoid looking too closely at the big picture, as the machinery of capitalism is lubricated by some rather unsavory substances. Does it make an imprint on any meaningful sphere of existence if you move 10 percent more units this quarter than last? For anyone living a conscious life, office culture inevitably brings the onset of a mild sort of existential despair. Call it the blahs if you'd like: What am I doing? Am I just flushing 40 hours a week down the toilet? And unless you're a heart surgeon or something, the answer is generally a resounding "yes."

I realized now why so many of the older people in the office kept some sort of discreet religious iconography at their desks. I'd only been working in an office for a few years; they'd been doing it for decades! I was still fighting it, but they'd long ago eagerly embraced their job as their all-encompassing identity. For them, existence had been leached of any meaning or consequence; all they had left was the promise of the immaterial. Whenever I found myself agonizing over an end-less day, I just thought about my elders in management. Their entire lives were essentially one never-ending day, only instead of a happy-hour-induced blackout to look forward to, all they had at the end was the sweet release of death.

One morning a few weeks later, I arrived to find an e-mail in my inbox reminding me that the movie picks for the product launch were due at noon. Since music was available all over the Internet, management had decided that we'd offer down-loadable movies as a "difference maker." The deal they'd struck with the studios was a million dollars to license a hun-dred movies. Back when I still cared, I'd convinced everyone that I was the man to compile the film library, anticipating that if the movie offerings turned out to be a big deal, I'd be well positioned for a promotion. But as time passed and the curtain was drawn back on the company's essential nature, I'd become less and less motivated until, in the long summer months, I'd forgotten about it entirely.

Now I had two hours to pick out a million dollars' worth of movies. I opened the spreadsheet catalog: it contained tens of thousands of titles. Just the A's went on for a hundred pages. Just then I got an e-mail from my office pal John: he had to take his car in for a tune-up that day, so our usual noontime burrito run would have to be moved up an hour. I looked at my watch: it was already ten thirty.

Shit, I only had thirty minutes! I'd have to pick three movies a minute in order to make the burrito run. I'd skipped break-fast that morning and I was already feeling light-headed with hunger, so forgoing lunch wasn't an option. I'd picked out maybe five movies when John showed up at my desk.

Ready to go?

You said I had until eleven!

He shrugged. The mechanic's place is farther away than I thought. We have to leave now.

I put my head down on my desk for a moment. Well, if Commotion was meant to fail from the beginning, who was I to stand in the way? I scrolled down the spreadsheet and randomly picked out ninety-five more movies. Months later, when I was coasting on unemployment and getting drunk in bars every night, I always concluded the above anecdote with, *and that's how I spent a million dollars in thirty seconds!* It was always a big hit with women. Ladies love a bad boy.

I showered one morning and afterward I stood in front of the foggy mirror flossing and shaving and sculpting my hair, the glass slowly clearing until right there in front of me was... holy fucking shit, how did Dad's body get inside my mirror?

All that perpetual cubicle snacking had caught up to me, all the pasta lunches and frappes and happy-hour pints. I stood there scrutinizing my body with lurid fascination; I'd always been underweight and thin, but somehow without my even noticing I'd become an ambulatory bean-bag chair. I looked seven months' pregnant, my stomach bloated and thighs jiggling, yes, visibly jiggling, and even my face was looking doughy. My god! All this time I'd thought my decay was just internal!

I put on my baggiest office clothes and spent the entire morning at my desk, researching area gyms, and before lunch I was a member, paid in full.

Have you ever wondered what it would be like to sit in the worst bar on earth, stone-cold sober? That's what the gym is like. Everyone pretending they're not checking each other out, harsh lighting, too much skin, bad music played too loud, total sausage party. I'd found a place near the subway stop I took to and from Commotion, and that night I dressed in my new shiny elastic-waisted synthetic fibers and commenced my first ever workout.

I decided to begin by lifting weights. The bench press, the

favored exercise of convicts and brutes. I loaded the bar, laid on my back, and pushed the weight up out of the brackets. Immediately I realized I'd made a mistake. The weight plummeted downward as if encountering no resistance whatsoever, indifferent to my anger and then my terror. Uh oh! With an audible thud, the bar hit my chest, and it took all my strength just to keep the weight from crushing the air out of my lungs. I began flailing my legs spasmodically, but this had the counterproductive result of rolling the bar back onto my throat, where it came to rest just below my Adam's apple. The idea of crying out for help occurred to me but I considered public embarrassment to be approximately on par with decapitation.

Just when I was beginning to fade out, a hirsute man wearing a weight belt appeared overhead and lifted the bar off my neck with an ease I found no less insulting given the circumstances.

You okay?

I nodded, still prone and gingerly rubbing my throat with both hands. The weight lifter tossed me a towel.

You pissed yourself, he said.

I went to the crowded locker room and stood in front of the full-length mirror, boiling over with humiliation. As I stood there and watched a wreath of rich, salmon-and-lavender-colored bruises appear on my neck, I heard my name called.

Franklin!

I turned to see one of the guys from Sales, a short cocky private-school bantam standing bemused in just a jockstrap.

Hey, I saw you out there, he said, grinning. How much was that, like fifty pounds?

Pff. More like three fifty!

He leaned toward me squinting. Those bruises look wicked, he said. I can't wait to tell everyone about this tomorrow.

Fuck you. You work in sales.

Yeah, but at least I can lift my body weight.

That's because you're a midget.

He dismissed me with a wave, and I exited the locker room. My first gym visit had been a public disaster, and I knew I was going to hear about it tomorrow. And not only was I still fat, now I looked like I'd been necking with a shop vac.

On the way home I stopped off at a department store and bought a week's worth of turtlenecks.

Still, my vanity won out and for several weeks I went directly from Commotion to the gym. But though everyone told me I was supposed to be enjoying my exercise, it seemed to me that the gym was just an annex of the office, with Nautilus machines instead of cubicles and mirrors instead of windows and a slightly nicer watercooler. (Ooh, cold, hot OR room temperature!)

Trudging from machine to machine in interminable circles, strolling along on the treadmill—the more I went, the more the gym seemed to be the perfect metaphor for what my life had become. "Runner's high" aside (a term by the way used un-derisively only by people who've never been actually, pharmaceutically, high), the pleasure I got from the gym wasn't pleasure exactly but the absence of suffering, or more accurately, a temporary cessation of the dread of suffering (getting fat, being out of shape, aging, etc.). And wasn't it ironic that in this bright ultramodern complex of steel and glass, all of us contemporary, urban, enlightened college graduates who scoffed reflexively at the very mention of religion were nonetheless engaged in our own evangelical pursuits? Like any medieval God-fearing peasant, we too were doing all we could to not necessarily embody virtue so much as avoid being contaminated by vice. (In this case, fat instead of sin.) Like the God-fearing peasant, we gladly suffered now for the promise of some distant ambiguous future reward, sweating away not for admission to the afterlife, but for "health." And weren't we also all bound to find that all our efforts had been in vain, as no matter how disciplined and high impact the yuppie's workouts were, he wasn't ever going to stave off decay and death, any more than the good Christian ever makes it through the pearly gates to recline and play the harp for eternity while surrounded by friends and family?

If I missed a workout or ate too many cookies I felt guilty. Guilty! And like the Catholic saying ten Hail Marys after confession to expiate some minor sin, I would likewise flee to the gym to ritually work off my own transgressions, monitoring calories burned and heart-rate elevation until I'd "made it right." It was all too creepy for me, and after a few months I swore off it.

Luckily, there's an entire segment of the clothes market aimed directly at lazy, paunchy office drones like myself. It wasn't until I got a little sloppy that I realized that the function of most men's clothes is to camouflage the deteriorating body. Say what you want about the false advertising of women wearing heavy makeup, but there's nothing more deceiving than the suit jacket. The stove pipe arms, the comedically constructed shoulders, the three-quarter's length that so stealthily conceals the expanding waist and ass. Throw in a tie that unsubtly points directly at the cock ("I'm a man, goddamnit!") and you can turn the saggiest milquetoast into a quasimilitary facsimile of a man's man, at least in outline.

And for the next year or so, until six months on the unemployment diet had melted off my love handles, I wore the cheesiest, boxiest menswear I could find, and the most depressing thing wasn't my appearance but how the other guys in the office immediately accepted me as one of them.

Every day I descended into the subway for my swaying, semiconscious commute, standing ass to crotch with the other zombies, pouring coffee into our mouths with pinched befuddled expressions in a fog of bad cologne and shampoo fumes. Those ubiquitous white earbuds nestled in almost every ear, and mine, too. One morning I forgot to grab my iPod on the

way out of the apartment, and I found myself standing undis-
tracted in the packed train car. Not even a discarded section
of the newspaper to peruse, not even a shitty cell phone game.
Without dynamic soundtrack accompaniment the commu-
ter's tableau revealed itself in all its squalid banality; the flickering lights, the stained carpeting, the resignation that was
almost hypnotic. I tried to look at something else, but there it
was, wherever I turned; my life! And just at the edge of my
hearing; the tinny strains of a half-forgotten punk anthem
from my adolescence. I turned to see a jowled, bespectacled
fellow in a bad suit and wingtips—he could've been thirty or
fifty—nodding along to his iPod; the ultimate company man
entertaining dreams of rebellion. I recoiled in disgust and
stumbled down the car, only to pull up next to a stony-faced
woman dressed in a sexless baglike Dress Barn number unconsciously soft-stepping to a sultry R&B sex joint; *my lumps,
my lady humps.* There really was no escape! A weak-chinned IT
guy in elevator shoes, his clothes pressed just so, clean shaven
and his ID lanyard carefully displayed as per regulation, wearing headphones like earmuffs, listening at tremendous volume
to a rap fantasy of homicide and fucking and Cristal-spraying.

It was horrifying, all the more so because I recognized my
own delusions there. I knew that these interludes weren't
escapes, but in their own minds, their real lives, their lives as
they wanted them to be and had convinced themselves they
were, and that when they reached their stop and took out
their earbuds and trudged to their cubicle, it wasn't as a
return to reality but as a reluctant digression from their
authentic, inner existence. The IT guy was in his own mind a
hard-fuckin' desperado, the corporate square actually a mav-
erick with middle fingers raised to the world, the chaste celi-
bate in sensible shoes actually a cauldron of white-hot lust.
Sure they were!

In this light, I couldn't possibly go back to my own "fuck
you" anthems. (I recall Danzig's "Mother" was one of my

favorites.) I put my iPod in the back of a drawer, and for good measure swore off television and movies and celebrity magazines. When I commuted I just sat there and took it in and in the office I sat un-head-phoned in my cubicle, receptive to all the non sequiturs and ringtones and acronyms. In my off hours, I laid on the sofa in my apartment staring off into space or took long walks or sat in bars that didn't have flat screens wherever you looked, that didn't serve wings or sliders or microbrews or any of that bullshit, just sat and nursed shitty beer and thought. All of this in an effort to perceive the Thing Itself, that is, my shitty life with no delusions or disguises or sugarcoating. And as the smoke screen dissipated and I gazed with increasing clarity into that unholiest of unholies, I knew that I'd proved my point, I'd hacked it long enough, and either this experiment was going to come to an abrupt end very soon, or I was.

After a month of shuffling around exuding indifference, Hilda summoned me into her office for a little talk. I showed up twenty minutes past the appointed time, unshaven and wearing the same clothes for the third consecutive day.

Hilda sat me down in front of her desk and then went back to typing.

I just have to finish this e-mail, she said.

She typed on for several minutes. It was obvious she was just making me wait to demonstrate who was in charge.

On her desk was a large photograph of her son Randy, an acne-bearded sailor with an overbite and slumped shoulders. He'd been reared with the assumption that he'd grow up to be a polymath genius but had dropped out of high school to join the navy. Upon his discharge she'd gotten him a job as a consultant at Commotion, where he was a figure of moderate ridicule. He perpetually lurked in the break room, where he put on elaborate air-bass performances for the janitorial staff and buttonholed unsuspecting coffee drinkers with navy-related anecdotes. One of his favorites revolved around him single-handedly detecting a hostile Russian submarine with his preternaturally acute hearing after his sub's sonar went down. They'd mistakenly ventured into Soviet waters, and if they'd been discovered, the result would've been nuclear war and mutually assured destruction, the straight-faced implication being that he'd single-handedly saved not only the day but also all of humanity.

His "job" required him to assemble an Excel spreadsheet aggregating all the information for the movies we'd purchased. It was never clear as to how exactly this spreadsheet was supposed to be useful. He used a freeware data-harvesting spider program to compile the document, for which his mother's department paid him twenty thousand dollars.

How is Randy, by the way? I asked, gesturing toward the photograph.

He's fine, said Hilda. He's getting married. He says they're going to have lots of kids.

Great! I said, the horror in my voice at the prospect of more Hilda-spawn perhaps insufficiently suppressed. Hilda stopped typing and pivoted in her chair to face me. She folded her hands on her desk and leaned forward.

So, she said.

So, I said.

Where to begin? It was obvious, she said, that my motivation was at "low ebb." I'd only been working eight hours a day, and I hadn't come in on a Saturday for weeks now. She'd also heard that I wasn't getting along with my coworkers. What incidents specifically was she referring to, I asked.

I heard that you dumped a trash can full of water on the graphic designer as he was smoking a cigarette in the parking garage. I also heard you held one of the writers down on the floor and squirted ketchup into his mouth until he choked on it.

This was all true, I told her. What could I say? Working at a failing company is stressful.

A lot of your team members say that you're very critical of their work, Hilda said, and that they don't feel they can depend on you for unconditional support.

Well, a lot of them aren't very good at their jobs.

You know what your problem is, Hilda said. Your standards are too high. You expect too much out of everything and everyone. Excellence is out of the reach of the vast majority of people, and so it's a corrosive, alienating element. Your life would be a lot easier if you'd just aim lower. Aim for good enough.

It took me a moment to absorb the full ramifications of her advice. I saw that it wasn't merely advice lightly offered but her actual life philosophy. The entire company was living testament to the fact that she didn't just preach mediocrity, she practiced it! Like most people (I think), I'd always assumed mediocrity to be an accidental outcome, the result of a good faith effort that merely fell short. To hear that it was actually an ideal in and of itself, something to be actively pursued—this was something to crack even my practiced cynicism.

I found that I was genuinely speechless. Coming into the meeting I'd been determined to bring up the founder's "meant to fail" confession, but now I saw I was up against forces much deeper and more systemic. We sat there for a full minute before she finally spoke.

You think I'm stupid, don't you? she asked.

It was a once-in-a-lifetime setup! Did I dare? I did.

Well, yes, I said.

Now it was Hilda's turn to be struck speechless. For a moment I thought she was going to fire me on the spot, but the moment passed. We sat regarding each other, and I saw for the first time that she sincerely hated me. She'd invested her entire life in enforcing and playing by the rules, pandering to her superiors, obsessively currying favor and clinging to a pay-check. In a way, Commotion was her worldview given sub-stance, her monument to resignation and mediocrity. It was the anti-meritocracy; the only qualification was knowing the right person and being sufficiently craven toward them. The barbarians weren't at the gates, they were the gatekeepers. To her, I must have appeared not just foolish but downright psy-chopathic. To roll my eyes at power, to scoff at authority, to treat a paying job not just with indifference, but contempt was an affront to her entire worldview.

There was a large jar of individually wrapped licorice ropes on Hilda's desk, and I leaned forward to take one. As I was withdrawing it from the jar, her hand jabbed out at cobra speed and seized it back.

Get out, she said.

I reached out as if to take another licorice rope, and she snatched them away with such force that the jar tumbled off the desk, strewing candies all over the floor.

Get out!

I went.

I guess BJ didn't like my articles, because he announced a day after our fateful meeting that all text-based content was dis-continued, effective immediately. In the "relaunch" meeting he showed us video of the man he wanted to bring on board to supervise our transition, a bumptious undergraduate in a gold-buttoned blazer and red bow tie who'd made millions selling air fresheners out of his dorm room. He seemed the type of person whose idea of "creativity" was to market books as doorstops.

Look, guys, BJ said as the lights went up and everyone jolted awake. Bottom line, I just want to make a billion dollars. I don't care how we do it.

This was clearly meant as a reassurance, but at that point

we were too savvy to swallow more robber-baron fantasies of limitless wealth. All we really wanted was a touch of sanity and candor, but I saw now that this was too much to ask. We walked out surer than ever that the company was dead in the water. The only question was, would I be fired or laid off?

I just couldn't figure out why I was still around. I'd backslid very comfortably into the role of the office malcontent, swaggering in an hour late, taking two-hour lunches, and leaving at 4:15 every day. I spent several weeks writing a scathing article about the company, which appeared on the front page of a local newspaper. I wanted to quit, but I couldn't—I hadn't endured a year of idiocy just to take orders from a new set of subnormals at some other cubicle Auschwitz. I needed a vacation, a long paid vacation, which meant I needed a relatively bloodless separation so I would qualify for unemployment checks. Every Friday I waited on tenterhooks to be called into the office for the pink slip—I had a long monologue rehearsed for the occasion—but it never happened. Some days I rode the bus home on the brink of tears: what more could I possibly do? Months passed and in my more paranoid moments I was sure they were keeping me on because they relished the sight of me slouching miserably from break room to cubicle and back, wasted youth as a salve for the bitter and old.

After the showdown with Hilda, I'd been disinvited from all future motivational jamborees on grounds of "incorrigibility." One afternoon as I sat in my cubicle the company assembled for a "spirit jam!" I listened as Hilda described the day's exercise: there would be ten teams, and each team would compose and choreograph a hip-hop song and dance routine. Each team would perform and then everyone would vote on whose was best. A sickly dead quiet met this announcement. Pinching my nose against a snicker, I rose off my chair to peer over my cubicle wall: the faces in the audience varied from shock to horror to undiluted contempt. These were engineers and graphic designers and IT engineers; not exactly a hip-hop song-and-dance crowd.

Don't worry, Hilda said, sensing the mutinous leanings. They do this at Harvard Business School.

Wow. I fell back into my chair, physically staggered by the sheer blind stupidity of this statement. So much suddenly made sense. All the stupid ideas, the jamborees, why I hadn't been fired, everything. Somehow I'd overestimated these people. Hilda and the rest of management were as credulous as toddlers: couch it in the right terms, brand it with a sexy logo, and they'd swallow anything, whole and without blinking. Colored strobe lights and silk tarps? On one hand, common sense would suggest that it was not an advisable way to treat adults; on the other hand, "Buckminster Fuller" has many syllables and sounds very distinguished. Subjecting a roomful of socially awkward, highly inhibited, overstressed and underpaid tech workers to a hip-hop song-and-dance recital? Hey, they do it at Harvard Business School, so it must be a good idea! These were not independent thinkers—these were not thinkers at all. These were people for whom questioning the face value of anything was tantamount to treason, for whom the application of critical faculties was the act of a subversive or terrorist—a "black knight"!

I'd been going about things all wrong. All wrong! I'd been strutting around the office with my head held high and a smirk curling my lip, acting as if I didn't have a care in the world. But they didn't see me as an impudent prick flouting their Mickey Mouse rules—they saw me as someone who wasn't going anywhere, who was sure he'd never be fired. And so it was! They could only make a literal one-to-one extrapolation between what they saw and what they thought. They'd gone to college, every last one of them, but their minds had been trained by nothing so much as television commercials: smiling man drinking beer? Beer = happiness!

If I wanted to get fired, I'd have to dumb-down my approach. I'd have to sell it.

The song-and-dance show went off better than I expected. The first team did a song about how they had a huge backlog of work to do but management was making them dance away the afternoon. The next team's song posited the question of why they couldn't get any raises even though we were receiving millions of dollars in funding, and so on. The applause was thunderous. Hilda watched the entire thing unfold stone-faced. In retrospect, I think that was the only exercise that actually cultivated any office unity, albeit not exactly in the way management had intended.

I started skulking around the office, looking nervous and guilty and fearful. I hunkered down and toed the line like a man trying to dig myself out of a hole, and wouldn't you know it—almost immediately I began hearing second- and third-hand rumors that I was on the chopping block. No wonder the business was failing—management was just as suggestible as the consumers they were trying to fleece.

All this craven playacting was hell on my ego—all the people I'd formerly scorned were now whispering when I walked past and shaking their heads disapprovingly. I just kept my eye on the prize—a six-month paid vacation, courtesy of unemployment. In my off hours, though, I made it a goal each night to drink until my memories of that day were thoroughly blacked out. My mornings became quite problematic, as I required several cups of strong coffee just to get dressed and out the door. Halfway though my two hour commute, my bladder would be full and painfully distended, and sitting on the vibrating plastic bus seat was like having your prostate jabbed with an electric cattle prod. One morning during the long stopless freeway segment of the bus ride I actually had to piss in my coffee cup (I was late as usual and there was no one else on the bus). Pinching my flaccid member between thumb and forefinger, I let go into my Starbucks cup while looking straight ahead and grinning maniacally. The bus driver never looked away from the road. I set the now-brimming cup on the floor and changed seats, but when the bus swerved onto the exit ramp, the cup tipped over and the stench of ammonia spread through the bus. I got off at the next stop and walked the last mile and a half to work. The Virginia exurbs are staunchly Republican and the penalty for public urination is, I think, death.

As soon as I walked in that morning, I could tell the office was on full alert. People who normally would've been napping under their desks, instant-messaging each other scat-porn screen caps, or playing Tetris with the sound all the way up were now sitting straight backed in their chairs and ostentatiously tap-tapping away at their keyboards. Were the VC people doing another walkthrough or something? I made a mental note to clean the vomit off my shoes, just as soon as I checked my eBay auctions.

But when I sat down I found a Post-it note on my computer monitor reading, "Report to Hilda's office ASAPP!!!!"

Ah boy. I have to admit, even when I'm actively trying to get fired, it still stings a little when it happens. The loss of a paycheck is always irritating (doubly so if it's money for nothing) and exile, even from a community of dolts, is still a blow to the ego. I knew Hilda was going to savor the moment, probably drawing it out with a lecture on the virtues of conformity and acceptance before letting me sign for my severance package. My only question was, why now?

When I arrived at Hilda's corner office (!), she was sitting stone-faced behind her desk, swaddled in her usual Nehru-collared boat tarp, her hair meticulously gelled down so that it resembled an arctic lichen.

You wanted to see me?

She pointed at an empty chair, closed the door behind me, and sat back down.

Were you in Evelyn's office yesterday?

I thought back through the fog of poisoned synapses. Yes, we'd had a meeting in her office the previous afternoon to discuss the latest "product concerns." Every time anyone expressed any degree of dissatisfaction with the product—whether it be an eighteen-year-old focus-group participant or a VP who thought you could get a virus on your laptop by sneezing on it—an emergency meeting was convened to draw up an action plan on how to incorporate this valuable new information. While the few people who still cared decisively decided on the wisest course of action (*Let's outsource the redesign to my brother-in-law!*), me and the rest of the malcontents sat in the back doodling on the huge foldout dry-erase board.

When the meeting broke up, we absentmindedly refolded the board and went back to our desks to eat free snacks and clock-watch. The next day, when Hilda dropped by the self-same office with a group of prospective investors and went to illustrate one of her nonsensical nonpoints on the dry-erase board, the group was treated to the sight of a drawing of a woman lying on her back, legs spread in the manner of giving birth, with only a question mark concealing the holiest of holies.

You're terminated, Hilda said. For sexual harassment.

What? I knew that if I went on record as having been fired for a serious transgression, my unemployment would be blocked. More important, Hilda knew it. I'd told a few people in the office that I hoped to get on unemployment, and word had gotten out.

Who did I harass, I asked.

The drawing was in Evelyn's office, Hilda said. Therefore, you harassed her.

Whew. Unbeknownst to the rest of the office, Evelyn and I

had been sleeping together for months, and she was one of
the few people in the office who I actually trusted. I went out
into the hallway and yelled for her to come down to Hilda's
office. She shuffled diffidently over and sat on the corner of
Hilda's desk.

What's up?

Did I sexually harass you? I asked.

What? Evelyn looked from Hilda back to me. No. No one
harassed me. What are you talking about?

The drawing on your dry erase board, I said. Hilda's saying I
harassed you.

Ha! You wish!

Hilda shuffled through a manila folder and drew out a form
with my signature on it.

This is the anti-harassment policy that you signed when
you started here. It clearly states that any instance of sexual
harassment will result in termination.

That's all well and good, I said. Except I didn't actually harass anyone.

Evelyn's jocularity was curdling into something else. Is this
for real, she asked.

Hilda turned to Evelyn. Did you at any point see the drawing
in your office? Did your eyes alight on it?

Yes.

Then you were harassed.

No, I wasn't!

Hush, Hilda told Evelyn. You've been traumatized.

I scoffed. You'll never make this one stick.

Hilda shrugged. We'll see in court, she said.

I cleaned out my desk and Hilda's assistant escorted me to
the elevators. He could barely contain his glee at my expulsion
and as I entered the elevator for the last time, he turned to me
with a smirk and extended his hand for a handshake. I knew it
was meant to be a gesture at my expense, but for some reason
I shook his hand anyway. I wondered for weeks afterward what

had possessed me in that moment, and even now it's my one regret from that period.

On balance, I'm not sure if my time at Commotion was good or bad for me. When I began working at Commotion, I'd started to reevaluate a lot of my assumptions about the world. After eight firings and various other debacles, I'd become poisonously cynical, and after much soul-searching I'd begun to consider the possibility that perhaps people weren't as ignorant and selfish and malicious as I thought, and that maybe the processes of the world were simpler and purer than I'd assumed. A year later, after being fired from Commotion, I realized that my error hadn't been in being too negative—quite the opposite, I'd been almost naïve! I'd given people too much credit; they were much, much worse than I'd imagined even at my most misanthropic, and the world a far poorer place. On my last day, riding the bus home, I thought back to the mangled fawn I'd seen on that same road, the day I'd signed the job offer. The comparison is, I admit, unsubtle, but it's inarguably appropriate.

CHAPTER 14

Unemployment Interlude

or, The Ugliest American

In a country where the twin gods are Money and Utility, it's not in anyone's best interests (save your own, and you don't matter) to have you idle, your earning potential untapped, not producing anything, not "generating wealth," an end and not a means to an end, someone else's end. They want you working, they need you working, and so they will do everything they can to take away your unemployment. When this happens, you have two choices: roll over or fight back.

I fought back, and if this was a Vietnam movie, this is the part where I'd stride out of the jungle bloody and stoic and dead eyed, wearing a necklace of human ears, and you the audience are supposed to realize that when a man fights monsters, he sometimes has to become a monster himself...or something.

After being fired from Commotion, Hilda kept her promise and protested my unemployment. This put my checks in escrow until a court hearing, after which point I'd either receive the entire massive backlog or receive nothing. This of course inconvenienced no one but me, and I was left to live off my meager savings while my old employer hounded my co-workers into giving unflattering statements about my character.

I consulted a pro bono labor lawyer for advice. A cagey courtroom brawler used to taking on the big boys, she knew the only thing that mattered was if you won the case or lost it.

If they don't show up for the hearing, you win by default, she told me in her office the morning of our appointment. If you can get them to not show up to the hearing, that's your best shot.

She gave me an implicative look that said, did I understand?

I did. If I lost the hearing, I'd get nothing, and I'd have wasted all this time and effort. If I won, by whatever means, I'd get all my backed-up checks. Even if I used unethical means to prevent their attendance, and they caught on (and one had to assume they would) and somehow wrangled another hearing, and won *that* hearing, the city's efforts to recover the money I'd already received would be unenthusiastic and largely toothless.

But how to prevent them from attending? I spent many hours pacing the hallways of my apartment, high-stepping over sleeping cats and errant couch cushions, hatching various questionable schemes. Bribe them? Set their cars afire the night before? String tire spikes across their driveways? Frame them as al-Qaeda sleeper agents? My friend Kyle knew an ex-con who took care of things for money. (This was the same person who supplied his illicit foodstamps.) We discussed having this person stomp the HR fellow spearheading my unemployment protest on the eve of the hearing, but ultimately decided against it, as the ex-con had a problem with impulse control (imagine that!), and once he drew blood he was liable to proceed directly to homicide.

At some point the simplest solution presents itself, and I realized that there was nothing I could do to keep my opponents from fulfilling their company-sanctioned duty to corn

hole me. Heaven and earth couldn't prevent them from showing up at that courtroom on the duly-appointed day. But what
if they got their dates mixed up?

I knew an amoral woman who'd done phone work before
and had an unimpeachably authoritative phone manner. She
agreed to help me and one afternoon, after a short rehearsal
and a *67 (untraceable!), she called up my ex-employer.

I'm calling from Judge John Doe's office, she said in the
clipped but weary monotone of a career bureaucrat. His
Honor has been diagnosed with Groat's syndrome, and all of
his cases have been delayed two months while he undergoes
treatment. Your hearing...let's see (shuffling of papers) case
#12345?...is now rescheduled for February 20. Is this accept-
able?

Let me check my calendar, said the HR lackey. Yes, that's
acceptable.

Listening on the other line, I did a silent little jig.

This court will send you a reminder letter one week before
your court date, said my pal.

Is the judge going to be okay? Is there anything we can do?

A silence on the line, and I briefly feared that my accomplice had been thrown off by this unforeseen query, but then I
realized it was all part of the act.

Thank you for your concern, but no, she said soberly. He's
in God's hands now.

We howled at that one after she'd hung up, and every time
our laughter wound down one of us would repeat the magical
line, mock-serious—*He's in God's hands now!*—and we'd be convulsed with glee all over again...

On the morning of the hearing I sauntered into the courtroom at the appointed time, freshly shaven and necktied, a
sheaf of papers under one arm, and sat at the defendant's
table. The plaintiff's table was unoccupied and remained so
right up until and past nine o'clock, when the judge started
the hearing. By nine fifteen I'd been officially declared victori-

ous, and within a week I received my first check—just over four thousand dollars.

But getting on unemployment is just the beginning. Staying on can be a challenge, primarily because people will try to give you jobs. The rules state that you're required to apply to two or three jobs a week, and if you're randomly picked for a checkup and the unemployment people find that you haven't been applying, or that you've turned down "suitable employment," they'll stop the checks and slap you with a bill for all the money you've received up to that point.

With a little ingenuity, though, it's quite easy to meet the letter of the law while defying its spirit. I remembered a job as an editor where I was tasked with hiring a staff writer. Among the deluge of responses from a Craigslist posting were a significant percentage—a quarter to a third—that consisted of an e-mail with no text in the body and nothing in the subject line. Just a résumé, attached as a Microsoft Word document. My general response to these was an incredulous "are you fucking kidding me?" followed by immediate deletion. I sent all my résumés out in the same manner, and almost never received any responses.

Almost never. This method backfired when some desperate department head actually opened my résumé one day, found it acceptable, and offered me a job. Upon reading the offer, I was chilled to the soul. It was a "good job"—staff writer for a website, very little editorial oversight, office right in the city a short bike ride from my house. The money was about twice as much as I made on unemployment at that time, but then one had to consider that if I took the job, my income would double but my quality of life would become nonexistent. I couldn't turn the job down cold, or I'd lose my unemployment. What was I to do? And then it hit me—I wrote him back and told him I wouldn't even consider the position if he didn't double the salary.

There are moments one remembers always. When he told me he'd talk to his superiors to see if he could authorize it, the pit of my stomach fell out and I nearly burst into tears. You moron, I wanted to scream, what earthly fucking reason would you have to pay me, *me*, almost six figures to write hacky fluff pieces for your shitty "webazine"?! I sat on my sofa shaken to the core, thinking that I was going to have to plunge back into the clock-punching nonlife, rising at dawn to don the uniform, nine-dollar bowls of soup for lunch surrounded by smiley eager beavers, long hours in a cubicle puzzling out where I'd gone wrong yet again despite all my pledges and promises, cashing big checks that I really had no interest in and yet felt obligated to spend.

When I received notice a few days later that he, regrettably, wasn't able to meet my salary requirements, I almost burst into hysterical tears of joy.

I'd been saved only by luck and I knew the next time I wouldn't be so lucky. I had to make sure I was never hired again. I was telling Kyle about my close shave one night when he told me he had a foolproof method to guard against job interviews.

Have you ever seen the average person's résumé? Kyle asked, opening his laptop. It looks like it was made by a third grader. It might as well be written in crayon. Typos, misspellings, stupid novelty fonts and exclamation points. Check this out.

In retrospect, I'm lucky that what he showed me next didn't just melt the flesh right off my skull, like when they open the Ark of the Covenant at the end of *Raiders of the Lost Ark*. That's how brilliant it was. I can't even really convey to you how great it was, so I'll just show you:

𝕶𝖞𝖑𝖊 𝕭. 𝕾𝖙𝖎𝖋𝖋

RESUME TO **WORK**: Professional, professional

1549 3rd St nw
Washington DC 20001
Phone 2024628616
prime_entertainer@mookfarm.com

Skills Summary

- ☐ **Quick** - Type 33 WPN and learn new soft ware ;)
- . **Excellent computer skills** - Proficient in Microsoft, Apple, IBM
- ☐ **Wants** to be the managre.
- ☐ **Turned** in my buddy for stealing! Known as the office snitch ;)

Objectives; To have a job at YOUR place of work! ;)

Education

-Illustration Major @ Ringling School an art school - - - - - - Sarasota FLorida
- ☐ Also went to the University of Life for almost 27 years old.

Work experience

March 2005 May 2006 Video American Washington DC
Helped customers right up then until it closed down. I went in the last day.

August 2004 - March 2005 Ben Edwards (real LIFE Artist")
Ben Edwards is @ Friendship Hieghts metro, turn right as you leave, within walking distance from metro.)

Helped him paint his art, which includes computer art and paint art.

July 2003 July/ September 2004

CB Richard Ellis Office @ Mclean Virginia
(This is the job were I turned someone in!!)

Only minutes away from CIAHQ, my favorite War memerial.

☐ Made the maps (ALL of them) for people I worked for.
Jerry said to not use our Philly office to help make the documents. Well
   why not? I called them often. It got the job DONE.

Never contributed to the fenomomenon of the "bathroom rush" at start
   of work day.

Did the "office thing" - you know! ;O

Emerald City Comic Books, Seminole, FL
Took charge of organizing thousands of comic book back issues. Top
   Five: Captain America, Punisher, Punisher Armory, Punisher War
   Zone.
☐ Help the customer.
   (turned in a coworker who steal.) ;)

Ref.:
See above. Ben Edwards, Jerry Harvey (the CB boss, please do not
contact this referense, and Chad @ Emerald Comics.

So you wanna get to now me?
Hard-working.
Dedication.
Stick to the job!
Satisfaction until I quit: thats when its DONE.
Need Sundays OFF (its just my rule.).

So when do I start?????????

"In the councilof the HOLY ONES G__d is greatly feared, HE is more AWE-
SOME than ALL who surround HIM. Psalm 89, 7-8. Awesome huh?

He'd been sending this masterpiece out every week for months and he slept easy, knowing his bounty would never be threatened by an untimely job offer. We opened my résumé next and looked it over. And therein lay the problem! It was far too effective, error-free and concise and thick with impressive job history. We huddled and added colored fonts, emoticons, and misspellings and from then on, that was the résumé I sent out to fulfill my weekly application requirements. I never received so much as a response or acknowledgment, let alone another offer.

A lot of people are weirdly guilty about going on unemployment, as if they're stealing or otherwise doing something wrong. I just don't understand this. Not only do I feel no guilt whatsoever about sucking from the state's teat, I feel that I'm absolutely entitled to it. Some people say that "the system doesn't owe me anything!" That's simply not true. Just peruse the lawbooks and you'll see that in fact they do. Yes, I feel entitled to the money, they call them fucking "entitlement programs," don't they? I paid money into the system and now I'm reaping the benefits. If you don't like living in a country where the government takes care of people, if you *hate* The United States of America—*God Bless It* ('scuse me I'm getting a little choked up here), then maybe you should just get the fuck out? I hear Afghanistan is really nice this time of year. Or Darfur. Or China. Traitor.

First of all, the employer that fired me pays for half of my unemployment, and fuck them. It's really my money in the first place. See, your employer never pays you what you're worth—there's a surplus, some of which goes toward overhead and various other business costs, and the rest of which is kept as profit. (This is what Marx was referring to when he talked about "exploitation of the workers.") A tiny fraction of this surplus—which, again, has been skimmed off of my labor—is put into a government-mandated account to go toward unemployment checks for fired workers. So yeah, it's my money. Give it back.

The other half of my unemployment is paid for by taxes. I pay taxes, but I don't have kids who go to public school, I don't have a car that depreciates the roads, Social Security (which I'm paying into) is going to be belly-up long before I retire, so my taxes are basically being taken from me and given to other people already anyway. And I hate to be "that guy," but we're flushing a trillion plus dollars a year down the toilet on exotic combat hovercraft and spent plutonium munitions and bunker busters and night vision goggles by the million, all to continually march off to war for uncertain, shifting reasons, against various third world countries whose standing armies consist of mule-mounted cavalry. And you're begrudging me a few hundred a week?

And really, am I doing something so wrong by not working? On the contrary, I'm doing no harm, which puts me far ahead of the vast majority of workers. I'm not making people fat, or stupid, or giving them cancer or making the rich richer or the poor poorer. In this oversaturated hyperaccelerated era, the last thing we need is more. The world doesn't need and would actually be better off without our contributions and our enthusiasm and our good intentions and opinions. It doesn't need a better mousetrap or a faster microchip or perkier customer service. You may think you're helping, but you're just throwing wood on the fire that's eventually going to consume us all.

But let me pause here. It may sound like I'm trying to justify myself, and I am, kind of. I think I'm perfectly justified in kicking back and living off the unemployment system, and that working is morally compromised and makes you no less dependent on other people than someone on the dole—it's just servitude to a different master. But yes, one could also make a compelling argument that on some level I'm taking advantage of the system. Shit, I'll even concede that point.

There is some element of pure unapologetic exploitation in my stance. But so what? I literally shrugged as I wrote that. So what, I say?

Our whole economy is based on exploitation! What, I can't turn around and do what was done to me every minute of every day I ever worked? The big rich corporate fat cats can lie, cheat, exploit, and steal, but I have to play by the rules? Turnabout isn't fair play when it's the little guy? Luckily there's nothing less American than fair play! And I'm the ugly fucking American, Horatio Alger for the twenty-first century, the ur-American, I eat the flag for breakfast and shit eagle feathers, hoo-ah motherfuckers! I don't vote (they're all the same, amirite?) and I don't stand for the national anthem at sporting events (fuck you pal, I paid for these seats) but I'm more American than George Washington's wooden teeth. You don't like me? You made me! You like money so fucking much? Me, too! Gimme some free checks.

Everyone likes to offer their macroeconomic analysis about why the economy crashed and burned; it was subprime derivatives, it was the bankers, it was cheap credit, and yes, it was all those things. But enabling all that was the American mindset of more, faster, bigger, better, and it made me sick to turn on the news and see all these self-righteous suburbanites calling for the bankers' heads on pikes when, excuse me, aren't those your his-and-hers Hummers in the driveway and didn't you just trade in your year-old sixty-eight-inch plasma screen for a new seventy-two-inch one? Which is to say, you may have noticed that this country's going down the shitter, and do you know why? It's not because of people like me. It's because of people like you.

That's right, high-earning workaholic assholes like you who felt entitled to buy big houses with gimmick mortgages and drive huge cars that force our government to subsidize gas prices, who run up credit card debt buying stupid blanket-shirts and all-purpose kitchen accessories you'll never use that you saw on your Chinese-made big-screen television at 3 a.m., and then vote Republican so you can pay less than your fair share of taxes. It's your fault, all you people who think second place is the first loser and he who dies with the most toys wins, anything popular must be good and its corollary, might makes right, and who bitches and whines if your home and your stock portfolio don't get more and more valuable every year as steady as clockwork, as if profit is your birthright. But no, you'd never acknowledge or probably even realize this, it can't be your fault, you're just reg'lar folks, salt of the earth, doin' the best you can with nothing more than the artificially-weathered name brand clothes on your back and eighteen maxed-out credit cards and an armload of celebrity gossip magazines! It's got to be the bankers! With their subprime derivatives! And the CEOs! And those bums in Congress! And illegal aliens! And homosexuals! And the Federal Reserve! And the Freemasons! And Muslamic terrorists working in tandem with Mossad and the vengeful panty-clad ghost of J. Edgar Hoover! Anyone but you! Because shit no, it can't possibly be Americans who are fuckin' up America, right?

Now who's un-American?! You are! And I'm the real patriot! Ironic, isn't it? I'm basically a bald eagle flying over Mount Rushmore while Hank Williams Jr. sings the Monday Night Football theme song in the background, and you're basically John Walker Lindh, American Taliban!

So who wants to drink to the red, white, and blue?

You're buying.

When Commotion received the letter informing them that I'd won the originally scheduled hearing by dint of their absence, they bombarded the court with aggrieved phone calls and letters and e-mails until another hearing was awarded. A friend of mine who still worked at my ex-employer's said that on the day of the letter's receipt, the head of HR had called a meeting with various VPs and the company attorney during which

there was much shouting and gesticulating and table pound-
ing, and concluded with the head of HR storming out of the
conference room screaming at the company attorney, *whatever
it takes, I want you to nail him!*

The morning of the hearing, we convened in a courtroom
downtown. I showed up alone with a few sheets of paper.
Commotion was represented by a party of three: the lackey
who'd smugly shaken my hand on the day of my firing, another HR bean-counter, and the company attorney, a middle-aged
steel-eyed Stanford-trained corporate shark. Each of them carried a foot-thick binder of documents, and in their deeply professional charcoal-gray finery were a striking contrast to me in
my encrusted black jeans and patchy unemployment beard.

Before the opening statements, as I slouched in my chair
and Commotion's attorney looked over a sheaf of index cards,
her lips moving silently, the judge asked if we had anything to
get out of the way.

I just have one thing, I said, raising a finger. Can you please
remove that woman from the room?

Commotion, in typical incompetent fashion, had failed to
list their lawyer on the proper form, and I'd been given a
heads-up from my pro bono lawyer that I could simply request
her removal.

The judge shrugged. You'll have to leave, she told the
lawyer.

She walked out dazedly as I did a little celebratory chair
dance. The smug handshaker and his fellow lackey looked at
each other wide-eyed. Oh shit!

After a brief huddle, the smug handshaker, Mitch, was designated as the stand-in lawyer. The first thing he did was present a series of statements, written by Hilda, that described
various incidents I'd been involved in at work—cubicle argu-
ments, meeting pranks. *I notified Franklin that it was unacceptable to body slam his coworker, and he acknowledged this as a
violation of office policy.* These were back-dated to give the im-

pression that I'd been a repeat offender who'd been given every chance to repent. If the employer can show a pattern of deliberate misbehavior, the ex-employee will almost always be denied unemployment, which is why HR usually keeps such meticulous records.

Hilda's statements, though, were just Word documents typed up and signed by her alone, most likely written out the night before. As the judge looked them over she seemed vaguely insulted at the quality of this deception.

These are just sheets of paper that says the plaintiff did so-and-so, she said. How do I know this was written out on the date given?

Mitch struck of pose of persecuted speechlessness. *No one told me there'd be a quiz!*

Next he presented the court with a copy of the newspaper story I'd written about the tradition of incompetence at Commotion, as well as a professional-looking transcription of a voicemail I'd left him a week earlier. Each side was obligated to present the other with copies of all the documents they were submitting to the court, and after I'd faxed mine to Commotion I'd left Mitch a notifying voicemail in which I called him, among other things, a dumbshit bootlicker.

The judge leafed through this evidence, looking unimpressed. But what does this have to do with the case, she asked Mitch. You contend the plaintiff neglected his obligations as an employee and sexually harassed a coworker. These documents have nothing to do with that.

Again Mitch seemed to be speechless. *B-but Your Honor,* his expression seemed to say, *Franklin called me bad names!*

My turn came up and I read aloud various statements I'd collected from other Commotion employees and ex-employees. All of management's bungling and false promises had left a lot of bad blood and disgruntlement behind, and people virtually lined up to help bring them down. My lawyer had told me that even if I acknowledged all the churlish behavior they accused me of—the cubicle rampages, the lewd drawing—I could still win if I could prove it was acceptable in context. My behavior would be judged in the light of Commotion's established standards, not of any sort of general community standards. So I told in graphic detail about Hilda speculating in meetings on which of the male employees were "sport fuckers," Horton the CEO's tendency to make bizarre non-sequitur references to sodomy and prostitutes, the snuff porn that regularly popped up in our company e-mail, sent as a prank. Unlike Hilda's "statements," mine were sworn and notarized and signed.

As I read on I could feel that I was winning the case, that the judge's sympathies were shifting to me and that Mitch and his sidekick were wilting. I was close, but there was still the matter of the dry-erase board drawing. Commotion's account of it made it sound like the most offensive thing since the Holocaust, and even my own acknowledged description of it sounded, out of context, pretty vulgar. *It was nothing much, Your Honor, just a close-up drawing of a woman lying on her back, legs spread, with a question mark over her vagina.* Mitch was Commotion's only eyewitness to the drawing and, company man that he was, he'd penned a statement swearing that he'd been irreversibly traumatized by my drawing, which he described in lavishly fabricated detail: (*I saw the labia...the anus...the clitoris...the vagina...the rectum...the urethra!*).

Luckily, Mitch was there in the courtroom, available for cross-examination, setting the stage for an exchange very possibly unprecedented in the history of litigation. I'd anticipated that it might come down to this, and I was prepared.

So you saw the drawing, I said casually, striding about the courtroom.

Yes, he said.

In your statement, you say that you saw an anus in the drawing. Is this true?

Yes, he said, unperturbed.

Are you sure?

Yes, he said.

It says you saw labia in the drawing. Is this true?

Yes.

It says you saw a urethra in the drawing. Is that correct?

Yes.

This was just the opening I was looking for.

Can you please describe to the courtroom what a urethra looks like?

A stunned silence settled on the courtroom. The female judge shifted uncomfortably in her seat but let me continue.

I don't understand, said Mitch, starting to flush.

In your sworn statement, you state that you saw a urethra in the drawing. Now. Can you *describe*...what a *urethra*...LOOKS LIKE?! I bellowed, doing my best Samuel L. Jackson. And may I remind you, sir, that you're under oath!

A long moment passed and then he slumped. No, he said, in an almost inaudible monotone. I can't.

Aha! Whether he was lying or just couldn't remember, his statement no longer had any credibility. I snuck a glance at the judge and she seemed to be thinking the same thing. I was sure I'd won. After the hearing adjourned, I tried to go over and reciprocate Mitch's smug handshake, but he and his colleague nearly ran from the courtroom before I got there. They looked angry but more than that, they looked puzzled. They just wanted to get back to the office, back through the looking-glass, where mediocrity would be rewarded, ignorance lauded, and reality rendered irrelevant once again.

I received a letter a few days later upholding my eligibility for unemployment. I was going to use the first check to send an expensive flower arrangement to Hilda, with a card bearing nothing but a tiny reproduction of the lewd drawing, but by that time, she herself had been fired from Commotion, and no one would tell me where she'd moved.

CHAPTER 15

Nonprofiteering

or, Nice People Suck, Too

Around the time my second run on unemployment petered out, my sister was laid off from her job at a nonprofit and dropped the entirety of her first unemployment check on a commemorative house party. When I arrived at her house that night, it was packed wall to wall with stoned-out dead-enders leaning against the walls and slouched in lawn chairs like gargoyles. I found Jennifer in the packed sauna-hot kitchen, attending with impatience an argument between several people on how best to consume a baggie of ambiguous powder, pipe or nasally or bong. Someone suggested making a tea, and everyone fell momentarily silent at this display of naïveté.

I just thank God the CEO got caught embezzling, she told me between draughts of piss-warm beer. I tried every trick in the book to get fired from that place, but no dice. I came in late, left early, rolled my eyes during meetings, stole people's lunches, wore headphones all day, took two-hour lunches.

You were definitely a bitch, said her office pal Karen, clad tonight in a skintight blue velour dress that nicely set off her bloodshot weed-stricken eyes. Everyone there hated you.

So why didn't they fire you, I asked.

Nonprofits, man, Jennifer said. It's a different world. It's like the Wild West, except with MEAN PEOPLE SUCK stickers everywhere. Everyone is so politically correct and sensitive that you can basically do what you please and no one will ever call you on it, for fear of offending some obscure sensibility or affiliation. You're not an insubordinate asshole; you're "spunky and spirited"! And if you ever get into a real bind, just start eating a bowl of rice or something to remind them you're half-Asian. Minorities get a free pass. As soon as they found out I was half-Korean I basically got job security for life. I could come in at 3 p.m. and be like, "I don't live by no white man's clock!" and they wouldn't blink an eye. They'd probably offer me a raise just out of guilt. Nonprofit isn't just a word, it's a totally different way of operating. No profit motive, no bottom line.

That sounds perfect, I said. Maybe I should start applying to nonprofits.

Why're you getting a job? Someone passed her a bong made out of an apple and she took a quick hit. Ugh, what is this shit?

PCP, someone said.

Jennifer shuddered. I just thank Our Lord Jesus Christ, she said, that that CEO was stupid enough to embezzle the place bankrupt, or I'd still be dragging my ass out of bed every morning to punch a clock.

My unemployment runs out next month, I said. And besides, from time to time I need to reassure myself that holding down a job-type job is an option, if worse comes to worst. I mean, if I'm flat-out incapable of maintaining employment, I better start stockpiling canned goods and spare shopping cart wheels for when I'm homeless.

Jennifer peered into my face looking slightly deranged. Who are you? Do I know you?

Oh boy, said Karen. Someone behind us lurched into our group, throttling a bottle of beer with his thumb tamped down over the neck and spraying a jet of foam over the room. You know, she said, I worked in HR at our nonprofit. If you really want to get hired at a nonprofit, I could tell you just what to say.

The upstairs apartment in my sister's row house was temporarily uninhabited and the painters had left the door open. We headed upstairs where it was quieter.

The more that I think about it, the more excited I am about this whole nonprofit job idea, I said as we climbed the dark stairwell. The profit motive is really what drives the whole cut-throat bottom-line aspect of office culture. Nothing matters except money—not people, not principles, not anything. It might be healthier to work toward something abstract, rather than moving more units or whatever. You think that's something I should stress in the job interview?

We were at the top of the stairs, and in the low light I could just make out Karen's silhouette leaning forward against the wall. Her dress was pulled up. She reached around behind her, took my hand, and put it between her legs.

Oh, I said.

It wasn't that hard to get hired. I really thought, or hoped, that it would be different, and I tapped into I think my last remaining reserves of hope. Sincerity gives you a glow just like pregnancy, and I received offers from most of the places I interviewed at. After all, on paper I looked like an ideal candidate, and if questions were asked, I knew just what to say. (*It looks like you were only at your last position for ten and a half months. Why did you leave? Well, I don't like to talk ill of my former employers, but quite frankly they didn't meet my own extremely high standards of professionalism.*)

I took a position at a prestigious national AIDS nonprofit, with a generous salary and benefits, no dress code, laid back office, and only one real responsibility—a weekly e-mail newsletter.

The office was situated in a remodeled firehouse, a brick warren of twisting hallways and cubbyholes. My boss, Theresa, was a blond Australian woman who was pleasant to an almost sinister degree. The first day she took me from office to office introducing me to my new coworkers. Handshakes, hugs, remarks on the weather, and so forth. After an hour my face ached from grinning ear to ear. When we'd bantered with the last employee, I was about to collapse at my new desk when Theresa emerged from her office wearing a coat.

Ready to go to the main office? she asked.

What?

This is just the satellite office. Most of the people work at the main office down the street, she said. She leaned in and whispered mock-conspiratorially. They just can't wait to meet you!

Jesus. The first day. The day you're actually least prepared for a barrage of insincerity and office banter and backslapping is when you've got to endure the worst of it. *The company was founded in 1984 by a courageous young group of visionaries…* A dizzying procession of names, faces, job descriptions, asses to kiss lined up from here to the far horizon. *We're not just about advocacy, we're about making a difference. We're about changing the world…* Yeah, but where's the shitter? Just point out the vending machines and I'm good. Am I starting a new job or becoming a goddamn Scientologist? Am I going to have to kiss the hem of Xenu's garment later?

It's like they're testing you, the first day as the integrity equivalent to doin' the limbo. *How low will he go? Will he bridle at the "changing the world" bit? No? Then how about the company logo baseball cap? If I give it to him, will he just carry it or… oh man, he actually put it on! He looks like a pedophile fleeing the country! How desperate is this guy for health insurance? Must have a pre-existing condition… I gotta parade this guy through the Member-ship section, they could use a laugh…*

Still, everyone seemed incredibly nice and the work was easy. My job consisted mainly of compiling an e-newsletter that was sent out by mass e-mail each Tuesday and was immediately deleted by every single recipient as spam. I also had to compose press releases that no one read to commemorate various CDC-sponsored awareness days. There are an insane number of these days, one for every possible permutation of ethnicity and disease: "February 30 is Inuit Gingivitis Awareness Day!" When one of these days approached, as they did several times a month, I would have to compose an announcement in a solemn, faux-biblical diction; "On this day of days, we, our eyes glistening with tears of compassion and fixed on the eternal flame of righteousness, would like to crisply salute our noble Eskimo comrades-in-arms, blah blah blah . . ." I would then have to fabricate quotations from the head man ("Forget al-Qaeda, forget global warming—gum disease in the sub-Arctic region is by far the most urgent problem facing human civilization today!") to make it sound like he was up all night every night agonizing over their situation when in fact he was on a beach in Brazil. Then, after hours of hemming, hawing, rewriting, rearranging, deleting commas, replacing those same commas, and acquiring the approval of several staff members, I would beam this meticulously constructed press release out into cyberoblivion where it would disappear without any trace, acknowledgment or effect whatsoever. Then I would go to Starbucks.

I asked the receptionist that first week why my predecessor had been fired.

Well, she said, she left the building once an hour every hour for maybe ten, fifteen minutes, which in itself may not have been so bad. But we noticed that she didn't smoke so one of us finally asked her where she was going all the time and she said she was going down the street to the bathroom. That seemed to be an acceptable answer, but after a few more days I wondered why she went all the way down the block. I mean, our bathroom isn't exactly luxurious, but it's got to beat the one at

Starbucks. So I asked her finally why she didn't use our bathroom. And she said, AIDS.

AIDS?

Yeah, she was afraid of catching AIDS from the toilet seat
here. Because some of the employees who use the bathroom
are gay.

Jesus.

Yeah, so obviously you can't have someone like that working at a national AIDS nonprofit. So we canned her ass.

I strolled back to my desk trying to quell my glee. I'd basically replaced a retarded person. Could the bar be any lower? I
must look like a goddamn superstar just for coming to work
with my shoes on the right feet! Could even I fuck this one up?
I felt so confident about my job security that I left an hour
early.

My sister was right, though. Nonprofits were just different.
Everyone was nice—very nice. Like, so nice that I very shortly
wanted to gather all the world's niceness in a big pit, douse it
in gasoline, and throw in a match. My desk was unfortunately
located on the way to the restrooms, so I was subjected to a
constant stream of banter. It wasn't like at other offices, just a
token hello and then they'd move on. These people seemed to
really care. Which in theory is nice, but in practice is just
weird. When my new coworkers asked me how I was, they
seemed to really care how I was. But why? Even I didn't care
how I was most of the time, and I was me! And when I said,
fine, without looking away from my computer screen, they
were disappointed, I'd deprived them of an opportunity for
genuine human contact, and I felt guilty knowing this,
because good intentions are after all quite rare in this world.
And before long I was spending long stretches at my desk just
concocting sincere answers for the inevitable "how are you?"
that I knew was imminent. ("My skin's a little dry today, but

I'm wearing my favorite pants, so I guess all in all I'm doing pretty well, say, eight out of ten.")

All the complaints I'd always heard about faceless heartless corporate offices where you were just a number and your boss's boss didn't even know your name seemed rather churlish now, considering my present circumstances. There's something far more sinister about the kind of job where there's no acknowledgment of the border between your real self and your work self. After all, I was only there because I didn't want to starve, because essentially I had to be there. I didn't want to be acknowledged as a person, because I wasn't there as a person—I was there as a square peg in a square hole, a producer of added value in biz-cazsh, and all that under duress. I didn't want to join a "family" or a "team" or anything else, I wasn't so insecure as to need to be valued as an individual by the people who signed my checks. If I hated working, it was because I resented the wasting of my time, not because company e-mails were short on smiley-face clip art attachments.

At other jobs the knell is money money money, everything is about the next product launch, the invoices, the messaging, the consumer. When they want you to work unpaid overtime or sign off on nonsense, they dangle the carrot of a raise or stock options or a bonus. Here, it was the opposite; instead of appealing to your greed, they appealed to your conscience. It's less vulgar for sure but more intrusive, as your values have been converted into a kind of behavioral lever. Now instead of *every weekend you work gets us that much closer to an IPO, and just imagine what kind of yacht you'll be able to buy with those stock options*, it was, *every hour you stay past five saves the life of another starving child in Africa*. Or, *how can you sit there and monitor eBay auctions when someone is being infected with HIV EVERY FOUR MINUTES?!*

Yeah, but this is a rare mint-condition Danzig concert T-shirt!!

This is an effective motivational tactic in offices like this because nonprofit employees are generally sensitized to the sufferings of the world and are under the illusion that they can do something about them. It even worked on me for a while, until I remembered that I could work dawn to dusk seven days a week for my entire life and children will still be starving by the millions, old men still huddling under bridges, nuclear families still imploding, dogs still howling at the cold white moon, and so on. Even worse, when you delve into pretty much any large-scale problem you generally find that all the real troubles emanate from the top down, the big boys who have power and seek mainly to consolidate it at all costs, and in doing so consign vast bodies of people to miserable clock-punching subsistence. And it's only natural to resent having to clean up the messes of the rich and powerful, and that your coworkers in their relentless narrow focus on "ground level" and "local action" seem to be willfully ignoring the root causes of the misery they so earnestly rail against, their labors essentially an exercise in futility, their heads in the sand. A dirty business full of compromises, this nonprofiteering, what with taking grants from the very corporations underwriting most of the miseries we were ostensibly trying to relieve, this insistence of working within the system, through proper channels, never mind that it's this very bottom-line dog-eat-dog system that sets us by default at each other's throat, the left hand throttling the right, and beneath all this matter-of-fact pragmatism one could sometimes detect a whiff of garden-variety cowardice. Because it's easier to file grant applications than throw stones, you can have your cake and eat it too, a warm pink glow of moral rectitude but also a warm apartment in the gallery district and a fifty-two-inch plasma. But then who am I to judge? I've always had the opposite problem—I'd love to throw stones but I just don't care about anything.

And of course I felt guilty for looking down on all the earnest do-gooding, but then what's more courageous, facing the unfortunate if immovable truth, or putting the blinders on and trudging forward? And when you think about it like that, Jesus Christ, the only thing that makes sense is to have a drink. And that's generally what I did at five sharp every day, after strutting out of the office, head held high, as my co-workers looked on with disapproval.

One morning as I was preparing another mass e-mail that no one would read except by accident, my boss dropped off an item she wanted included. It was a blurb soliciting volunteers for a study on incest and sexual abuse—a serious and worthy cause indeed—but upon first read it seemed a little awkward. I reread it several times and then aloud before I detected the source of the weirdness.

I walked back to my boss's office with the copy. Are you sure you want me to put this in as is?

Sure. Why wouldn't I?

You know it rhymes, don't you?

Does it? Well, this woman gets very sensitive about us changing her submissions. Just put it in as is.

I blinked. You're the boss, I said. And that week the e-mail newsletter was headlined by an incest study volunteer solicitation that read, in part: *Dad pump your rear? Please click* here!

It was while I was working at the nonprofit that a problem from my past returned with a vengeance. I'd noticed in the past that working generally made me stupider, but usually I wrote it off as a combination of sleep deprivation and depression. This time around I was getting plenty of sleep, thanks to a flexible start time, and wasn't really any more depressed than usual, but for some reason I'd been reduced to a near-mute cretin. I'd be in the break room and the girl from Membership would turn to me and ask what I thought of, say, *this crazy weather we're having?* I would open my mouth but nothing would come out. After an excruciating pause I might gather my wits enough to stutter, *I-I like it…I guess?* as my conversation partner flashes a sympathetic smile. But I'm not a cretin, I would want to scream, shaking her by her magenta-cashmere-wrapped shoulders. But wasn't I? Why couldn't I speak?

I finally had a breakthrough one day in the break room. The girl from Membership tottered in on her too-tall spike heels, her calves bulging like grapefruit, while I was making a cup of hot cocoa. When she turned her somewhat chilling smile on me I found that I was too hungover and tired to make my usual attempt at conversation. Without the slightest conscious thought, I opened my mouth, and the first thing that came out was, "I like cocoa."

The effect was immediate. A slow flush spread up her face, and as her posture relaxed I realized that she'd been hunched defensively. She squared her shoulders to me and her smile widened, a genuine smile now. Her misgivings about me had been dissolved, I was okay now, perhaps a bit strange still but I was on the right track now and that's what really counted.

Me too! she chirped, with immense satisfaction.

Aha! Before I'd even gotten back to my desk I'd cracked the proverbial code. In my head I replayed all the things I heard around the office each day: *How 'bout this weather? That Britney sure is kerr-azy! Working hard or hardly working? Ready for the weekend? Another day, another dollar!* Nominally interrogative, these statements nevertheless don't require answers. In fact, they're of such zenlike vacuity that they seem to preclude the very possibility of an answer. All they require is an acknowledgment. *Yes! Sure! Ha ha!* And as much as I racked my brain, I couldn't think of a single office interaction I'd had or witnessed, perhaps in years, that didn't fit that template.

Innocuous, meaningless statement?

Acknowledgment!

It's like this in all modern offices, what with the general contemporary atmosphere of well-scrubbed neo-Victorian political correctness. This radical dumbing-down of discourse was perfectly in line with the rest of the culture at large, with its emphasis on the straightforward, uncomplicated, unironic, and declarative. In the American manner this is probably seen as some sort of virtue, but really all it had done was to strip away all the layers and complication and intrigue that makes real adult interpersonal dialogue interesting. And it made sense, as this mode of office discourse has become the default mode for the white-collar middle and upper classes, which in a nutshell is why squares are boring.

That said, the nonprofit was particularly bad. Aside from the utopian vibe there was a relentless Stepfordian positivity so that even that last traditional bastion of critical thought—gossipping about coworkers—was well out of bounds. There was really nothing for me to do but just go with it, to turn off the brain and just babble on like some malfunctioned Dockers-clad Furby. It got to the point where I had to bite my tongue against responding to innocuous office banter with a loud, monotone exclamation of "Acknowledgment!"

Eventually I even came to grudgingly admire my coworkers, after my own attempts at meaningless office Zen bon mots (*Earth is a planet!*) fell flat during test runs. (*Yeah, Earth is… what did you just say?*) As in everything, I guess, there's an art to it.

Another vexing aspect of this cheery atmosphere is that you couldn't say no to anything. No one even really asked you questions, they just stated what you were going to do for them with the clear assumption that your answer was yes. This wasn't as aggressive as it sounds; it was just a natural by-product of a culture of YES, of positivity and smiles and unironic thumbs-up and embracing, no, bear-hugging, the brighter side of life. Most of the time this was harmless; an add-on for the coffee run, an overwillingness to borrow staplers, and so on. But slowly it began to extend in other directions. I was "asked" to work an hour later, and then "asked" to do this and that, until somehow I'd started working twice as many hours and doing the work of two people.

On the eve of my weeklong vacation, my boss asked if I could spend one of my vacation days compiling the e-mail newsletter. I consulted my schedule.

Sorry, I told her, I'm going to be at the beach that day.

She insisted that I "find a way." I explained to her that there was just no way I could get to a computer in the Iowa hinterlands...I suggested that I send out the e-mail newsletter the day afterward, when I'd be closer to civilization, but she found this unacceptable. God forbid we send out the spam one day late! I felt like dropping a dictionary on her desk and telling her to look up "vacation."

I ended up agreeing to "try to get it done," which of course meant that I did not try even a little bit to get it done. In truth, I totally forgot about the stupid e-mail newsletter until I got back to the office and was called in to see my boss.

I should have seen it coming. The one rule in that world was, never say no, and I'd broken it. Even before she said those magic words, *I hate to say this but I'm not sure if this is working,* I was already racking my brain for an out. It wasn't so much that I wanted to keep my job, as much as I didn't want to face the possibility that I was downright unemployable. As she continued on about all the valuable contributions I'd made, I remembered my sister's advice: *If you ever get in a bind, just remind them you're half-Asian. Minorities get a free pass.* But how? It's not like I carry a bowl of rice around with me (though maybe I should start). I racked my brain. Perhaps a quick karate chop to the top of her desk? But what if I broke my hand (quite likely) and failed to change her mind (also likely)? Then I'd have a broken hand and no more medical insurance. I remembered doing some tai chi in high school gym; maybe I should just stand up, fall into a stance, and start doing "pushing hands"? *I make better, boss! Rejoin heaven and earth most ricky-tick!*

She'd finished up and was now waiting for me to say something. Could I? I opened my mouth and even subtly crinkled my eyes, but in the moment of truth I just couldn't lower myself to the yellow minstrel routine.

You're probably right, I said finally. This is all for the best.

I gathered my things at my desk, walked out, and went home and back to bed. It was true after all—I was a loser, a zero. This was much less stinging than I'd anticipated. In fact, considering the winners, this felt like a staggering victory.

That was three years ago, and I haven't worked since.

Not surprisingly, the rest of the world didn't agree that being unemployable was something to be proud of. In the aftermath of this fateful firing, my parents didn't hide their chagrin at my failures and plenty of people I knew began treating me like damaged goods. At first I always tried to convince them otherwise, laid out my argument point by point on how the working world rewarded mediocrity and punished certain virtues and that being finally deemed unemployable was more of an emancipation than an exile, but they would just shake their heads and look pained. I never changed anyone's mind and after a few months I stopped trying.

I was visiting my sister in Seattle for the holidays and at eleven on New Year's Eve I was elected to go on a beer run with her ex-boyfriend Mark. We'd been arguing all night about the pride I took in my unemployability and as we walked to the store we took up this line of discussion once again.

Just face it, he said. You're a loser.

What?! What does that make you, a winner? Just because you've worked at the same assembly-line job for, what, almost ten years?

That's right.

What's so "win" about that?

I'm contributing. To, like, society and stuff.

What does that even mean?

It means I'm a winner. And you're a loser.

I was drunk and I had no idea how to rebut this hazy circular logic so we walked on in silence. After several minutes of seemingly random turns we passed a house party for what I was sure was the second time.

Do you know where we are, I asked Mark.

Kind of, he muttered. As he said this he stumbled and I realized that he was far too drunk to find his way anywhere.

Voices floated down from an apartment balcony above us, and I yelled up to them, asking for directions back to my sister's street. In response someone threw a glass of beer down on us. Mark found an empty bottle in the gutter and threw it up at the party and then we had to run when several fellows expressed a keen interest in coming down for a face-to-face discussion.

We ran until we came to a highway, which seemed to stir some note of recognition in Mark's half-lidded eyes.

We've got to get across this highway, he said.

He weaved out across the three lanes of traffic and leaped to grasp the top of the concrete retaining wall that separated the two halves of the highway. He was short and drunk and the leap seemed to exhaust the entirety of his resources; he simply hung by his arms, limp and wheezing with his feet suspended perhaps six inches above the pavement. After a moment he began to scrabble with both feet against the wall, but his worn shoes couldn't gain any purchase and he went back to hanging.

Maybe we should find a way around, I said.

Just come here and give me a boost!

But if I boost you over, how do I get over?

Don't be such a loser.

During this exchange, a steady flow of traffic shot past us. Emerging from around a curve a hundred feet or so uphill from us I could almost see the whites of the drivers' eyes as they saw us there in the highway, Mark hanging primate-like from the median wall and myself standing hands in pockets watching, and then veered around us at the last moment, laying on the horn or cursing out their windows. It was New Year's Eve and it seemed inevitable that one of these drivers would be drunk and wouldn't see us until it was too late. After Mark had failed twice to get over the wall, I retreated to the sidewalk and urged him to give up.

Come on, I said. We'll find an overpass.

He ignored me and flung himself anew at the retaining wall, this time hanging for just an instant before falling back onto his ass. A tow truck flew by, its horn blaring.

It's probably not a good idea to be out in the middle of the highway, I said.

Shut up, loser!

At that moment, a voice rang out behind me. *Boy, get out of that road right now!* This statement was delivered with such unimpeachable authority that without hesitating Mark trotted over to the sidewalk, and stood looking sheepishly at his feet

I turned and saw a fifty-something black man in sweatpants, carrying a brown bag of tallboys, regarding Mark with evident disgust.

What's wrong with you, he asked Mark.

I dunno.

You could've died out there.

Mark shrugged.

We're lost, I said. We're trying to get back to Ballard.

Ballard? Ballard's not even over there.

Oh. Can you tell us where it is?

I'm not sure myself, but my friend Carl can tell you. Why don't you boys come over to my room and we'll give you directions.

We went with him to a decaying motel down the block. His name was Roy and he and Carl lived in a room on the ground floor with two twin beds, a few lawn chairs, and a nine-inch black and white television. When we came in, Carl was watching Dick Clark on the tiny screen with a teenage girl sitting on his lap.

I found these boys trying to cross the highway, said Roy. They were trying to climb over the wall in the middle.

Carl was a bit older than Roy and wore sunglasses and was dressed in head-to-toe red. He looked at Mark and me and shook his head.

We're trying to get back to Ballard, I said.

Carl gave us directions which we both nodded at but neither of us retained. It's almost midnight, he told us. Why don't you two have a drink here before you go?

We agreed and Roy poured us paper cups of beer. I sat on a bed and Mark sat in a rickety lawn chair. He looked at his cup of malt liquor and the bare walls and our hosts and I could tell he found the situation immensely novel.

So what's your name, ma'am, Mark asked the girl.

Don't talk to her, said Carl flatly. She's mine.

The girl continued to look at the television, unaware that she'd been addressed.

We sat sipping our beers for a moment and then Mark said, you guys have any weed?

Carl and Roy looked at each other and sighed and then Roy brought out a joint from the pocket of his t-shirt. He passed it to Mark, who lit it, took a long drag, held it for several seconds, and then let the smoke waft from his mouth. Then he took another drag, held it, and exhaled. He took a third drag, held it, and went off on a coughing fit.

Pass that anytime, said Carl.

Mark reluctantly gave up the joint and then reclined in his chair. I can't believe you guys live here, he said.

What's that supposed to mean, asked Roy.

This place is a dump!

We all watched the ball of lights descend in Times Square as crowds chanted in the background.

What do you guys do?

What do we "do"?

Yeah, you know. Where do you work?

We don't work.

You don't have jobs?

Nope.

This guy doesn't have a job either!

Roy and Carl looked over at me and I nodded to them and they nodded back.

Mark giggled. You guys are losers, he said.

Carl stood up from his chair, dumping the girl soundlessly onto the floor. I heard a click like an eggshell cracking or the last piece of a puzzle being put into place, and I saw a switch-blade in his hand. He walked across the room and stood over Mark, on whose lap I could see a dark stain spreading.

Don't call me a loser, said Carl.

C
H
A
P
T
E
R
16

A Delightful Party

or, The Sufferings of Young Franklin

Waking up in agony one December morning at some indeterminate hour atop my filthy unsheeted IKEA crib mattress (it was half the price of the twin mattress, though half the size, but then what did I care if my feet hung off the bottom? And any morningtime discomfort was well worth all the street-cred-rich anecdotes I'd banked about *The Three Years I Was on Unemployment and Slept on a Crib Mattress* and *You Should've Seen Her Face When She Saw My Bed, Vols. 1–35*), and what time was it? Grainy light coming through the window and it could've been either dawn or dusk. I couldn't make out the red letters of the clock radio without my glasses, and I fumbled around for them for a few seconds before abruptly giving up, because what does it matter if it's dawn or dusk or anytime in between? I'd been coasting on unemployment for three years now and I was so thoroughly unmoored from the "real" world that I rarely knew what day of the week or even month it was, because what did it matter? I lived by my own schedule, sleeping when I was tired and eating when I was hungry, and I'll admit I even felt a secret pride when someone said to me, *what do you mean Valentine's Day is coming up, it's March!* Or I went to

the bank to deposit my latest unemployment check and rattled the locked doors, puzzled, and a well-scrubbed man in
fine clothes walks by and says, *It's Sunday morning, asshole.*

A dim memory from the previous night of speeding home
on my bike after bar close, praying that I'd reach my toilet
before the mounting disturbance in my stomach forced me to
stop and vomit curbside. I'd almost made it. Just a few blocks
from home and hurtling down the deserted early-morning
boulevard, I'd felt a hitch in my stomach and then a full-on
uprising and I didn't even have time to stop, I just put my
head down and vomited at full speed, steering the bike perfectly straight with a queer dexterity even as I convulsed atop
the saddle retching PBR and Ol' Grandad and semidigested
Indian food down onto my whirring bicycle chain, which flung
it in every direction like a little vertical lawn sprinkler of
throw up. And marveling at that wondrous disgusting vomit
pinwheel was the last thing I remembered before waking up
just now at dawn or dusk or whenever with a prodigious hangover.

On these mornings I always took an ice-cold shower for
relief and I groaned my way down the passage of my apartment, my head throbbing. The apartment seemed unusually
cold and I half-expected to see my breath. I started a cold
shower and, holding my breath, scooted under the water. In
an instant, I couldn't move, couldn't breathe, I was seeing
spots as my blood rushed everywhere at once, my arms and
legs flexing spasmodically and I nearly bit the tip of my tongue
off in a fit of teeth chattering, my scrotum shrinking so quickly it felt like my testicles were being squeezed in a vise. I gritted my teeth and counted to ten and then quickly spun off the
cold water and went full-on hot.

Waiting...waiting...nothing. I bent over, blinking through
tears at the spigots. There was no hot water! I scampered out
of the shower and into the kitchen. There was a palpable draft
bisecting the room, and as I pulled the utility closet open to

reveal the water heater I could feel my eyes trying to roll back in their sockets. I bent dripping and miserable and dancing dementedly from foot to foot over the water heater for a good half-minute before realizing that I had no idea what I was looking for. Fuck.

I guess I'd have to settle for a hot bath. I filled all my pots and pans with water and put them on the stove, shivering so furiously that I was basically having an extended seizure. But when I turned the burner knobs, nothing happened. Ah. The gas had been turned off. I hadn't paid the bill in months and in fact last winter's four-figure bill was still outstanding, but I figured that they wouldn't cut me off in the dead of winter. For Christ's sake, what if I had my old frail grandmother living with me? Would they cut off my heat then? I decided to ask them.

I put on longjohns, jeans, snowpants, shirts, sweater, parka, hat and gloves, piled all my blankets on the bed, and burrowed underneath. As soon as my shivering had subsided, I called up the gas company customer service line.

You'll have to address your outstanding balance before we can turn your service back on, sir, the rep told me.

You know, I said, my grandmother is living with me. She's ninety years old. If she gets a chill, that's basically it. Pneumonia. Do you want a sweet old lady's death on your conscience? Is that what you want?

Your bill is severely past due, sir.

Okay, I said. I'll just tell Grandma to go ahead and die now because God forbid you don't get your money. Because that's what's really important in life, money, and not sweet old ninety-year-old ladies who knit sweaters and cook fantastic multicourse dinners all by themselves with no visible effort and get a little drunk on cider at Christmas every year and do the Charleston in front of the fireplace like she's still twenty. You know, she was going to bake some cookies today, but I guess she'll just die instead.

I just work here, sir.

And why do I even have to pay for heat, I asked. Isn't heat a basic human right? If this is the richest most advanced country in history, isn't it kind of a shitty deal that our betters can't even guarantee basic necessities like food and heat and shelter? That they could quite easily give it to us for free but would rather sell it off to regional robber barons? Hey, I have an idea for you, why don't you install tiny meters in everyone's lungs and charge them for how much oxygen they consume, and if they don't pay their bill you can just close off their windpipe? Didn't pay your bill? Now you die slowly of suffocation!

There was a brief silence on the line. That's actually not a bad idea, sir.

I awoke hours later, weak and hungry in the sickly light of winter dusk. I trudged through the frigid wreckage of my apartment and stood blowing into my cupped hands as I waited for the coffeemaker to heat water for oatmeal. I took the bowl back to my room and ate while being half-crushed under a foot of covers. For a night person, daytime is weakening. I found half a flat beer within arm's reach and I took sips from it as I laid there reading some Henry Miller. As the evening fell, doubts began to take hold in my heart. Were they right, and I wrong? What the hell was I doing? To what end was this marginal outlawry? As I laid there on my crib mattress in my frigid garret, I felt the same sort of undirected anomie that I'd felt when I was trapped in the fluorescent-lit cubicle farm. I'd gone full circle!

I was in a bad place, and I surveyed my options. The proposal for this book was circulating at this time, and my agent had assured me that I'd receive some sort of advance. I remembered a proposal from a few years before to move overseas with my pal Jacob, a fellow writer and layabout, so we could write our respective literary masterpieces. He and I had been close friends since childhood, but had grown apart in the past year or so. We used to dress and talk and even look alike, but now he was gainfully employed and engaged to his girlfriend, a property owner with a closet full of fine-ish suits, and I was, well, me. He worked somewhere doing something— he'd told me more than once, but I'd refused to let the information nest in my brain. In school, we'd both wanted to be writers, but he'd listened to various parental voices of reason and studied business, the logic being that he could make money hand over fist in the corporate arena and write "on the side." He of course never quite got around to putting pen to paper and, approaching thirty and seeing his childhood dreams receding into the void, he'd pitched a move to Berlin for a life of Henry Miller–esque debauchery—writing during the day in a dirt-cheap cavernous East Berlin warehouse loft and setting out at dusk for gallery openings and unmarked nightclubs full of blond frauleins enchanted by our accents. At the time I'd been tempted but declined, partly out of laziness and partly because it sounded too good to be true. Now I was seized with sudden motivation and called Jacob.

Hey, I said when he picked up his phone. We should talk.

There was a silence on that line. It had been almost a year since we'd last seen each other. About what, he asked.

Maybe I should come by and tell you about it, I said. I can come by tonight. Is that cool?

Of course, said Jacob. Kate and I are having some people over for dinner tonight, we'd love to have you. You remember where we live?

I did. Historically, my neighborhood had been the realm of the lower classes, the servant and workingman, and it was built of narrow cracker-box row houses with low ceilings and few windows and no yards, just entire blocks of concrete dwellings crammed in together. Jacob's neighborhood was where the gentry had lived, the foreman and manager and the administrator, and the houses were sprawling affairs with wraparound porches and landscaped terraces and balconies and skylights and bay windows. I had to ride my bike over; public transportation didn't go where he lived, everyone drove.

When I entered the house, I was struck by the odors of fine cooking and firewood. Conversation paused as everyone assessed this latest arrival, and then continued after they'd turned away...

A man and two women about my age were standing by the fireplace and I sauntered over to join them.

Hello, said the man. You're a friend of Jacob's, aren't you?

Yes, that's right.

What do you do?

Pass, I said. He laughed, thinking it was a joke.

Fine, I'll go first, he said. I'm a compliance officer at a consulting firm.

Yes, I gathered that, I said, gesturing at the laminated photo ID that hung around his neck.

Oh, did I forget to take it off again, he said unconvincingly. But he made no move to take it off.

I'm a lawyer, said one of the women. She made a cursory gesture toward her own lanyard.

Sweet card, I said.

I like your jacket, said the other girl, fingering the lapel.

Thank you.

What brand is it? Is it Marc Jacobs?

No.

Where'd you get it?

I got it at the Salvation Army for five dollars.

No, that's impossible. I saw someone on TV wearing one just like it. I mean, the exact same jacket, and he said it was Gucci.

Well, that's what they do, I said to the girl. Designers steal their ideas from starving marginal artist-types and third world naifs and homeless people, gloss them up a little bit, and then sell them to rich people who think they can buy authenticity.

That's how culture works now. Music, literature, fashion, everything. That's what "everything sacred was once criminal" means. The elite get rich by coopting ideas from the margins and selling watered-down versions to the masses. That's why white people imitate black people and you pay hundreds of dollars for artificially weathered denim.

She was clearly horrified. No, I don't believe it! She turned toward the corner of the room where I now saw Jacob and Kate, huddled in conference.

Kate! Jacob! Do fashion designers get their ideas from poor people?

Kate curled her upper lip in disgust. No! Of course not! Gross!

Jacob?

Well, he said. Yes. I thought it was obvious. He shrugged. Hello, Franklin.

What do you know, snarled Kate, and sunk back into her chair, arms crossed. The girl next to me turned slowly back, looking down at her own clothing with mistrust now, horrified at the prospect that she might be the object of some sort of cosmic practical joke, tricked into dressing like a poor person.

Jacob came over and took my arm and led me across the room.

Sorry about that, he said. Do you want a beer? Bourbon?

I'll take both, I said.

We stood by the fireplace with our drinks, and Jacob caught me up on the latest developments. He'd gotten a promotion, mutual friends from college had become this or that, doctors and lawyers and parents and whatnot. As he talked I nodded but I was savoring the warmth of the fire, standing as close as I could without actually bursting into flames.

You look great, said Jacob, patting me on the arm. He grabbed an alarming handful of paunch through his shirt. I can't stop putting on weight, he said. Kate and I go out to dinner too much, and I drink. How do you stay so goddamn thin?

I'm poor, I said.

He laughed thinly and downed the rest of his whiskey.

So what's this you have to talk to me about?

Do you remember when we talked about moving to Berlin to write?

He smiled and nodded, but I could see before I said a word that he wasn't going to go for it. I'd come all this way and the whiskey was spreading through my brain and so I went for it anyway, gave him the full-on hard sell—*the frauleins! The warehouse loft!*—but as he talked I could see him shutting down, recoiling, his life wasn't something to escape from anymore, at least not in his mind. And who knows, maybe he was right? The doubts of earlier welled up again and as I looked at his fine house, the gleaming woodwork and double-malt whiskey and the fireplace, I felt a twinge of despair as I allowed myself to consider the possibility that I had it all wrong, that I'd taken a wrong turn at some distant moment in the past and had been drifting farther and farther off course all these years. I think these thoughts must have manifested in my speech because Jacob placed a hand on my shoulder, cutting off my pitch in midsentence.

It sounds great, it always did, he said. But I just couldn't do it anymore.

Why not?

He shrugged. It's hard to explain...

A commotion erupted in the next room. Jacob reluctantly separated himself from the mantel and we peered around the corner to see the source of the disturbance. His fiancée, Kate, was berating a guest for putting an uncoastered glass on their Danish coffee table, as the woman stood by with her hands clasped to her face, almost in tears. Kate was dressed in her usual outfit of blue button-up and gray pants. The previous year she'd thrown out her entire wardrobe and gotten all new interchangeable separates at J. Crew; she was sick of making decisions, she was sick of trying. Now she looked like someone who worked at a cell phone kiosk in the mall. But her mornings were so simple!

This was a familiar sort of scene in their household and before long, Jacob and I and the rest of the guests wandered back to the living room, where we resumed our various conversations as her harangue unwound in the background.

Jacob and I sat on the sofa and talked about people we'd known in college and recalled various whimsical incidents from those days as I tried to conceal my disappointment. Eventually the conversation circled around to his impending nuptials and I couldn't resist.

How are things with Kate?

Jacob shrugged. I dunno, he said. He paused and rubbed his chin. We're engaged. So that's something. Our families are excited.

Still good though, yeah, I asked. At the beginning of their relationship they'd been virtually conjoined, oblivious to anyone else and exuding raw sensuality. I raised my eyebrows and he finally caught the implication.

Well, he said. He muttered something about gaining weight, being really busy, always tired, and as his voice trailed off, the implication was clear.

What about you, he asked. How are things going for you in that department?

What to say to him? Is it cruel to tell a starving man about the feast you just left? I listed off a few of the recent anecdotes, the dead man in the porta potty, the princess on the pile of dirty laundry. As I sketched out these encounters, Jacob listened with a cool equanimity that I at first took for resentment but finally realized was simply puzzlement. Our lives were so divergent that he could barely conceive of the sorts of things I was describing. I tried to goose him awake with a few ribald details, but he just sat and nodded like a man watching lions couple on a nature show. This instantly depressed me and I changed the subject.

Where's Hubert, I asked. Hubert had been his beloved puppy, who I calculated was by now just about six years old.

Ah, Hubert. We had him put to sleep because he kept scratching up the furniture.

Jacob and I sat in embarrassed silence, looking into our glasses. I was just concocting an excuse to leave when Kate announced that dinner was ready.

As the other guests filed into the dining room I lagged behind until I was alone in the room. In one hand I had an empty beer bottle, in the other an empty highball glass, both sweating beads of condensation. I made sure no one was looking and then placed them very carefully on the Danish table.

Half the guests were Jacob's coworkers and half were Kate's. As we picked at our pork medallions and asparagus, conversation proceeded in fits and starts, as our hosts fumblingly searched for a rhetorical common ground. *Brr, sure is cold out there, yes?... Yes, brr, freezing. Everyone see the show last night on TV? Yes, sure, no, I TiVoed it, for God's sake don't spoil it for me! The neighborhood is changing, isn't it? Yes, but it still has a few rough edges, last month someone threw a lawn mower through the window of the house down the street in the middle of the night.*

There was a moment of silence as everyone struggled to digest this report of our ongoing cultural disintegration, and then someone made a remark about work that day and they were off, one camp and then the other, all of a sudden talking over each other a mile a minute.

Did you hear, the lead-ins were cut and now Pam is threatening to fire Corey!

If he thinks he can dump the viral marketing costs onto the discretionary budget, he better think twice.

They're always saying we're in content delivery but no, I keep telling them, we're in customer satisfaction. Big difference.

If we can make it to IPO next year, it would change everything. Obviously!

When this downturn finally ends, we're going to be positioned to expand our market share big time. Big time. Huge time.

I fixed my eyes down onto my plate but I couldn't help but notice the woman next to me giving me a solicitous look. I tried to ignore her, but eventually decided she couldn't be all that bad if she wasn't participating in the shop talk. I looked over and raised my eyebrows.

So what do you do, she asked.

Fuck! I had to bite back an urge to slap my forehead. Nothing, I said.

Well, you must do something. What do you do for money?

I'm on unemployment, I said.

Ah. For how long?

For three years.

My God, she said. Is it that bad out there?

I don't know, I said. I haven't really been looking. You see, I have this special résumé filled with typos and emoticons and novelty fonts that I send out, to make sure no one will offer me a job. That happened once with my previous résumé and I had to demand that they double my salary so they'd withdraw the offer. That was a close one, let me tell you.

She narrowed her eyes as she began to understand the implications of what I was telling her. She'd opened her mouth to speak when Jacob, who'd been eavesdropping, leaned over.

He's only kidding, he said. Franklin is a writer.

No, I'm not, I said.

Yes, he is, said Jacob. He's writing a book on unemployment.

No, I'm not, I said firmly. I'm just unemployed. I don't do anything.

Even though at this point my book deal was all but finalized. Because I hated more than anything the moment when people asked what I did, and I told them, and they nodded and half-smiled a little smirk of unsought approval that said yes, I was okay, I was one of the good ones, I did something, I didn't just exist, no, because life was not for living, it was for doing, and I was a doer. As if working was anything commendable, as if taking the path of least resistance was something to be praised. No, I didn't want them thinking for even a moment that I was anything like them, and if someone would ever have pressed the issue and asked for proof that I really was an unproductive layabout and nothing more, asked to search my home for traces of constructive activity, I would've gladly taken them to my door and then skipped ahead to burn all my notes and wipe all my hard drives, just to prove a point.

The woman looked from Jacob to me and back to Jacob again.

Okay, I was wrong, he's nothing, said Jacob, sighing and holding his hands out, palms up, in a gesture of concession.

Have you really not worked in three years?

Darling, I said, grinning and leaning close, my elbows on the table. Up close she smelled like coffee and industrial carpet disinfectant. I made eight thousand dollars last year, and most of that came out of your taxes.

She curled her upper lip and scooted her chair closer to Jacob.

I could never do something like that, she said.

I'm sure there are a lot of things you couldn't do.

It's wrong. It's not right.

You know, I agree that the system could be better, I said. For example. Think of all the administrative costs associated with putting all that tax money in a big pot and then splitting it up and sending out checks to people like me. I've been thinking of writing my congressperson and proposing a setup where we'd cut out the middleman entirely and pair unemployed people up with employed people, and instead of the employed people's paychecks having money deducted and put through all these chutes and funnels, the person with the job would just pay their unemployed buddy directly out of their paycheck. All those bureaucrats and databases, cut out in a single stroke! Think of the savings to the average taxpayer! Isn't that what it's all about? And if you'll just write your Social Security number on this napkin here I'd be happy to propose the two of us as a pilot project.

You're a disgusting man, she said. She took her plate in one hand and stood and went over and sat alone on the sofa, picking at her food.

I was in a contemplative mood and I remembered a game Jacob and I had played since we were young. Let's say, we'd begin, that a silver capsule materialized out of thin air and a hatch opened in the side and out walked your own childhood self, come to the present in this time machine. Upon seeing you, his present-day self, and your life, what would he do? Would he rejoice or despair? When things were bad, we would joke that our younger selves would take one look at us and shoot themselves in the head, their future being too dreadful to contemplate. It was a way of regaining some perspective on where we were in our lives, in the context of what we'd once envisioned and hoped.

Remember the time machine question? I asked Jacob.

He smiled and nodded. Of course, he said.

Well? What would he think?

Oh God.

Jacob and I laughed and then our laughter petered out and then we sat watching the rest of the guests gesticulating and exchanging declarative statements.

I think he'd be all right with how things turned out, as long as he didn't dig too deep, said Jacob after a moment, smiling ruefully. What about your younger self?

I imagined my younger self sauntering on stubby legs down the silver ramp of the time machine, looking around with wide eyes at his future, taking a tour of my unheated dumpy apartment, the dim dive bars, the frozen tableau of these over-earnest dinner guests in their pastel-colored finery, and his face falling and shoulders sagging until he finally couldn't take any more.

How did this happen, he asks finally. He stamps a galoshed foot for emphasis and stands with hands on hips in imitation of various authority figures.

What do you mean?

This isn't what we planned at all! First of all, what's this about not even having a job? All grown-ups have to have a job!

Well, we've had a few jobs. But we get fired a lot.

For what?

For various things. You know how you get in trouble a lot at school? Remember how you got in trouble every day for the first week of third grade for reading ahead and talking to your friends and just generally being bored stiff, until the teacher told you to just move your desk back to the corner permanently, and that's where you sat for the entire rest of the year? It's a lot of stuff like that.

But that was just stupid rules for kids.

It never really changes.

Well...did we go to college?

Sure.

And?

It was bullshit.

What does that mean?

You'll see.

We're so good at tests and school and stuff, why don't we have a cool job, like jet pilot or actor or president or something?

Being good at stuff doesn't get you ahead in the grown-up

world. One of our last firings was because we "strove for excellence." Our boss told us to "aim lower" and "embrace mediocrity" and when we didn't, we got fired.

So what do we do for money then?

We're on unemployment right now. It's great, we just kind of hang out and cash free checks.

But that's not a plan! That won't last forever!

Oh, stop being such a scared little baby.

Well, what are we going to do?

I've got a plan. I'm going to write a book, a book about not working.

A book? That's your money-making plan, writing a *book*?! Oh, we're so screwed...

I have no response to this and I stand meekly and wait for him to change the subject. He senses an opening and plunges ahead.

Why'd you tell that girl we only made eight thousand dollars last year? You can't say things like that to a girl, you have to be nice and impress them so they'll be your girlfriend and then marry you!

Ugh, just put that out of your mind right now.

Why?

You know how Mom and Dad are so clearly sick to death of each other and Jimmy's parents get in screaming matches and his dad storms out and doesn't come back for a few days and sometimes he comes home smelling and talking weird and sleeps on his front lawn? That's what happens when you get married.

Yeah, but it'll be different for me.

That's what everyone says.

Well, it's true.

What do you know about it?

I know plenty!

Everything they ever told you, about women and life and right and wrong and everything else, is wrong. You'll see.

Why would they lie?

I rubbed my chin. It's kind of a long story.

Young Franklin takes a licorice whip out of his back pocket and saunters through the dining room where Jacob and his guests sit frozen and oblivious. He looks at each person at the table in turn and I can see his disappointment and his incredulity. *But there's more to life*, he's thinking, *there has to be!* He was so sure of it and I knew he was because I had been, I was sure at that understimulated age, subject to an endless matrix of arbitrary authority figures and rule enforcers, that when I got older I'd escape, that life would blossom and deepen just like all the greeting cards and television commercials promised. But of course it never happened, it was just more work and more rules and rooms like these, an endless procession of them, offices and conference rooms and happy hours all filled with people like these, these embalmed fucking Martians who talked about television and furniture and promotions and real estate, who laughed before the punchline to every joke, who didn't have much sex but watched a lot of porn, who talked about their jobs even on weekends, who hated their bosses only because they themselves wanted to call the shots, they didn't hate the throne, they only coveted it, they wanted so badly to love life but didn't know how and were afraid to try, were just afraid, scared to fucking death, of everything, and hated you if you weren't.

And God, it's exhausting day after day and it wears you down until you get to the point where you're shuffling home sleep deprived and caffeine frazzled one night and the eye alights on the third rail. It would be so easy! But I always found reasons to hold off for another day; a piece of ass on the horizon or a drinking spree, and sometimes the only thing that kept me from it was the possibility that at the funeral my boss would be asked to say a few words—a not-so-improbable prospect—and he'd get up and tell all the usual lies people tell about the dead, that Franklin was a fine decent fellow, a company man through and through, hardworking and punctual and a team player, clean-cut and always took the initiative and stayed late without complaint. And in the back row, enemies and ex-girlfriends I hadn't seen in years, listening to this line of bullshit and not knowing any better and thinking, *so the spineless bastard gave up the ghost after all, I always knew he'd sell out, he was all talk all along.* (And my eternal spirit floating above it all, protesting unheard—*no, it's not true! I showered once a week and came to work still drunk from the previous night and tried to fuck all the interns and abused the sick leave system and never gave up the good fight!* But like George in *It's a Wonderful Life,* no one can hear me, and if there is a hell I think this would be my custom fate, to float endlessly above as my boss eulogizes me as a virtuous and upstanding citizen.)

But of course I can't tell him all this, though I want to, because hope is what gets us from day to day. Which is to say, ignorance is bliss.

Are these your friends? Young Franklin asks, waving his licorice stub at the dinner guests.

Not really. They're Jacob's.

I don't like them.

Why not?

They're fakers.

Well, you better get used to it. When you grow up, everyone's like this. And it's their world, their rules, their values and virtues ascendant. We're just guests in it, and unwelcome ones at that.

What? Why?

That's just the way it is.

That's not fair!

Don't whine. It's undignified.

Why do we have to do everything the hard way? I don't want

to live in that cold little apartment! I want to live in a house like this, with a big TV and fancy bed and nice stuff.

I would, too, I said. But everything has a price, and the price is always too high. That's kind of part of it, too. You'll see...

My younger self looks around impotent and horrified one more time and then his eyes become cold slits and I realize that this is not just some kid, this is me, and that assholes are born and not made, and this is the same ruthless Franklin who stuffed his underwear full of marijuana and embezzled thousands of dollars one quarter at a time and charged some old man in Tennessee a five hundred dollar switching fee and then sent him a check for a dollar fifty and who shredded a hundred million dollars' worth of high-priority construction proposals and then erased the backups and who spent a million dollars in ten minutes on shitty movies like *Leonard 6* and had an accomplice impersonate a judge's clerk to trick my ex-employer into missing their court date and sent out fake résumés for three years to milk the system dry, in defiance of all good counsel and advice and man's law and God's law and everything else, the Franklin who his whole life would cut off his nose to spite his face, would cut off his fucking *head* to spite his face. I've pushed him too far too soon, he wasn't ready for all that at once, after all most people go their whole lives without ever being ready, and as I stand there smirking and knowing-it-all he reaches into the front pocket of his Oshkosh overalls, the ones with the giraffes on the legs that I remember so well, and what does he pull out but a gleaming steel-gray Ortgies 7.65 caliber automatic pistol, the snubnose drawing out for what seems like an impossible length of time, like a tiny jalopy disgorging a hundred clowns and why not, after all this is all just a passing musing, and he puts the pistol to his child's head and gives me a mirthless gap-toothed smile and shows me my own tiny middle finger and says, *No thanks, motherfucker!* And then he blows his brains, our brains, all over the far wall and my older self, me, I blink out of existence and I guess theoretically so does this book and these words and—

I jolt out of my reverie and Jacob is sitting there waiting for my answer.

He'd definitely kill himself, I said. But hey, what do kids know?

We laughed and he seemed to know exactly what I meant, and I leaned forward to try again on the Berlin thing, but right then Kate stood up at the other end of the table and clinked her glass with a fork and asked for our attention. All the talk of jobs and promotions and bosses and salaries quelled, and Jacob got very sober and I sat back in my chair and we waited to hear what she had to say.

Everyone, she says, it's been a long time coming, but Jacob and I are thrilled to announce that we're pregnant!

A general squeal goes up around the table, and my eyebrows crawl up my forehead and I understand now why Jacob can't go to Berlin. I look over at him to offer whatever congratulations I can muster but when we make eye contact he just shrugs as if to say I'm sorry, I tried, I went as far as I could and then I couldn't go any further, it's over for me now and it's all up to you. And it broke my heart.

A few minutes later I'm standing at the mantel now drinking in earnest, removed from the general tumult, and Jacob has recovered and is now playing the part of the proud father, accepting handshakes and well-wishes. I'd been close to faltering, but in a stroke all my confidence had been renewed. There is a certain quantity of life to be lived and, as in a poker game, as more players fold the pot gets richer and the stakes higher for the players who remain. *If only you've got the guts.* I'd finish my book and flee the country and then who knows? Perhaps I'd run for president, as I'd joked the other night, the other chapter. It was a long way off, but the key to life is endurance, and I think that if I can imprint this night in my memory, I could go on forever.

As I stood there savoring this clarity, I felt my cell phone vibrate in my pocket. It was a message from the girl who'd thrown my previous cell phone off her balcony. She was out on the town, and did I want to meet up for a drink? Jesus Christ, did I fucking ever. We'd been seeing each other for the past few weeks, every night or every other night because why not? We didn't have anything to do in the morning and the bar tabs weren't paid with real money, it was just unemployment. She was smart and witty and didn't suffer fools and talked in a derisive monotone and rolled her eyes at babies and couples and read books and liked to half-joke that she hated life, to which I usually rolled my eyes but at that moment I understood. Her present stint on unemployment was her first time off the hamster wheel—she'd worked nonstop since college— and that was all she knew of life, so of course it was something to be hated. But as long as the economy stays in the toilet, she has a chance. And to be honest, I like her chances, because if there's one thing I've learned in the last ten years, the last ten jobs, it's that you can always count on the men in charge to fuck things up.

I sent her a text saying I'd be there in thirty minutes and then started to say good-bye to Jacob but then realized I didn't have much to say to him anymore. No one noticed as I sidestepped toward the door, and why would they, and then I turned and fled out into the night.